F. (Franz) Swediaur

The Philosophical Dictionary

Or, the Opinions of Modern Philosophers on Metaphysical...: Vol. II.

F. (Franz) Swediaur

The Philosophical Dictionary
Or, the Opinions of Modern Philosophers on Metaphysical...: Vol. II.

ISBN/EAN: 9783337069827

Printed in Europe, USA, Canada, Australia, Japan

Cover: Foto ©Thomas Meinert / pixelio.de

More available books at **www.hansebooks.com**

THE
PHILOSOPHICAL
DICTIONARY:

OR, THE

OPINIONS

OF

MODERN PHILOSOPHERS

ON

METAPHYSICAL, MORAL,

AND

POLITICAL SUBJECTS.

IN FOUR VOLUMES.

VOL. II.

LONDON:
PRINTED FOR G. G. J. AND J. ROBINSON;
AND
FOR C. ELLIOT, EDINBURGH.
M,DCC,LXXXVI.

CONTENTS

OF THE

SECOND VOLUME.

A 2

iv CONTENTS.

On

LIBERTY

MIRA-

NATURE

                                    PAIN

THE

THE

PHILOSOPHICAL

DICTIONARY.

H.

HABIT.

WE are what we are made by the objects that surround us: To expect that a man who sees other objects, and who leads a life different from mine, should have the same ideas that I have, would be to require contradictions. Why does a Frenchman resemble another Frenchman more than a German, and a German much more than a Chinese? Because these two nations, by their education, and the resemblance of the objects presented to them, have an infinitely greater connection with each other than with the Chinese.

HELVETIUS.

On the same Subject.

The influence of habit arises from the natural
indolence of man; and this indolence increases in
proportion as he indulges himself in it: it is eafier to do as we have done before, than to strike
out any thing new.   The influence of habit is
great over old men and indolent persons; it seldom affects youth.   Habit is convenient only to
weak minds, which it enfeebles daily more and
more.

Habit in every thing destroys the powers of the
imagination; these are excited only by the novelty of the object.   The imagination is never
employed on those objects which are familiar to
us; these affect only the memory: and hence
we see the reason of the axiom, *Ab assuetis non
fit passio;* for the passions are lighted only at the
fire of the imagination.   Rousseau.

On the same Subject.

General states of mind, turns of thought,
and fixed habits which are the consequences of
them, arise from education and the circumstances
men are placed in.   It is a necessary effect of the
principles of association, that the mind grows cal-
lous to new impressions continually; it being already

ready occupied with ideas and fenfations which render it indifpofed to receive others, efpecially of an heterogeneous nature. In confequence, we feldom fee any confiderable change in a perfon's temper and habits after he is grown to man's eftate; nothing fhort of an entire revolution in his circumftances and mode of life can effect it.

PRIESTLEY.

MORAL AND MECHANICAL HABITS, AND THEIR INLUENCE IN POLITICAL SOCIETY.

THE end of every individual is his own good. The rules he obferves in the purfuit of this good are a fyftem of propofitions, almoft every one founded in authority; that is, derive their weight from the credit given to one or more perfons, and not from demonftration.—And this in the moft important, as well as the other affairs of life, is the cafe even of the wifeft and philofophical part of the human fpecies; and that it fhould be fo is the lefs ftrange, when we confider that it is perhaps impoffible to prove that being, or life itfelf, has any other value than what is fet on it by authority.—A confirmation of this may be derived from the obfervation, that in every country in the univerfe happinefs is fought upon a different plan; and, even in the fame country, we fee it placed, by different ages, profeffions, and ranks of men, in the attainment of enjoyments utterly

unlike-

unlike.——Thefe propofitions, as well as others
framed upon them, become habitual by degrees;
and, as they govern the determinations of the
will, I call them moral habits. There are another fet of habits that have the direction of the
body, that I call therefore mechanical habits. Thefe
compofe what we commonly call the arts; which
are more or lefs liberal or mechanical, as they
more or lefs partake of affiftance from the operations of the mind.—The cumulus of the moral
habits of each individual is the manners of that
individual; the cumulus of the manners of individuals makes up the manners of a nation.—The
happinefs of individuals is evidently the ultimate
end of political fociety; and political welfare, or
the ftrength, fplendour, and opulence of the ftate,
have been always admitted, both by political writers and the valuable part of mankind in general,
to conduce to this end; and are therefore defirable.—The caufes that advance or obftruct any
one of thefe three objects are external or inter-
ternal. The latter may be divided into phyfical,
civil, and perfonal; under which laft head I comprehend the moral and mechanical habits of mankind. The phyfical caufes are principally climate,
foil, and number of fubjects; the civil are government and laws; and political welfare is always in a ratio compofed of the force of thefe particular caufes; a multitude of external caufes,

and

and all thefe internal ones; and not only control and qualify, but are conftantly acting on, and thereby infenfibly, as well as fenfibly, altering one another both for the better and the worfe; and this not excepting the climate itfelf.

FRANKLIN.

HAPPINESS.

A CONSIDERABLE part of our happinefs confifts in the defire itfelf. It is with happinefs as with the golden bird fent by the fairies to a young princefs: The bird fettles at thirty paces from her; fhe goes to catch it, advances foftly, is ready to feize it; the bird flies thirty paces further; fhe paffes feveral months in the purfuit, and is happy. If the bird had fuffered itfelf to be taken at firft, the princefs would have put it in a cage, and in one week would have been tired of it. This is the bird of happinefs which we inceffantly purfue; we catch it not, and are happy in the purfuit, becaufe we are fecure from difguft. If our defires were to be every inftant gratified, the mind would languifh in inaction, and fink under difquietude. Man muft have defires. Few men, however, acknowledge they have this want; it is neverthelefs to a fucceffion of their defires they owe their happinefs.

HELVETIUS.

THE

HAPPINESS of different Stations from the different Employment of Time.

MEN hunger and thirst; they require to lie with their wives, to sleep, &c. Of the twenty-four hours of the day they employ ten or twelve in providing for these several wants. As soon as they are gratified, from the dealer in rabbit-skins to the monarch, all are equally happy. It is in vain to say that the table of wealth is more delicate than that of mediocrity. When the labourer is well fed, he is content. The different cookery of different people proves only that good cheer is that to which we have been accustomed.—If labour be generally regarded as an evil, it is because, in most governments the necessaries of life are not to be had without excessive labour; from whence the very idea of labour constantly excites that of pain. Labour, however, is not pain in itself: habit renders it easy; and when it is pursued without remarkable fatigue, is in itself an advantage. How many artisans are there who when rich still continue their occupations, and quit them not without regret when age obliges them to it? There is nothing that habit does not render agreeable.—The busy man is the happy man. To prove this, I distinguish two sorts of pleasures. The first are *the pleasures of*

the

the senses. Thefe are founded on corporeal wants, are enjoyed by all conditions of men; and at the time of enjoyment all are equally happy. But thefe pleafures are of fhort duration. The others are *the pleafures of expectation.* Among thefe I reckon all the means of procuring corporeal pleafures; thefe means are by expectation always converted into real pleafures. When a joiner takes up his plane, what does he experience? All the pleafures of expectation annexed to the payment for his work. Now thefe pleafures are not experienced by the opulent man. He is therefore always uneafy, always in motion, continually rolling about in his carriage, like the fquirrel in his cage, to get rid of his difguft. The wealthy idler experiences a thoufand inftances of anxiety, while the labouring man enjoys the continual pleafure of frefh expectations.—In general, every ufeful occupation fills up in the moft agreeable manner the interval that feparates a gratified from a rifing want; that is, the ten or twelve hours of the day, when we moft envy the indolence of the rich, and think they enjoy fuperior happinefs. Employment gives pleafure to every moment; but is unknown to the great and idle opulent. The meafure of our wealth, whatever prejudice may think, is not therefore the meafure of our happinefs. Great treafures are the appearance of happinefs, not the reality: fo that the workman in

in his shop, or the tradesman behind his counter,
is often more happy than his sovereign. The condition of the workman who can by a moderate labour provide for his wants and those of his family, when the habit of labour has been early contracted, is nearly as happy as it can be, nay, is
perhaps of all conditions the most happy. The
want that compels his mind to application, and
his body to exercise, is a preservative against dis-
content and disease: now these are evils; joy and
health, advantages. Therefore, without being e-
qual in wealth and dignity, individuals may be
equal in felicity.—It was not on the tomb of Crœ-
sus, but on that of Baucis, this epitaph was engraved, *His death was the evening of a beautiful
day.*   HELVETIUS.

HELL.

WHEN men came to live in society, they could
not but perceive that many evil-doers escaped the
severity of the laws: these could affect only open
crimes; so that a curb was wanting against clan-
destine guilt, and religion alone could be such a
curb. The Persians, the Chaldeans, the Egyptians, and the Greeks, introduced a belief of punishments after this life; and, of all ancient nations we are acquainted with, the Jews alone
admitted only temporal punishments. At length
the

HELL.

Not long fince, an honeft well-meaning Hugenot
print, that there would be a day of grace to the

HEREDITARY Succession in Governors.

THE higheft offices of all in a ftate ought to be

intereſt of men to extend them, and when ſo flattering an object is kept ſo long time in view, opportunities will be found for the purpoſe. What
nation would not have been enſlaved by the un-
controverted ſucceſſion only of three ſuch princes
as Henry IV. of France, Henry VII. of England,
or the preſent king of Pruſſia? The more accom-
pliſhed and glorious they were as warriors or
ſtateſmen, the more dangerous would they be as
princes in free ſtates. It is nothing but the continual fear of a revolt in favour of ſome rival, that
could keep ſuch princes within any bounds; *i. e.*
that could make it their intereſt to court the favour of the people. Hereditary nobles ſtand in
the ſame predicament as hereditary princes. The
long continuance of the ſame parliaments have all
the ſame tendency. But though it be evident
that no office of great power or truſt ſhould
be ſuffered to continue a long time in the ſame
hands, the ſucceſſion might be ſo rapid, that the
remedy would be worſe than the diſeaſe. But
though the exact medium of political liberty, with
reſpect to the continuance of men in power, be
not eaſily fixed, it is not of much conſequence to
do it; ſince a conſiderable degree of perfection in
government will admit of great varieties in this
reſpect.   PRIESTLEY.

HERE-

HEREDITARY SUCCESSION IN GOVERN-MENT.

. OF all the various forms of government which have prevailed in the world, an hereditary monarchy seems to present the fairest scope for ridicule. Is it possible to relate, without an indignant smile, that, on the father's decease, the property of a nation, like that of a drove of oxen, descends to the infant son, as yet unknown to mankind and to himself; and that the fairest warriors and the wisest statesmen, relinquishing their natural right to empire, approach the royal cradle with bended knees, and protestations of inviolable fidelity? Satire and declamation may paint these obvious topics in the most dazzling colours; but our more serious thoughts will respect an useful prejudice that establishes a rule of succession independent of the passions of mankind; and we shall cheerfully acquiesce in any expedient which deprives the multitude of the dangerous, and indeed the ideal, power of giving themselves a master. In the **cool** shade of retirement, we may easily devise imaginary forms of government, in which the sceptre shall be constantly bestowed on the most worthy, by the free and incorrupt suffrage of the whole community. Experience overturns these airy fabrics; and teaches us, that, in

a]

a large fociety, the election of a monarch can never devolve to the wifeft or to the moft numerous
part of the people. The army is the only order of
men fufficiently united to concur in the fame
fentiments, and powerful enough to impofe them
on their fellow-citizens; but the temper of foldiers, habituated at once to violence and flavery,
renders them very unfit guardians of a legal, and
even civil conftitution. Juftice, humanity, or
political wifdom, are qualities they are too little
acquainted with in themfelves to appreciate them
in others. Valour will acquire their efteem, and
liberality will purchafe their fuffrage; but the
firft of thefe merits is often lodged in the moft
favage breafts: the latter can only exert itfelf at
the expence of the public; and both may be turned againft the poffeffor of the throne by the ambition of a daring rival.—The fuperior prerogative
of birth, when it has obtained the fanction of
time and popular opinion, is the plaineft and leaft
invidious of all diftinctions among mankind. The
acknowledged right extinguifhes the hopes of fac-
tion, and the confcious fecurity difarms the cruelty of the monarch. To the firm eftablifhment
of this idea we owe the peaceful fucceffion and
mild adminiftration of European monarchies; to
the defect of it we muft attribute the frequent civil wars through which an Afiatic defpot is obliged to cut his way to the throne of his fathers.

GIBBON.

THE MIRACULOUS AND MARVELLOUS IN
HISTORY.

IT is the busine∫s of hi∫tory to di∫tingui∫h between the miraculous and marvellous; to reject the fir∫t in all narrations merely profane and human; to ∫cruple the ∫econd; and when obliged by undoubted te∫timony to admit of ∫omething extraordinary, to receive as little of it as is con∫i∫tent with the known facts and circum∫tances.

HUME.

FOUNDLING HOSPITALS.

HOSPITALS for foundlings ∫eem favourable to the increa∫e of numbers; and perhaps may be ∫o when kept under proper re∫trictions. But when they open the door to every one without di∫tinction, they have probably a contrary effect, and are prejudicial to the ∫tate. It is computed that every ninth child born at Paris is ∫ent to the ho∫pital; though it ∫eems certain, according to the common cour∫e of human affairs, that it is not a hundredth child who∫e parents are altogether incapacitated to rear and educate him. The great difference for health, indu∫try, and morals, between the education in an ho∫pital and that in a private family, ∫hould induce us not to make the entrance

VOL. II.   C   †   into

into an hofpital too eafy and engaging. To kill one's own child is fhocking to nature, and muft therefore be fomewhat unufual; but to turn over the care of him upon others is very agreeable to the natural indolence of mankind.

HUME.

HUMANITY.

Born without ideas, without vice, and without virtue, every thing in man, even his humanity, is an acquifition: it is to his education he owes his fentiment. Among all the various ways of infpiring him with it, the moft efficacious is to accuftom him from childhood, in a manner from the cradle, to afk himfelf when he beholds a miferable object, by what chance he is not expofed in like manner to the inclemency of the feafons, to hunger, cold, poverty, &c. When the child has been ufed to put himfelf in the place of the wretched, that habit gained, he becomes the more touched with their mifery; as in deploring their misfortunes it is for human nature in general, and for himfelf in particular, that he is concerned. An infinity of different fentiments then mix with the firft fentiment; and their affemblage compofes the total of the fentiment of pleafure felt by a noble foul in fuccouring the diftreffed; a fentiment that he is not always in a fitua-

tion

tion to analyfe.—We relieve the unfortunate to avoid the pain of feeing them fuffer. To enjoy an example of gratitude, which produces in us at leaft a confufed hope of diftant utility; to exhibit an act of power, whofe exercife is always agreeable to us, becaufe it always recalls to the mind the images of pleafure attached to that power; and, laftly, becaufe the idea of happinefs is conftantly connected, in a good education, with the idea of beneficence; and this beneficence in us, conciliating the efteem and affection of men, may, like riches, be regarded as a power or means of avoiding pains and procuring pleafures:——In this manner, as from an affinity of different fentiments, is made up the total fentiment of the pleafure we feel in the exercife of beneficence.

HELVETIUS.

ON THE SAME SUBJECT.

IN order to love mankind, little muft be expected from them. In order to view their faults without afperity, we muft accuftom ourfelves to forgivenefs; to a fenfe that indulgence is a juftice which frail humanity has a right to require from wifdom. Now nothing has a greater tendency to difpofe us to indulgence, to clofe our hearts againft hatred, and to open them to the principles of an humane and mild morality, than a

profound

profound knowledge of the human heart. Accordingly, the wifeſt men have always been the moſt indulgent. What beautiful maxims of morality are ſcattered through their works! It was the ſaying of Plato, " Live with your inferiors " and domeſtics as with unfortunate friends." " Muſt I always," ſaid an Indian philoſopher, " hear the rich crying out, Lord, deſtroy all who " take from us the leaſt parcel of our poſſeſſions ; " while the poor man, with a plaintive voice, and " eyes lifted up to heaven, cries, Lord, give me a " part of the goods thou dealeſt out in ſuch pro- " fuſion to the rich ; and if others leſs happy de- " prive me of a part, inſtead of imprecating thy " vengeance, I ſhall conſider theſe thefts in the " ſame manner as in ſeed-time we ſee the doves " ranging over the fields in queſt of their food."

HELVETIUS.

ON THE SAME SUBJECT.

THE folly and wickedneſs of human nature does not fill a man of ſenſe and humanity with indignation : he, like Democritus, ſees in them none but fools ; or children, againſt whom it would be ridiculous to be offended, and who are more worthy of pity than of anger. There are ſome men who are not humane becauſe they have been impoſed upon, and whoſe humanity decrea-

ſes

fes in proportion as they obtain more knowledge;
but the man of genuine fenfe and humanity is
conftantly the friend of mankind, becaufe he alone
is acquainted with the nature of man. He confiders men with the eye of a mechanic; and, without infulting humanity, complains that nature has
united the prefervation of one being to the deftruction of another; that, to afford nourifhment,
he orders the hawk to feize in his talons the
dove; made it neceffary for the infect to be devoured; and rendered every being an affaffin.

HELVETIUS.

HYPOCRISY.

TO act the part of a hypocrite is a tafk at once
fo painful and fo difficult, that nothing but the
moft violent effort of patience and artifice can
fupport a long and fuccefsful performance of it.
Let us always be fearful of giving too much to
the mind, by taking too much away from the
heart. If we enjoy fome talents wherewith we
deceive others, how many more talents do we not
poffefs which feduce us to impofe upon ourfelves?
The willingnefs with which we are apt to credit
the fuppofed exertions of hypocrify may perhaps
arife from the not having fufficiently reflected on
the nature of the human heart. All who have
obferved the empire which our intereft maintains

C 3
over

over our opinions, muft have met with ample
reafon to be convinced that its own fuccefles foon
prove the means of its deftruction. We lead off
by difhoneftly affecting certain practices and fentiments; and when this impofture hath brought
us within the reach of applying fome great part,
of commanding mankind, and of receiving from
them riches and confequence, we begin to repofe
in it more truft; and it at length happens, that
by little and little our intereft attains to the power
of confolidating in our mind the bafis of our authority. It is an old remark, that gamefters begin by being dupes, and end by being knaves: in
matters of opinion, the cafe is reverfed; and we
begin by being knaves, and end by being dupes.

CHATELLUX.

I.

I.

IDEA OF BODY EQUALLY OBSCURE AS THAT OF SPIRIT.

IF any one fay, he knows not what it is that thinks in him, he means he knows not what the fubftance is of that thinking thing. If he fays, he knows not how he thinks; I anfwer, neither knows he how he is extended, how the folid parts of body are united, or cohere together to make extenfion. For though the preffure of the particles of air may account for the cohefion of feveral parts of matter, that are groffer than the particles of air, and have pores lefs than the corpufcles of air; yet the weight or preffure of the air will not explain, nor can be a caufe of, the coherence of the particles of air themfelves. And if the preffure of the ether, or any fubtiler matter than the air, may unite and hold faft together the parts of a particle of air, as well as other bodies; yet it cannot make bonds for itfelf, and

hold

hold together the parts that make up every the least corpuscle of that *materia subtilis*. So that that hypothesis, how ingeniously soever explained, by showing that the parts of sensible bodies are held together by the pressure of other external insensible bodies, reaches not the parts of the ether itself: and by how much the more evidently it proves that the parts of other bodies are held together by the external pressure of the ether, and can have no other conceivable cause of their cohesion and unity; by so much the more it leaves us in the dark concerning the cohesion of the parts of the corpuscles of the ether itself; which we can neither conceive without parts, they being bodies, and divisible; nor yet how their parts cohere, they wanting that cause of cohesion which is given of the cohesion of the parts of all other bodies.

But, in truth, *the pressure of any ambient fluid, how great soever, can be no intelligible cause of the cohesion of the solid parts of matter*. For though such a pressure may hinder the avulsion of two polished superficies one from another in a line perpendicular to them, as in the experiment of two polished marbles; yet it can never in the least hinder the separation by a motion in a line parallel to those surfaces; because the ambient fluid, having a full liberty to succeed in each point of space deserted by a lateral motion, resists such a motion of bodies

dies

dies fo joined, no more than it would refift the
motion of that body were it on all fides environed
by that fluid, and touched no other body: And
therefore, if there were no other caufe of cohefion, all parts of bodies muft be eafily feparable
by fuch a lateral fliding motion. For if the preffure of the ether be the adequate caufe of cohefion, wherever that caufe operates not, there can
be no cohefion. And fince it cannot operate
againft fuch a lateral feparation, therefore in every
imaginary plane, interfecting any mafs of matter,
there could be no more cohefion than of two po-
lifhed furfaces, which will always, notwithftanding any imaginary preffure of a fluid, eafily flide
one from another. So that perhaps, how clear an
idea foever we think we have of the extenfion of
body, which is nothing but the cohefion of folid
parts, he that fhall well confider it in his mind,
may have reafon to conclude, that it is as eafy for
him *to have a clear idea how the foul thinks, as
how the body is extended.* For fince body is no
further nor otherwife extended than by the union
and cohefion of its folid parts, we fhall very ill
comprehend the *extenfion* of body, without underftanding wherein confifts the union and cohefion of its parts; which feems to me as incomprehenfible as the manner of thinking, and how
it is performed.

I allow it is ufual for moft people to wonder
how

how any one fhould find a difficulty in what they
think they every day obferve. Do we not fee,
will they be ready to fay, the parts of bodies ftick
firmly together? Is there any thing more common? and what doubt can there be made of
it? And the like I fay concerning *thinking* and
voluntary motion : Do we not every moment experiment it in ourfelves? and therefore can it be
doubted? The matter of fact is clear, I confefs:
but when we would a little nearer look into it,
and confider how it is done, there, I think, we
are at a lofs both in the one and the other; and
can as little underftand how the parts of body cohere, as how we ourfelves perceive or move. I
would have any one intelligibly explain to me,
how the parts of gold or brafs (that but now, in
fufion, were as loofe from one another as the particles of water or the fands of an hour-glafs) come
in a few moments to be fo united, and adhere fo
ftrongly one to another, that the utmoft force of
mens arms cannot feparate them. Any confider-
ing man will, I fuppofe, be here at a lofs to fatisfy his own or another man's underftanding.

The little bodies that compofe that fluid we call
water, are fo extremely fmall, that I have never
heard of any one who, by a microfcope, pretended to perceive their diftinct bulk, figure, or motion; and the particles of water are alfo fo perfectly loofe one from another, that the leaft force
fenfibly

senfibly feparates them: nay, if we confider their perpetual motion, we muſt allow them to have no cohefion one with another: and yet let but a ſharp cold come, and they unite, they confolidate; thefe little atoms cohere, and are not, without great force, feparable. He that could find the bonds that tie thefe heaps of loofe little bodies together fo firmly; he that could make known the cement that makes them ſtick fo faft to one another, would difcover a great and yet unknown fecret; and yet, when that was done, would be far enough from making the extenfion of body (which is the cohefion of its folid parts) intelligible, till he could ſhow wherein confifted the union or confolidation of the parts of thofe bonds, or of that cement, or of the leaft particle of matter that exifts. Whereby it appears, that this primary and fuppofed obvious quality of body will be found, when examined, to be as incomprehenfible as any thing belonging to our minds; and a folid extended fubftance as hard to be conceived as a thinking immaterial one, whatever difficulties fome would raife againſt it.

In the communication of motion by impulfe, wherein as much motion is loft to one body as is got to the other, which is the ordinarieft cafe, we can have no other conception but the paffing of motion out of one body into another; which, I think, is as obfcure and inconceivable as how our

3   minds

minds move or stop our bodies by thought, which
we every moment find they do. The increase of
motion by impulse, which is observed or believed
sometimes to happen, is yet harder to be understood. We have by daily experience clear evidence of motion produced both by impulse and
by thought : but the manner how, hardly comes
within our comprehension; we are equally at a
loss in both. So that, however we consider motion and its communication either from body or
spirit, *the idea which belongs to spirit is at least
as clear as that which belongs to body.* And if we
consider the active power of moving, it is much
clearer in spirit than body; since two bodies, placed by one another at rest, will never afford us
the ideas of power in the one to move the other,
but by a borrowed motion : whereas the mind af-
fords ideas of an active power every day of moving bodies; and therefore it is worth our confideration, whether active power be not the proper
attribute of spirits, and passive power of matter.
Hence may be conjectured, that created spirits
are not totally separate from matter, because they
are both active and passive. Pure spirit, viz. God,
is only active; pure matter is only passive : those
beings that are both active and passive, we may
judge to partake of both. But be that as it will,
I think we have as many and as clear ideas belonging to spirit as we have belonging to body,
the

the fubftance of each being equally unknown to
us; and the idea of thinking in fpirit as clear as
extenfion in body; and the communication of motion by thought, which we attribute to fpirit, is
as evident as that by impulfe, which we afcribe
to body. Conftant experience makes us fenfible
of thefe, though our narrow underftandings can
comprehend neither.

Senfation convinces us, that there are folid extended fubftances; and reflection, that there are
thinking ones. Experience affures us of the
exiftence of fuch beings, and that the one hath a
power to move the body by impulfe, the other by
thought: this we cannot doubt of. Experience,
I fay, every moment furnifhes us with the clear
ideas both of the one and the other; but beyond
thefe ideas, as received from their proper fources,
our faculties will not reach. If we would inquire
further into their nature, caufes, and manner, we
perceive not the nature of extenfion clearer than
we do that of thinking. If we would explain them
any further, one is as eafy as the other; and there
is no more difficulty to conceive how a fubftance
we know not fhould by thought fet body into motion, than how a fubftance we know not fhould
by impulfe fet body into motion. So that we are
no more able to difcover wherein the ideas belonging to body confift, than thofe belonging to
fpirit.   LOCKE.

IDEAS DERIVED FROM QUALITIES IN BODIES.

WHATSOEVER the mind perceives in itfelf,
or is the immediate object of perception, thought,
or underftanding, that I call *idea* ; and the power
to produce any idea in our mind, I call *quality* of
the fubject wherein that power is. Thus a fnow-
ball having the power to produce in us the ideas
of white, cold, and round, the powers to produce
thofe ideas in us as they are in the fnow-ball, I
call *qualities* ; and as they are fenfations or perceptions in our underftandings, I call them *ideas*.

Qualities thus confidered in bodies, are, *firft*,
Such as are utterly infeparable from the body, in
whatfoever ftate it be; fuch as in all the alterations
and changes it fuffers, all the force that can be
ufed upon it, it conftantly keeps; and fuch as
fenfe conftantly finds in every particle of matter,
which has bulk enough to be perceived, and the
mind finds infeparable from every particle of matter, though lefs than to make itfelf be perceived by
our fenfes : *v. g.* Take a grain of wheat; divide
it into two parts; each part has ftill folidity, extenfion, figure, and mobility ; divide it again, and
it retains ftill the fame qualities; and fo divide
it on till the parts become infenfible, they muft
retain ftill each of them all thefe qualities. For

D   divifion

divifion (which is all that a mill or peftle, or any
other body, does upon another in reducing it to
infenfible parts), and never take away either folidity, extenfion, figure, or mobility from any body,
but only makes two or more diftinct or feparate
maffes of matter of that which was before but
one; all which diftinct maffes, reckoned as fo
many diftinct bodies, after divifion make a certain number. Thefe I call original or *primary*
qualities of body; which I think we may obferve
to produce fimple ideas in us, viz, folidity, extenfion, figure, motion, or reft, and number.

Secondly, Such qualities, which in truth are nothing in the objects themfelves but powers to produce various fenfations in us by their primary
qualities, *i. e.* by the bulk, figure, texture, and
motion of their infenfible parts; as colours,
founds, taftes, &c. Thefe I call *fecondary* qualities.

The next thing to be confidered is, how bodies
produce ideas in us; and that is manifeftly by *im-*
pulfe; the only way which we conceive bodies
operate in.

If, then, external objects be not united to our
minds when they produce ideas in it, and yet we
perceive *thefe original qualities* in fuch of them
as fingly fall under our fenfes; it is evident that
fome motion muft be thence continued by our
nerves or animal fpirits, by fome parts of our bo-

dies, to the brain, or the feat of fenfation, there *to produce in our minds the particular* ideas *we have of them.* And fince the extenfion, figure, num-ber, and motion of bodies of an obfervable big-nefs, may be perceived at a diftance by the fight, it is evident fome fingly imperceptible bodies muft come from them to the eyes, and thereby convey to the brain fome *motion*, which produces thefe ideas which we have of them in us.

After the fame manner that the ideas of thefe original qualities are produced in us, we may conceive that the *ideas of fecondary qualities* are alfo produced, viz. *by the operation of infenfible particles on our fenfes :* For it being manifeft that there are bodies, each whereof are fo fmall that we cannot by any of our fenfes difcover either their bulk, figure, or motion, as is evident in the particles of air and water, and others ex-tremely fmaller than thefe, perhaps as much fmaller than the particles of air or water are fmaller than peafe or hailftones; the different motions and figures, bulk and number of fuch particles affecting the feveral organs of our fenfes, produce in us thofe different fenfations which we have from the colours and fmell of bodies; *v. g.* that a violet, by the impulfe of fuch infenfible particles of matter of peculiar figures and bulks, and in different degrees and modifications of their motions, caufes the ideas of the blue colour

and

and fweet fcent of that flower, to be produced in our minds.

From whence I think it is eafy to draw this obfervation, That the ideas of primary qualities of bodies are *refemblances* of them, and their patterns do really exift in the bodies themfelves; but the ideas produced in us by thefe fecondary qualities have *no refemblance* of them at all. There is nothing like our ideas exifting in the bodies themfelves. They are in the bodies we denominate from them, only a power to produce thofe fenfations in us; and what is fweet, blue, or warm in idea, is but the certain bulk, figure, and motion of the infenfible parts in the bodies themfelves, which we call fo.

Flame is denominated *hot* and *light;* fnow, *white* and *cold;* and manna, *white* and *fweet,* from the ideas they produce in us: which qualities are commonly thought to be the fame in thofe bodies that thofe ideas are in us; the one the perfect refemblance of the other, as they are in a mirror. But whoever confiders that the fame *fire,* that in one diftance *produces* in us the fenfation of *warmth,* does, at a nearer approach, produce in us the far different fenfation of *pain,* will have no reafon to fay, that his *idea of warmth,* which was produced in him by the fire, is actually *in the fire:* and his *idea of pain,* which the fame fire produced in him the fame way, is not in the fire.

The

The particular bulk, number, figure, and motion of the parts of fire or fnow, are really in them, whether one's fenfes perceive them or not; and therefore may be called *real qualities*, becaufe they really exift in thofe bodies. But light, heat, whitenefs, or coldnefs, are no more really in them, than ficknefs or pain is in manna. Take away the fenfation of them; let not the eyes fee light or colours, nor the ears hear founds; let the palate not tafte, nor the nofe fmell; and all colours, taftes, odours, and founds, as they are fuch particular *ideas*, vanifh and ceafe, and are reduced to their caufes, *i. e.* bulk, figure, and motion of parts.

Pound an almond, and the clear white colour will be altered into a dirty one, and the fweet tafte into an oily one. What real alteration can the beating of the peftle make in any body, but an alteration of the *texture* of it?

Ideas being thus diftinguifhed and underftood, we may be able to give an account how the fame water, at the fame time, may produce the idea of cold by one hand, and of heat by the other; whereas it is impoffible that the fame water, if thofe ideas were really in it, fhould at the fame time be both hot and cold. For if we imagine *warmth*, as it is *in our hands*, to be *nothing but a certain fort and degree of motion in the minute particles of our nerves or animal fpirits*, we may

underftand

underſtand how it is poſſible that the ſame water
may at the time produce the ſame ſenſation of heat
in one hand, and cold in the other; which yet figure
never does, that never producing the idea of a ſquare
by one hand which has produced the idea of a globe
by another. But if the ſenſation of heat and cold
be nothing but the increaſe or diminution of the
motion of the minute parts of our bodies, cauſed
by the corpuſcles of any other body; it is eaſy to
be underſtood, that if that motion be greater in
one hand than in the other; if a body be applied
to the two hands, which has in its minute particles a greater motion than in thoſe of one of the
hands, and a leſs than in thoſe of the other, it
will increaſe the motion of the one hand, and leſ-
ſen it in the other; and ſo cauſe the different ſen-
ſations of heat and cold that depend thereon.

LOCKE.

IDEAS OF SENSATION CHANGED BY THE JUDGMENT.

THE ideas we receive by ſenſation are often
altered by the judgment, without our taking notice of it. When we ſet before our eyes a round
globe, of any uniform colour, *v. g.* gold, alaba-
ſter, or jet, it is certain that the idea thereby imprinted in our mind is of a flat circle, variouſly
ſhadowed, with ſeveral degrees of light and bright-
neſs

nefs coming to our eyes; but we having by ufe
been accuftomed to perceive what kind of appear
ance convex bodies are wont to make on us, what
alterations are made in the reflections of light by
the difference of the fenfible figure of bodies, the
judgment prefently, by an habitual cuftom, alters
the appearances into the caufes; fo that from that
which is truly variety of fhadow or colour, collecting the figure, it makes it pafs for a mark of figure, and frames to itfelf the perception of a convex figure, and an uniform colour, when the idea
we receive from thence is only a plane varioufly
coloured; as is evident in painting. Suppofe a
man born blind, and now adult, and taught by
his touch to diftinguifh a cube and a fphere of the
fame metal, and nighly of the fame bignefs, fo as
to tell, when he felt one, and when the other,
which is the cube, which the fphere. Suppofe
then the cube and fphere placed on a table, and
the blind man be made to fee: Query, Whether
by his fight, before he touched them, he could
now diftinguifh and tell which is the globe, which
the cube? It may be anfwered, No: For though
he has obtained the experience how a globe, how
a cube affects his touch; yet he has not yet attained the experience, that what affects his touch
fo or fo, muft affect the fight in the fame manner; or that a protuberant angle in the cube, that
                                        preffed

preffed his hand unequally, fhall appear to his eye
as it does in the cube.

But this I think is not ufually in any of our
ideas but thofe received by fight; becaufe fight,
the moft comprehenfive of all our fenfes, convey-
ing to our minds the ideas of light and colours,
which are peculiar only to that fenfe; and alfo
the far different ideas of fpace, figure, or motion,
the feveral varieties whereof change the appearance of its proper object, viz. light and colours,
we bring ourfelves by ufe to judge of the one by
the other. This in many cafes, by a fettled habit
in things whereof we have frequent experience,
is performed fo conftantly, and fo quick, that we
take that for the perception of our fenfation which
is an idea formed by the judgment: fo that one,
viz. that of fenfation, ferves only to excite the
other, and is fcarce taken notice of itfelf; as a
man who reads or hears with attention or underftanding, takes little notice of the characters or
founds, but of the ideas that are excited in him by
them.

Nor need we wonder that this is done with fo
little notice, if we confider how very quick the
actions of the mind are performed; for as itfelf
is thought to take up no fpace, to have no extenfion, fo its actions feem to require no time, but
many of them feem to be crowded into an inftant.
I fpeak this in comparifon to the actions of the
body.

body. Any one may eafily obferve this in his own
thoughts, who will take the pains to reflect on
them. How, as it were, in an inftant, do our
minds with one glance fee all the parts of a demonftration, which may very well be called a long
one, if we confider the time it will require to put
it into words, and ftep by ftep fhow it another?
We fhall not be fo much furprifed that this is done
in us with fo little notice, if we confider how the
facility which we get of doing things by a cuftom
of doing, makes them often pafs in us without
our notice. *Habits*, efpecially fuch as are begun
very early, come at laft to *produce actions in us,
which often efcape our obfervation*. How frequently do we in a day cover our eyes with our
eye-lids, without perceiving that we are at all in
the dark? Men, that by cuftom have got the ufe
of a by-word, do almoft in every fentence pronounce founds, which, though taken notice of by
others, they themfelves neither hear nor obferve;
and therefore it is not fo ftrange that our mind
fhould often change the idea of its fenfation into
that of its judgment, and make one ferve only to
excite the other, without our taking notice of it.

LOCKE.

Asso-

ASSOCIATION OF IDEAS.

IT is evident that there is a principle of connection between the different thoughts and ideas
of the mind; and that in their appearance to the
memory or imagination, they introduce each
other with a certain degree of regularity and method. In our more serious thinking and discourse,
this is so observable, that any particular thought
which breaks in upon this regular track or chain
of ideas, is immediately remarked and rejected:
And even in our wildest and most wandering re-
veries, nay, in our very dreams, we shall find, if
we reflect, that the imagination ran not altogether
at adventures, but that there was still a connection upheld among the different ideas which succeeded each other. Were the loosest and freest
conversation to be transcribed, there would immediately be observed something which connected it in all its transitions. Or where this is wanting, the person who broke the thread of the discourse might still inform you, that there had se-
cretly revolved in his mind a succession of thought,
which had gradually led him away from the subject of conversation. Among the languages of
different nations, even where we cannot suspect
the least connection and communication, it is
found, that the words expressive of ideas, the
most

moſt compounded, do yet nearly correſpond to
each other. A certain proof, that the ſimple ideas,
comprehended in the compound ones, were bound
together by ſome univerſal principle, which had
an equal influence on all mankind. The principles of connection among ideas appear to be
only three in number, viz. *Reſemblance, contiguity* in time and place, and *cauſe* and *effect :* Con-
traſt or contrariety is a connection among ideas,
which may perhaps be conſidered as a mixture of
cauſation and reſemblance. Where two objects
are contrary, the one deſtroys the other, i. e. is
the cauſe of its annihilation; and the idea of the
annihilation of an object implies the idea of its
former exiſtence. A picture naturally leads our
thoughts to the original: this depends on the principle of *reſemblance.* The mention of one apart-
ment in a building naturally introduces an inquiry or diſcourſe concerning the others: this ori-
ginates from the *contiguity* of the apartments. If
we think of a wound, we can ſcarcely forbear reflecting on the pain which follows it: this ariſes
from the connection between cauſe and effect.
This ſubject is copious; and many operations of
the human mind depend on the connection, or
aſſociation of ideas, which is here deſcribed: particularly the ſympathy between the paſſions and
imagination will, perhaps, appear remarkable;
while we obſerve that the affections, excited by

2   one

one object, pass easily to another connected with it; but transfuse themselves with difficulty, or not at all, along different objects which have no manner of connection together. By introducing into any composition, personages and actions foreign to each other, an injudicious author loses that communication of emotions, by which alone he can interest the heart, and raise the passions to their proper height and period. That this enumeration of the principles of the association of ideas is complete, and that there are no other except these, may be difficult to prove to the reader's satisfaction, and even to a man's own satisfaction.

HUME.

THE ORIGIN OF IDEAS.

ALL the perceptions of the mind may be divided into two species, distinguished by their different degrees of force and vivacity. The less forcible and lively are denominated *ideas*; the other species we shall call *impressions*. By the term *impression*, may be understood all our more lively perceptions; when we hear, or see, or feel, or love, or hate, or desire, or will. There is a considerable difference between the perceptions of the mind, when a man feels the pain of excessive heat, or the pleasure of moderate warmth, and when he afterwards recalls to his memory this sensation,

or anticipates it by his imagination. These faculties may copy the perceptions of the senses;
but the utmost we say of them, even when they
operate with the greatest vigour, is, that they re-
present the object in so lively a manner, that we
could almost say we feel, or see it: but except the
mind be disordered by disease or madness, they
never can arrive at such a pitch of vivacity, as to
render these perceptions altogether undistinguish-
able. A man in a fit of anger, is actuated in a
very different manner from one who only thinks
of that emotion. If you tell me of a person in
love, I easily understand your meaning, and form
a just conception of his situation; but never can
mistake that conception for the real disorders and
agitations of that passion.

All our ideas are copies of our impressions.
When we analyse our thoughts or ideas, we always find, that they resolve themselves, however
compounded, into such simple ideas, as were copied from a precedent feeling or sentiment. If it
happen from a defect of the organ, that a man is
not sensible of any species of sensation, we always
find that he is as little susceptible of the correspondent ideas. A blind man can form no notion
of colours; a deaf man of sounds. The case is
the same, if the object, proper for exciting any
sensation, has never been applied to the organ.
A Laplander or Negro has no notion of the re-   lish

lifh of wine. A man of mild manners can form no idea of inveterate revenge. There is a phenomenon, which may prove it not to be impoffible for ideas to arife independent of impreffions. The feveral ideas of colours and of founds are really different from each other, though refembling. If this be true of different colours, it muft be fo of the different fhades of the fame colour; each fhade produces a diftinct idea. Suppofe a perfon to have enjoyed his fight thirty years, and to have become acquainted perfectly with colours of all kinds, except one particular fhade of blue. Let all the different fhades of that colour, except that fingle one, be placed before him, defcending gragually from the deepeft to the lighteft; it is plain that he will perceive a blank where that fhade is wanting; and it feems poffible for him, from his own imagination, to fupply this deficiency, and raife up to himfelf the idea of that particular fhade, though it had never been conveyed to him by his fenfes. Simple ideas, therefore, are not always, in every inftance, derived from correfpondent impreffions.

HUME.

HEATHEN IDOLATRY.

THE Heathen idolatry is a common topic of declamation and abufe on occafions of this nature.

It

It ftands, with modern abfurdity and folly, in the
fame circumftances with a woman who has been
beautiful, but whofe charms are faded, and who
is ever the object of the moft malignant fatire to
another who is diftinguifhed with a native and
original uglinefs.   The fuperftitions of the ancients, like their beautiful edifices, are defaced
only by time and violence.   The communities of
antiquity, in their decline, feem to have been like
fome great minds in the decline of life; who are
faid to retain their former conclufions, while they
have totally forgotten the premiffes and calculations which had led them to them.   The Heathen
mythology is natural philofophy allegorifed and
abufed by poets and priefts : Jupiter and Juno,
and Minerva and Neptune, were perfonifications
of real principles in nature; whereas the phantoms of modern fuperftition are reprefentations of
no true objects in heaven or earth.   The former
were in the ftate of all fimilies, metaphors, and
poetical ornaments, liable to be mifunderftood
and abufed; but they were alfo ufeful, and fur-
nifhed the moft elegant entertainment and pleafure : the latter, being the produce only of per-
verted and gloomy imaginations, are never ufeful,
never pleafing; but merely the inftruments of impofture, to intimidate and injure mankind.   Idolatry, therefore, was to be reftrained, as all exceffes of natural paffions are to be reftrained. For,

by

by fixing the attention wholly on poetical perfons, men were led away from nature, the only fource of truth; they eafily wandered into follies and vices; and their whole fyftem fell a facrifice to more extravagant and myfterious inftitutions. The emperor Julian feems to have had thefe ideas; and he lived at the very period of this remarkable revolution. He probably thought, that men were not at fo great diftance from the real principles of nature and truth, and would not require fo much trouble to lead them back to thofe principles, while they adhered to the Heathen idolatry, as when the ambitious Chriftian priefts had plunged them into the fathomlefs abyfs of myfteries; awed them with heavenly and infernal phantoms; bound them down to unintelligible and ufelefs dogmas; and reduced them to the worft fpecies of flavery. Succeeding events proved that he judged rightly. Men, by refigning their faculties to pretended heavenly commiffioners, and becoming the tools of their ambition, exhibited a fcene of ignorance, barbarifm, cruelty, and villany, beyond any thing which had ever difhonoured the annals of the world. This wretched ftate remained until fome fragments of ancient learning were recovered; and fome perfons were tempted, by manly thoughts and fine writing, into reafon, into herefies, and rebellions.

WILLIAMS.

E 3

ILL

ILL-HUMOUR.

NOTHING concerns me more than to see people in ill-humour; to see men torment one another; particularly when, in the flower of their age, in the very season of pleasure, they waste their few short days of sunshine in quarrels and disputes, and only feel their error when it is too late to repair it.

We are apt to complain that we have but few happy days; and it appears to me that we have very little right to complain. If our hearts were always in a proper disposition to receive the good things which Heaven sends us, we should acquire strength to support the evil when they come upon us. But, you will perhaps say, we cannot always command our tempers; so much depends on the constitution; when the body is ill at ease, the mind is so likewise. Well, let us look upon this disposition as a disease, and see if there is no remedy for it. I think, indeed, a great deal might be done in this respect. Ill-humour may be compared to sloth. It is natural to man to be indolent; but if once we get the better of our indolence, we then go on with alacrity, and find a real pleasure in being active. If you object, that we are not masters of ourselves, and still less of our feelings; I must answer, that we don't know how

far

far our ftrength will go till we have tried it; that
the fick confult phyficians, and fubmit to the moft
fcrupulous regimen, and the moft naufeous medicines, to recover their health.

Is it not enough that we are without the power
to make one another happy, but muft we deprive
each other of that fatisfaction, which, left to ourfelves, we might often be capable of enjoying?
Show me the man who has ill-humour, and who
hides it; who bears the whole burden of it himfelf,
without interrupting the pleafures of thofe about
him. No; ill-humour arifes from a confcioufnefs
of our own want of merit; from a difcontent
which always accompanies that envy which fool-
ifh vanity engenders. We diflike to fee people
happy, unlefs their happinefs is the work of our
own hands. Wo unto thofe who make ufe of
their power over a human heart to deprive it of
the fimple pleafure it would naturally enjoy! All
the favours, all the attention in the world, cannot for a moment make amends for the lofs of that
happinefs which a cruel tyranny deftroys.

We fhould fay to ourfelves every day, What
good can I do to my friends? I can only endeavour not to interrupt them in their pleafures, and
try to augment the happinefs which I myfelf partake of. When their fouls are tormented by a violent paffion, when their hearts are rent with grief,
I cannot give them relief for a moment.

And

And when at length a fatal malady seizes the unhappy being, whose untimely grave was prepared by thy hand—when, stretched out and exhausted, he raises his dim eyes to heaven, and the damps of death are on his brow—then thou standest before him like a condemned criminal; thou seest thy fault, but it is too late; thou feelest thy want of power; thou feelest, with bitterness, that all thou canst give, all thou canst do, will not restore the strength of thy unfortunate victim, nor procure for him a moment of consolation.

GOETHE.

WORKS OF IMAGINATION GENERALLY PLEASING.

WORKS of imagination are more generally admired, because there are few who have not experienced some passion. Most persons are better pleased with the beauty of a description, than with the depth of an idea; because they have felt more than they have seen, and seen more than they have reflected. From hence we may conclude, that the paintings of the passions must be more generally agreeable than those of natural objects; and a poetical description of the same objects must find more admirers than philosophical works.　　HELVETIUS.

INDIANS.

INDIANS JUSTLY INCREDULOUS WITH
REGARD TO ICE.

THE Indian prince, who refused to believe the first relations concerning the effects of frost, reasoned justly; and it naturally required very strong testimony to engage his assent to facts that arose from a state of nature with which he was unacquainted, and bore so little analogy to those events of which he had had constant and uniform experience. Though they were not contrary to his experience, they were not conformable to it. No Indian, it is evident, could have experience that water did not freeze in cold climates. This is placing nature in a situation quite unknown to him; and it is impossible for him, *à priori*, to tell what will result from it. It is making a new experiment; the consequence of which is always uncertain. One may sometimes conjecture from analogy what will follow; but still this is but conjecture. And it must be confessed, that in the present case of freezing, the event follows contrary to the rules of analogy; and is such as a rational Indian would not look for. The operations of cold upon water are not gradual, according to the degrees of cold; but whenever it comes to the freezing point, the water passes in a moment from the utmost liquidity to perfect hardness. Such

an

an event may be denominated *extraordinary*, and requires a pretty ftrong teftimony to render it credible to people in a warm climate : but ftill it is not *miraculous*, nor contrary to uniform expe- rience of the courfe of nature, in cafes where all the circumftances are the fame. The inhabitants of Sumatra have always feen water fluid in their own climate, and the freezing of their rivers ought to be deemed a prodigy: but they never faw water in Mufcovy during the winter; and there- fore they cannot reafonably be pofitive what would there be the confequence.

Hume.

The Exposition of INFANTS.

The practice of expofing children in their early infancy was very common among the ancients; and is not mentioned by any author of thofe times with the horror it deferves, or fcarcely even with difapprobation. Plutarch, the humane, good-na- tured Plutarch, recommends it as a virtue in At- talus, king of Pergamus, that he murdered, or, if you will, expofed all his own children, in order to leave his crown to the fon of his brother Eu- menes; fignalizing in this manner his gratitude and affection to Eumenes, who had left him his heir preferably to that fon. It was Solon, the moft celebrated of the fages of Greece, that gave

parents

parents permission by law to kill their children. And, perhaps, by an odd connection of causes, this barbarous practice of the ancients increased the population of those times. By removing the terrors of too numerous a family, it would engage many people in marriage; and such is the force of natural affection, that very few, in comparison, would have resolution enough, when it came to the push, to carry into execution their former intentions; though Plutarch, it must be owned, speaks of it as a general practice of the poor. China, the only country where this practice of exposing children prevails at present, is the most populous country we know; and every man is married before he is twenty. Such early marriages could scarcely be general, had not men the prospect of getting rid of their children.

HUME.

ON THE SAME SUBJECT.

THE exposition, that is, the murder, of new-born infants, was a practice allowed of in almost all the states of Greece, even among the polite and civilized Athenians; and whenever the circumstances of the parent rendered it inconvenient to bring up the child, to abandon it to hunger or to wild beasts was regarded without blame or censure. This practice had probably begun in the

times

times of the moſt ſavage barbarity. The imaginations of men had been firſt made familiar with
it in that earlieſt period of ſociety, and the uniform continuance of the cuſtom had hindered
them afterwards from perceiving its enormity.
We find at this day, that this practice prevails
among all ſavage nations; and in that rudeſt and
loweſt ſtate of ſociety it is undoubtedly more par-
donable than in any other. The extreme indi-
gence of a ſavage is often ſuch, that he himſelf is
frequently expoſed to the greateſt extremity of
hunger; he often dies of pure want; and it is frequently impoſſible for him to ſupport both himſelf and his child. We cannot wonder, therefore, that, in this caſe, he ſhould abandon it.
One who, in flying from an enemy whom it
was impoſſible to reſiſt, ſhould throw down his
infant becauſe it retarded his flight, would ſurely
be excuſable; ſince by attempting to ſave it, he
could only hope for the conſolation of dying with
it. That in this ſtate of ſociety, therefore, a parent ſhould be allowed to judge whether he can
bring up his child, ought not to ſurpriſe us ſo
greatly. In the latter ages of Greece, however,
the ſame thing was permitted from views of remote intereſt or convenience, which could by no
means excuſe it. Uninterrupted cuſtom had by
this time ſo thoroughly authoriſed the practice,
that not only the looſe maxims of the world tole-

2   rated

rated this barbarous cuſtom, but even the doctrine
of philoſophers, which ought to have been more
juſt and accurate, was led away by the eſtabliſhed
practice; and upon this, as upon many other occaſions, inſtead of cenſuring, ſupported the horrible abuſe, by far-fetched conſiderations of public utility. Ariſtotle talks of it as of what the
magiſtrate ought upon many occaſions to encourage. The humane Plato is of the ſame opinion;
and, with all that love of mankind which ſeems
to animate all his writings, no where marks this
practice with diſapprobation. When cuſtom can
give ſanction to ſo dreadful a violation of humanity, we may well imagine that there is ſcarce any
particular practice ſo groſs which it cannot authoriſe. Such a thing, we hear men every day
ſaying, is commonly done; and they ſeem to think
this a ſufficient apology for what in itſelf is the
moſt unjuſt and unreaſonable conduct.

A. SMITH.

INGRATITUDE.

INGRATITUDE would be more rare, if benefits
upon uſury were leſs common. Nothing can be
more natural than to love thoſe who do us ſer-
vice. The heart of man is ſelf-intereſted, but
never ungrateful; and the obliged are leſs to be
charged with ingratitude, than their benefactors

VOL. II.   †   F   with

with felf-intereft. If you fell me your favours,
let us fettle the price; but if you pretend to give,
and afterwards expect to make terms with me,
you are guilty of fraud: it is their being given
gratis which renders them ineftimable. The heart
will receive laws only from itfelf: by endeavouring to enflave it, you give it liberty; and by leaving it at liberty, it becomes your flave. When
the fiflerman throws his bait into the water, the
fifh affemble and continue round him without fufpicion; but when, caught by the concealed hook,
they perceive him draw the line, they then endeavour to efcape. Is the fifherman their benefactor, or are the fifh ungrateful? Do we ever fee
a man, who is forgotten by his benefactor, forget
that benefactor? On the contrary, he fpeaks of
him with pleafure, and never thinks of him without emotion: and if by chance he has it in his
power to make any return for the favours he has
received, with what joy he fnatches the opportunity; with what rapture he exclaims, *Now it is
my turn to oblige!* Such is the true voice of nature. A real benefit can never produce ingratitude.

ROUSSEAU.

THE

The important Precept of Morality, do no INJURY to any one.

The most important lesson of morality is, *Never to do any injury to any one.* Even the positive precept of doing good, if not made subordinate to this, is dangerous, false, and contradictory. Who is there that doth not do good? All the world, even the vicious man, does good to one party or the other: he will often make one person happy at the expence of making an hundred miserable. Hence arise all our calamities. The most sublime virtues are negative; they are also the most difficult to put in practice, because they are attended with no ostentation, and are even above that pleasure so flattering to the heart of man, that of sending away others satisfied with our benevolence. O! how much good must that man necessarily do his fellow-creatures, if such a man there be, who never did any of them harm! What intrepidity of soul, what constancy of mind, are necessary here! It is not, however, by reasoning on this maxim, but by endeavouring to put it in practice, that all its difficulty is to be discovered. The injunction of doing no harm to any one, infers that of doing the least possible harm to the community in general; for in a state of society, the good of one man necessarily becomes

F 2 the

the evil of another. The relation is essential to
the thing itself, and cannot be changed. We may
inquire on this principle, Which is best; man in
a state of society, or in a state of solitude? A certain noble author hath said, *None but a wicked
man might exist alone:* for my part, I say, *None but
a good man might exist alone.* If the latter proposition be less sententious, it is more true, and more
reasonable, than the former. If a vicious man
were alone, what harm could he put in practice?
It is in society only that he finds the implements
of mischief. ROUSSEAU.

INTENTIONS NOT THE OBJECTS OF HUMAN JUDGMENT.

WE cannot judge of intentions. How is it possible? It is seldom or never that an action is the
effect of a sentiment; we ourselves are often ignorant of the motives by which we are determined. A rich man bestows a comfortable subsist-
ence on a worthy man reduced to poverty. Doubtless he does a good action; but is this action simply the desire of rendering a man happy? Pity,
the hopes of gratitude, vanity itself; all these different motives separately, or aggregately, may
they not, unknown to himself, have determined
him to that commendable action? Now if a man
be, in general, ignorant himself of the motives of
his

his own generous actions, how can the public be
acquainted with them? Thus it is only from the
actions of men that we can judge of their virtue.
A man, for inftance, has twenty degrees of paffion for virtue; but he has thirty degrees of love
for a woman; and this woman would inftigate
him to be guilty of murder. Upon this fuppofi-
tion, it is certain, that this perfon is nearer guilt
than he who, with only ten degrees of paffion for
virtue, has only five degrees of love for fo wicked
a woman. Hence we may conclude, that of two
men, the more honeft in his actions has fometimes the leffer paffion for virtue. The virtue of
men greatly depends on the circumftances in
which they are placed. Virtuous men have too
often funk under a ftrange feries of unhappy
events. He who warrants his virtue in every poffible fituation, is either an impoftor or a fool;
characters equally to be diftrufted.

HELVETIUS.

JUSTICE.

JUSTICE has two different foundations, viz.
that of *intereft*, when men obferve that it is impoffible to live in fociety without reftraining themfelves by certain rules; and that of *morality*, when
this intereft is once obferved, and men receive a
pleafure from the view of fuch actions as tend to

the

the peace of society, and an uneasiness from such as are contrary to it. It is the voluntary convention and artifice of men which makes the first interest take place; and therefore those laws of justice are so far to be considered as artificial. After that interest is once established and acknowledged, the sense of morality in the observance of these rules follows *naturally*, and of itself: though it is certain, that it is also augmented by a new *artifice*; and that the public instructions of politicians, and the private education of parents, contribute to the giving a sense of honour and duty in the strict regulation of our actions with regard to the properties of others. Though justice be artificial, the sense of its morality is natural. It is the combination of men, in a system of conduct, which renders any act of justice beneficial to society. But when once it has that tendency, we *naturally* approve of it; and if we did not so, it is impossible any combination or convention could ever produce that sentiment.

Most of the inventions of men are subject to change. They depend upon humour and caprice. They have a vogue for a time, and then sink into oblivion. It may, perhaps, be apprehended, that if justice were allowed to be a human invention, it must be placed on the same footing. But the cases are widely different. The interest on which justice is founded is the greatest imaginable; and

justice

juftice extends to all times and places. It cannot poffibly be ferved by any other invention. It is obvious, and difcovers itfelf on the very firft formation of fociety. All thefe caufes render the rules of juftice ftedfaft and immutable; at leaft as immutable as human nature: And if they were founded on original inftinct, could they have any greater ftability?   HUME.

ON THE SAME SUBJECT.

THERE is one virtue, of which the general rules determine with the greateft exactnefs every external action which it requires. This virtue is *Juftice*. The rules of juftice are accurate in the higheft degre; and admit of no exceptions or modifications, but fuch as may be afcertained as accurately as the rules themfelves, and which generally, indeed, flow from the very fame principles with them. The man therefore who, in this virtue, refines the leaft, and adheres with the moft obftinate ftedfaftnefs to the general rules themfelves, is the moft commendable, and the moft to be depended upon. Though the end of the rules of juftice be, to hinder us from hurting our neighbour, it may frequently be a crime to violate them, though we could pretend, with fome pretext of reafon, that this particular violation could do no hurt. A man often becomes a villain the moment he he begins, even in his own heart, to chicane in this manner. The moment he thinks of departing from the most staunch and positive adherence to what those inviolable precepts prescribe to him, he is no longer to be trusted; and no man can say what degree of guilt he may arrive at. The thief imagines he does no evil when he steals from the rich what he supposes they may easily want, and what possibly they may never even know has been stolen from them. The adulterer imagines he does no evil when he corrupts the wife of his friend, provided he covers his intrigue from the suspicion of the husband, and does not disturb the peace of the family. When once we begin to give way to such refinements, there is no enormity so gross of which we may not be capable.

A. SMITH.

THE ORIGIN OF JUSTICE AND PROPERTY.

IT has been asserted, that justice arises from *human conventions*, and proceeds from the voluntary choice, consent, and combination of mankind. If by *convention* be here meant a promise (which is the most usual sense of the word) nothing can be more absurd than this position. The observance of promises is itself one of the most considerable parts of justice; and we are not surely bound to keep our word, because we have given

our

our word to keep it. But if by convention be meant a fenfe of common intereſt, which fenfe each man feels in his own breaſt, which he remarks in his fellows, and which carries him, in concurrence with others, into a general plan or fyſtem of actions, which tends to public utility; it muſt be owned, that in this fenfe juſtice ariſes from human conventions. For if it be allowed (what is indeed evident), that the particular conſequences of a particular act of juſtice may be hurtful to the public as well as individuals; it follows, that every man, in embracing that virtue, muſt have an eye to the whole plan or fyſtem, and muſt expect the concurrence of his fellows in the fame conduct and behaviour. Did all his views terminate in the confequences of each act of his own, his benevolence and humanity, as well as his felf-love, might often prefcribe to him meafures of conduct very different from thofe which are agreeable to the ſtrict rules of right and juſtice.

Thus two men pull the oars of a boat by common convention, for common intereſt, without any promife or contract: Thus gold and filver are made the meafures of exchange: Thus fpeech, and words, and language, are fixed by human convention and agreement. Whatever is advantageous to two or more perfons if all perform their part, but what lofes all advantage if only one

one perform, can arife from no other principle. There would otherwife be no motive for any one of them to enter into that fcheme of conduct.

This theory concerning the origin of property, and confequently of juftice, is, in the main, the fame with that hinted and adopted by Grotius. (*De jure belli et pacis*, Lib. ii. cap. 2. § 2. art. 4, & 5.)

The word *natural* is commonly taken in fo many fenfes, and is of fuch a loofe fignification, that it feems to little purpofe to difpute, if juftice be natural or not. If felf-love, if benevolence, be natural to man; if reafon and fore-thought be alfo natural; then may the fame epithet be applied to juftice, order, fidelity, property, fociety. Mens inclinations, their neceffities, lead them to combine; their underftandings and experience tell them, that this combination is impoffible where each governs himfelf by no rule, and pays no regard to the poffeffions of others. And from thefe paffions and reflections conjoined, as foon as we obferve like paffions and reflections in others, the fentiment of juftice, through all ages, has infallibly and certainly had place, to fome degree or other, in every individual in the human fpecies. In fo fagacious an animal, what neceffarily arifes from the exertion of the intellectual faculties may juftly be efteemed natural.

Natural may be oppofed, either to what is *unufual*

uſual, miraculous, or *artificial.* In the two former ſenſes, juſtice and property are undoubtedly
natural. But as they ſuppoſe reaſon, fore-thought,
deſign, and a ſocial union and confederacy among
men, perhaps that epithet cannot be ſtrictly, in
the laſt ſenſe, applied to them. Had men lived
without ſociety, property had never been known;
and neither juſtice nor injuſtice had ever exiſted.
But ſociety among human creatures had been impoſſible without reaſon and fore-thought. Inferior animals that unite, are guided by inſtinct,
which ſupplies the place of reaſon. But all theſe
diſputes are merely verbal.

The rules of equity and juſtice depend entirely
on the particular ſtate and condition of men in ſociety; and owe their origin and exiſtence to that
utility which reſults to the public from their ſtrict
and regular obſervance. Reverſe in any conſiderable circumſtance the condition of men; produce extreme abundance, or extreme neceſſity;
implant in the human breaſt perfect moderation
and humanity, or perfect rapaciouſneſs and ma-
lice: by rendering juſtice totally uſeleſs, you thereby totally deſtroy its eſſence, and ſuſpend its obligation on mankind.

The common ſituation of ſociety is a medium
among all theſe extremes. We are naturally partial to ourſelves and to our friends; but are capable of learning the advantage reſulting from a
more

more equitable conduct. Few enjoyments are given us from the open and liberal hand of nature;
but by art, labour, and industry, we can extract
them in great abundance. Hence the ideas of
property become neceſſary in all civil ſociety;
hence juſtice derives its uſefulneſs to the public;
and hence alone ariſe its merit and moral obligation. Examine the writers on the laws of nature, and you will always find, that whatever
principles they ſet out with, they are ſure to terminate here at laſt; and to aſſign as the ultimate
reaſon for every rule which they eſtabliſh, the convenience and neceſſities of mankind. A confeſ-
ſion thus extorted, in oppoſition to ſyſtems, has
more authority than if it had been made in pro-
ſecution of them. Does any one ſcruple, in extraordinary caſes, to violate all regard to the private property of individuals, and ſacrifice to public intereſt a diſtinction which had been eſtabliſhed for the ſake of that intereſt? The ſafety
of the people is the ſupreme law. All other particular laws are ſubordinate to it, and dependent
on it: And if, in the *common* courſe of things,
they be followed and regarded, it is only becauſe
the public ſafety and intereſt *commonly* demand ſo
equal and impartial an adminiſtration.

All queſtions of property are ſubordinate to the
authority of civil laws; which extend, reſtrain,
modify, and alter the rules of natural juſtice, ac-

2   cording

cording to the particular convenience of each
community. The laws have, or ought to have,
a conftant reference to the conftitution of government, the manners, the climate, the religion, the
commerce, the fituation of each fociety. *What
is a man's property?* Any thing which it is lawful
for him, and for him alone, to ufe. *But what
rule have we by which we can diftinguifh thefe objects?* Here we muft have recourfe to ftatutes,
cuftoms, analogies, precedents, and a hundred
other circumftances; fome variable and arbitrary.
But the ultimate point in which they all profef-
fedly terminate is, the intereft and happinefs of
human fociety.   HUME.

K.

The KNOWLEDGE
Of historical Facts and of speculative Opinions is not propagated in the same Manner.

AN hiſtorical fact, while it paſſes by oral tradition from eye-witneſſes and cotemporaries, is diſguiſed in every ſucceſſive narration, and may at laſt retain but very ſmall, if any, reſemblance of the original truth on which it was founded. The frail memories of men, their love of exaggeration, their ſupine carelefsnefs; theſe principles, if not corrected by books and writing, ſoon pervert the accounts of hiſtorical events; where argument or reaſoning has little or no place, nor can ever recal the truth which has once eſcaped thoſe narrations. It is thus the fables of Hercules,

cules, Thefeus, Bacchus, are fuppofed to have
been originally founded in true hiftory, corrupted
by tradition. But with regard to fpeculative opinions, the cafe is far otherwife. If thefe opinions
be founded in arguments fo clear and obvious as
to carry conviction with the generality of mankind, the fame arguments which at firft diffufed
the opinions will ftill preferve them in their original purity. If the arguments be more abftrufe,
and more remote from vulgar apprehenfion, the
opinions will always be confined to a few perfons; and as foon as men leave the contemplation of the arguments, the opinions will be immediately loft and buried in oblivion.

HUME.

SENSITIVE KNOWLEDGE of PARTICULAR EXISTENCE.

THERE can be nothing more certain, than that
the idea we receive from an external object is in
our minds; this is intuitive knowledge. But whether there be any thing more than barely that idea
in our minds, whether we can thence certainly
infer the exiftence of any thing without us which
correfponds to that idea, is that whereof fome
men think there may be a queftion made; becaufe men may have fuch ideas in their minds
when no fuch thing exifts, no fuch object affects

G 2

their.

their senses. But yet here, I think, we are provided with an evidence that puts us past doubt-
ing: For I ask any one, whether he be not invin-
cibly conscious to himself of a different perception, when he looks on the sun by day, and thinks
on it by night; when he actually tastes worm-
wood, or smells a rose, or only thinks on that favour or odour? We as plainly find the difference
there is between an idea revived in our minds
by our own memory, and actually coming into
our minds by our senses, as we do between any
two distinct ideas. If any one say, a dream may
do the same thing, and all these ideas may be
produced in us without any external objects; he
may please to dream that I make him this answer: 1. That it is no great matter whether I remove this scruple or no; where all is but dream,
reasoning and arguments are of no use, truth and
knowledge nothing. 2. That I believe he will
allow a manifest difference between dreaming of
being in the fire, and being actually in it. But
yet if he be resolved to appear so sceptical as to
maintain, that what I call being actually in the
fire is nothing but a dream, and we cannot
thereby certainly know that any such thing as fire
exists without us; I answer, that we certainly
finding that pleasure or pain follows upon the application of certain objects to us, whose existence
we perceive, or dream that we perceive, by our
                                              senses;

fenfes; this certainty is as great as our happinefs or mifery, beyond which we have no concernment to know, or to be.

Locke.

KNOWLEDGE, PARTLY NECESSARY, PARTLY VOLUNTARY.

IF our knowledge were altogether necessary, all mens knowledge would not only be alike, but every man would know all that is knowable: and if it were wholly voluntary, fome men fo little regard or value it, that they would have extremely little or none at all. Men that have fenfes cannot choofe but receive fome ideas by them; and if they have memory, they cannot but retain fome of them; and if they have any diftinguifhing faculty, cannot but perceive the agreement or difagreement of fome of them one with another: as he that has his eyes, if he will open them by day, cannot but fee fome objects, and perceive a difference in them. But though a man, with his eyes open in the light, cannot but fee; yet there may be certain objects which he may choofe whether he will turn his eyes to; there may be in his reach a book containing pictures and difcourfes capable to delight or inftruct him, which yet he may never have the will to open, never take the the pains to look into.

G 3

Thera

There is also another thing in a man's power, and that is, though he turns his eyes sometimes toward an object, yet he may choose whether he will curiously survey it, and with an intent application endeavour to observe accurately all that is visible in it. But yet what he does see, he cannot see otherwise than he does. It depends not on his will to see that black which appears yellow; nor to persuade himself, that what actually scalds him feels cold. The earth will not appear painted with flowers, nor the fields covered with verdure, whenever he has a mind to it: in the cold winter, he cannot help seeing it white and hoary if he will look abroad. Just thus is it with our understanding; all that is voluntary in our knowledge is the employing or with-holding any of our faculties from this or that sort of objects, and a more or less accurate survey of them : but they being employed, our will hath no power to determine the knowledge of the mind one way or other; that is done only by the objects themselves, as far as they are clearly discovered. And therefore, as far as mens senses are conversant about external objects, the mind cannot but receive those ideas which are presented by them, and be informed of the existence of things without : and so far as mens thoughts converse with their own determined ideas, they cannot but, in some measure, observe the agreement or disagreement
ment

ment that is to be found amongſt ſome of them; which is ſo far knowledge: and if they have names for thoſe ideas which they have thus conſidered, they muſt neceſſarily be aſſured of the truth of thoſe propoſitions which expreſs that agreement or diſagreement they perceive in them, and be undoubtedly convinced of thoſe truths. For what a man ſees, he cannot but ſee; and what he perceives, he cannot but know that he perceives.

Thus he that hath got the ideas of numbers, and hath taken the pains to compare one, two, and three to ſix, cannot chooſe but know that they are equal: he that hath got the idea of a triangle, and found the ways to meaſure its angles and their magnitudes, is certain that its three angles are equal to two right ones; and can as little doubt of that, as of this truth, " that it is impoſſible for " the ſame thing to be, and not to be."

He alſo that hath the idea of an intelligent, but frail and weak being, made by and depending on another, who is eternal, omnipotent, perfectly wiſe and good, will as certainly know that man is to honour, fear, and obey God, as that the ſun ſhines when he ſees it. For if he hath but the ideas of two ſuch beings in his mind, and will turn his thoughts that way, and conſider them, he will as certainly find that the inferior, finite, and dependent, is under an obligation to obey the ſupreme and infinite, as he is certain to find, that

three,

three, four, and seven are less than fifteen, if he
will consider and compute these numbers; nor
can he be surer in a clear morning that the sun is
risen, if he will but open his eyes and turn them
that way. But yet these truths, being ever so certain, ever so clear, he may be ignorant of either,
or all of them, who will never take the pains to
employ his faculties as he should, to inform himself about them.

LOCKE.

L.

L.

LABOUR.

IT is neceſſary for the happineſs of man, that pleaſure ſhould be the reward of labour; but of a moderate labour. If nature had of itſelf provided for all his wants, it would have made him the moſt pernicious of all preſents; he would have paſſed his days in languor; the idly rich would have been without reſource againſt *l'Ennui*. What palliative could there have been to this evil? None: if all the people were without wants, all would be equally opulent. Where then would the wealthy idler find men to procure him amuſement?—The labour to which man was formerly, they ſay, condemned, was not a puniſhment of heaven, but a benefaction of nature. Labour ſuppoſes deſire; and the man without deſire vegetates without any principle of activity: the body and the ſoul remain, if I may uſe the expreſſion,

in

in the same attitude. Occupation is the happinefs of man. Habit renders labour eafy: if we
do that always without pain which we are always
doing, and if every means of acquiring pleafure
ought to be reckoned among the pleafures, labour
always fills up, in the moft agreeable manner, the
time that feparates a gratified want from the next
that fhall arife, and confequently the twelve only
hours of a day in which we fuppofe the greateft
inequality in the happinefs of men. But to be
occupied and ufe exercife, what is neceffary? A
motive: and of all others that of hunger is the
moft powerful, and moft general. It is this that
commands the peafant to labour in the fields, and
the favage to hunt and fifh in the foreft.—A want
of another kind animates the artift and man of
letters: the defire of reputation, of the public
efteem, and of the pleafures they reprefent. E-
very want, every defire, compels men to labour;
and when they have contracted an early habit, it
becomes agreeable. For want of that habit, idlenefs renders labour hateful; and it is with aver-
fion that men fow, reap, or even think.—One of
the principal caufes of the ignorance and floth of
the Africans, is the fertility of that part of the
world; which fupplies almoft all neceffaries without culture. The African therefore has no motive for reflection; and in fact he reflects but
little. The fame may be faid of the Caribbs. If
they

they be lefs induftrious than the favages of North
America, it is becaufe they have lefs occafion to
labour for fubfiftence.

HELVETIUS.

ON NATIONAL LABOUR.

THE annual labour of every nation is the fund
which originally fupplies it with all the neceffaries and conveniences of life which it annually
confumes, and which confift always either in the
immediate produce of that labour, or in what is
purchafed with that produce from other nations.

According therefore as this produce, or what
is purchafed with it, bears a greater or fmaller
proportion to the number of thofe who are to con-
fume it, the nation will be better or worfe fupplied with all the neceffaries and conveniences
for which it has occafion.

But this proportion muft in every nation be regulated by two different circumftances; firft, by
the fkill, dexterity, and judgment with which its
labour is generally applied; and, fecondly, by the
proportion between the number of thofe who are
employed in ufeful labour, and that of thofe who
are not fo employed. Whatever be the foil, climate, or extent of territory of any particular nation, the abundance or fcantinefs of its annual

supply muſt, in that particular ſituation, depend upon thoſe two circumſtances.

The abundance or ſcantineſs of this ſupply, too, ſeems to depend more upon the former of thoſe two circumſtances than upon the latter. Among the ſavage nations of hunters and fiſhers, every individual who is able to work, is more or leſs employed in uſeful labour, and endeavours to provide, as well as he can, the neceſſaries and conveniences of life, for himſelf, or ſuch of his family or tribe as are either too old, or too young, or too infirm, to go a-hunting or fiſhing. Such nations, however, are ſo miſerably poor, that, from mere want, they are frequently reduced, or, at leaſt, think themſelves reduced, to the neceſſity ſometimes of directly deſtroying, and ſometimes of abandoning, their infants, their old people, and thoſe afflicted with lingering diſeaſes, to periſh with hunger, or to be devoured by wild beaſts. Among civilized and thriving nations, on the contrary, though a great number of people do not labour at all, many of whom conſume the produce of ten times, frequently of a hundred times, more labour than the greater part of thoſe who work; yet the produce of the whole labour of the ſociety is ſo great, that all are often abundantly ſupplied; and a workman, even of the loweſt and pooreſt order, if he is frugal and induſtrious, may enjoy a greater ſhare of the neceſſaries and conveniences

veniences of life than it is poffible for any favage
to acquire.

Whatever be the actual ftate of the fkill, dexterity, and judgment, with which labour is applied
in any nation, the abundance or fcantinefs of its
annual fupply muft depend, during the continuance of that ftate, upon the proportion between
the number of thofe who are annually employed
in ufeful labour, and that of thofe who are not fo
employed. The number of ufeful and productive
labourers is every where in proportion to the quantity of capital ftock which is employed in fetting
them to work, and to the particular way in which
it is fo employed.

Nations tolerably well advanced as to fkill, dexterity, and judgment, in the application of labour, have followed very different plans in the
general conduct or direction of it; and thofe plans
have not all been equally favourable to the great-
nefs of its produce. The policy of fome nations
has given extraordinary encouragement to the induftry of the country, that of others to the induftry of towns. Scarce any nation has dealt equally
and impartially with every fort of induftry. Since
the downfal of the Roman empire, the policy of
Europe has been more favourable to arts, manufactures, and commerce, the induftry of towns;
than to agriculture, the induftry of the country.

Though thofe different plans were, perhaps,

firſt introduced by the private intereſts and prejudices of particular orders of men, without any
regard to, or foreſight of, their conſequences upon
the general welfare of the ſociety; yet they have
given occaſion to very different theories of political œconomy : of which ſome magnify the importance of that induſtry which is carried on in
towns, others of that which is carried on in the
country. Thoſe theories have had a conſiderable
influence, not only upon the opinions of men of
learning, but upon the public conduct of princes
and ſovereign ſtates.

THE LAW OF NATURE.

THERE are ſome who ſay, that at the moment
of our birth God engraves on our hearts the precepts of the natural law. Experience proves the
contrary. If God is to be regarded as the author
of the laws of nature, it is as being the author of
corporeal ſenſibility, which is the mother of human reaſon. This ſort of ſenſibility at the time
of the union of men in ſociety, obliged them to
make among themſelves conventions and laws;
the aſſemblage of which compoſes what is called
the laws of nature. But have thoſe laws been the
ſame among different nations? No: their greater
or leſs perfection was always in proportion to the
progreſs of the human mind; to the greater or

leſs

lefs extent of knowledge that focieties acquired of what was ufeful or prejudicial; and this knowledge has been in all nations the produce of time, experience, and reflection.

HELVETIUS.

On the same Subject.

NATURAL right prefuppofes a law of nature which has eftablifhed that right. But where is this law of nature to be found? Who has produced it? Law is the expreffion of will. The law of nature then muft be the expreffion of will; but of whofe will?—Of nature's? But what is nature? Or is it the expreffion of the will of God, who is fometimes called the Author of nature? But if this be the cafe, where is the difference between this and what is called the law of revelation?

Right is a mere legal term. Where no law is, there is no tranfgreffion, has been faid; with equal truth it might be faid, Where no law is, there is no right. A man acquires a right or property in a thing by the declaration of the legiflator, that he may ufe and enjoy that thing; joined to a promife of the legiflator, expreffed or implied, that he will reftrain every other perfon from depriving him of that thing, or from troubling him in the ufe or enjoyment of it. How is it that a man acquires a right to do or forbear any act? By the de-

claration

claration of the legiſlator, that he may do or forbear it; joined to a promiſe of the legiſlator, expreſſed or implied, that he will reſtrain every other perſon from conſtraining him to forbear the one or to do the other.—As to things antecedently to law, a man may have the uſe and enjoyment of them, but he cannot have the right to them; that is, he may have poſſeſſion, but he cannot have property. As to acts, he may be in the habit of doing or forbearing, but he cannot have the right of exerciſing that habit. For until there is ſome law, tacit or expreſſed, he cannot be ſure that others will be reſtrained from troubling him in the exerciſe of it. He may be free, but without law he cannot have the right of freedom. When men talk of a law of nature, they mean only certain imaginary regulations, which appear to them to be fit and expedient. When they ſay that a man has a natural right to the uſe and enjoyment of any thing, or to do or forbear any act, I am apt to conceive they mean no more, than that it appears to them to be fit and expedient that ſuch a right ſhould be eſtabliſhed. LIND.

LAWS.

THE general object of legiſlature ſhould be variouſly modified in different countries, agreeable to local ſituation, the character of the inhabitants,

bitants, and thofe other circumftances which require that every people fhould have a particular
fyftem of laws, not always the beft in itfelf, but
the beft adapted to that ftate for which it is calculated.——Befides the maxims common to all
nations, every people are poffeffed in themfelves
of fome caufe which influences them in a particular manner, and renders their own fyftem of
laws proper only for themfelves. It is thus that,
in ancient times among the Hebrews, and in
modern times among the Arabians, religion
was made the principal object of national concern; among the Athenians this object was lite-
rature; at Carthage and Tyre it was commerce;
at Rhodes it was navigation, at Sparta war, and
at Rome public virtue. ROUSSEAU.

ON THE SAME SUBJECT.

EVERY law that is not armed with force, or
which from circumftances muft be ineffectual,
fhould not be promulgated. Opinion which reigns
over the minds of men, obeys the flow and in-
direct impreffions of the legiflator, but refifts
them when violently applied; and ufelefs laws
communicate their infignificance to the moft falutary, which are regarded more as obftacles to
be furmounted, than as fafe-guards of the public
good. But, further, our perceptions being limited,

H 3   by

by enforcing the obfervance of laws which are evidently ufelefs, we deftroy the influence of the moft falutary.   Beccaria.

Civil and Ecclesiastical LAWS.

NO ecclefiaftical law fhould be in force till it has received formally the exprefs fanction of the civil government: By this it was that Athens and Rome never had any religious quarrels.—Thofe quarrels appertain only to barbarous nations.—To permit or prohibit working on a holdiay fhould only be in the magiftrate's power; it is not the fit concern of priefts to hinder men from cultivating their grounds.—Every thing relating to marriages fhould depend folely on the magiftrate; and let the priefts be limited to the auguft function of the folemnization.—Lending at intereft ought to be entirely within the cognizance of the civil law, as by it commercial affairs are regulated —All ecclefiaftics whatever fhould, as the ftate's fubjects, in all cafes be under the control and animadverfion of the government.—No prieft fhould have it in his power to deprive a member of fociety of the leaft privilege on pretence of his fins: for a prieft being himfelf a finner, is to pray for finners; he has no bufinefs to try and condemn them.——Magiftrates, farmers, and priefts, are alike to contribute to the expence of the

the ftate, as alike belonging to the ftate.—One
weight, one meafure, one cuftom. The punifhments of criminals fhould be of ufe: when a man
is hanged, he is good for nothing; whereas a man
condemned to the public works ftill benefits his
country, and is a living admonition.—Every law
fhould be clear, uniform, and precife; explana-
tions are for the moft part corruptions.—The
only infamy fhould be vice.—Taxes to be propor-
tionate.—A law fhould never clafh with cuftom;
for if the cuftom be good, the law muft be faulty.

VOLTAIRE.

INTERPRETATION OF LAWS.

THERE is nothing more dangerous than the
common axiom, *The fpirit of the laws is to be confidered.* To adopt it, is to give way to the tor-
rent of opinions. This may feem a paradox to
vulgar minds, which are more ftrongly affected
by the fmalleft diforder before their eyes, than by
the moft pernicious, though remote, confequences
produced by one falfe principle adopted by a nation.—Our knowledge is in proportion to our
ideas. The more complex thefe are, the greater
is the variety of pofitions in which they may be
confidered. Every man hath his own particular
point of view, and at different times fees the fame
objects in very different lights. *The fpirit of the
laws*

laws will then be the refult of the good or bad logic of the judge: and this will depend on his good or bad digeftion; on the violence of his paffions; on the rank and condition of the accufed, or on his connections with the judge; and on all thefe little circumftances which change the appearances of objects in the fluctuating mind of man. Hence we fee the fate of a delinquent changed many times in paffing through the different courts of judicature, and his life and liberty victims to the falfe ideas or ill-humour of the judge, who miftakes the vague refult of his own confufed reafoning for the juft interpretation of the laws. We fee the fame crimes punifhed in a different manner at different times in the fame tribunals; the confequence of not having confulted the conftant and invariable voice of the laws, but the erring inftability of arbitrary interpretation. The diforders which may arife from a rigorous obfervance of the letter of penal laws, are not to be compared with thofe produced by the interpretation of them. The firft are temporary inconveniences, which will oblige the legiflator to correct the letter of the law; the want of precifenefs, and uncertainty of which, has occafioned thefe diforders : and this will put a ftop to the fatal liberty of explaining; the fource of arbitrary and venal declamations. When the code of laws is once fixed, it fhould be obferved

in

in the literal fenfe; and nothing more is left to
the judge than to determine, whether an action
be or be not conformable to the written law.
When the rule of right is a matter of controverfy,
not of fact, the people are flaves to the magiftrates.—Thefe are the means by which fecurity of perfon and property is beft obtained;
which is juft, as it is the purpofe of uniting in
fociety; and it is ufeful, as each perfon may cal-
culate exactly the inconveniences attending every
crime.   BECCARIA.

THE CONTINUNACE OF LAWS DEPENDS ON THE SILENCE OF THE LEGISLATURE.

THE principle of political life lies in the fovereign authority. The ftate doth not fubfift by
virtue of the laws, but by the legiflative power.
The ftatutes of yefterday are not in themfelves
neceffarily binding to-day; but the tacit confirmation of them is prefumed from the filence of
the legiflature, the fovereign being fuppofed inceffantly to confirm the laws not actually repealed. Whatever is once declared to be the will of
the fovereign, continues always fo, unlefs it be
abrogated.

Wherefore then is there fo much refpect paid
to ancient laws? Even for this reafon: It is rational to fuppofe, that nothing but the excellence
of

of the ancient laws could preferve them fo long
in being ; for that, if the fovereign had not found
them always falutary and ufeful, they would have
been repealed. Hence we fee, that the laws, inftead of lofing their force, acquire additional authority by time in every well formed ftate : the
prepoffeffion of their antiquity renders them every
day more venerable ; whereas, in every country
where the laws grow obfolete, and lofe their force
as they grow older, this alone is a proof that the
legiflative power is decayed and the ftate extinct.

ROUSSEAU.

THE EFFECT OF LEGAL RESTRAINTS ON HUMAN NATURE.

THE regularity and induftry we find in common life are the effects of neceffity ; and that
neceffity is occafioned by fear. Hence that diffa-
tisfaction and gloom which ever attend them.
Man is not made to be forced even into happinefs ; and that fociety is ever ineffectual and
miferable in proportion to the number and feverity of its legal reftraints. The mechanic regularity and order, which are the confequences
of fubmitting all actions to the direction of laws,
and to the influence of penalties, never produce
happinefs : they even deftroy the firft principle of
its

it. This, however, is the confequence of public vices in communities which have been originally ill conftituted; and which, from many caufes not immediately arifing from their conftitution, have had their exiftence continued for many ages. This feems to be the cafe of China, where the government has furvived the ufual periods of profperity, luxury, and vice; and has fettled into an univerfal dominion of law, without moral virtue, and even at the expence of real wifdom and happinefs. It would be difficult for a Chinefe to perform an action which has not been referred to by fome law, or fome regulation. A wife and virtuous Chinefe muft of confequence be a phenomenon.   WILLIAMS.

LEGISLATURE and its OMNIPOTENCE.

IF any one fhould afk, What is the civil liberty of a nation or community? I fhould lead him to anfwer himfelf, by putting this other queftion in return: What are the civil reftraints by which a community can be bound? If this community is the whole of an independent nation, the idea of civil liberty feems not at all applicable to it, becaufe it can be under no civil reftraints. Being independent, it muft make its own laws to be governed by: but thefe laws cannot bind the whole

as one body; for this one body can certainly repeal the whole at pleasure: and it is an inconsistency to say, that any person, individual or col-
lective, is bound by a law which he can at pleasure repeal. I do not say that a nation cannot
bind itself by a treaty or a promise made to a distinct nation: but this is not a civil tie; this tie
has its strength from the laws of nature, from
that branch of them called the laws of nations.
If a part of an independent nation obtains the
name of a community, it is evident that such community may be subject to civil laws; those made
by the legislative power of the whole nation,
wherever that resides. That the legislature is not
omnipotent, as opposed to the whole people, is
clear enough; for the whole people must include
the members of the legislature: and it would be
absurd to say, that the voice of the legislature
alone should prevail over that which is the voice
of the legislature and the rest of the people taken
together. But this voice of the whole people
cannot be had; it is as to practice an absolute
chimera: and when once it is allowed to dispense
with the actual unanimous consent of all individuals because we are under a necessity of dispensing with it, we must go on where the necessity
of human affairs leads us; and that is, if I mistake not, to this point, that those to whom the
ordinary powers of legislation in any state are

com-

committed, muft be confidered as unconfined in
the power of making laws.——What! Were the
Britifh parliament to enact a law, that no one,
on pain of death, fhould tafte food for a month;
would every Englifhman be bound to fubmit to
fuch a law ?—Extreme cafes like this always bring
with them all the remedy they are capable of. It
is to no purpofe to lay down rules about them beforehand: for when they happen, all rules and
laws ceafe; violence alone has place. In vain
would a man, in any particular circumftances, fay
at the time, This is an extreme cafe; and attempt
to juftify himfelf by arguments, in acting as if it
really was fo. It is trifling to argue about fuch
cafes; not merely becaufe thofe who are involved
in them will always act from feelings which pre-
clude the effect of arguments, but becaufe the
cafes cannot be reduced to any diftinct general
ideas, fo as to become a proper fubject for argu-
mentation. Therefore, in all fpeculations, we
may ftill confider the legiflature as unbounded in
its powers. HEY.

ON THE SAME SUBJECT.

THE fupreme power is not limited in itfelf;
nor can it be faid to have any affignable, any certain bounds, unlefs where limited by exprefs convention. That to fay, there is any act they can-

not do;—to speak of any thing of theirs as being illegal—as being void ;—to speak of their exceeding their authority (whatever be the phrase)—their power—their right—is, however common, an abuse of language. The legislature cannot do it: the legislature cannot make a law to this effect. Why cannot? What is there that should hinder them? Why not *this* as well as many other laws murmured at, perhaps as inexpedient, yet submitted to without any question of the right? With men of the same party, with men whose affections are already listed against the law in question, any thing will go down; any rubbish is good that will add fuel to the flame. But with regard to an impartial bystander, it is plain that it is not denying the right of the legislature, their authority, their power, or whatever be the word, —it is not denying that they *can* do what is in question ;—it is not that, I say, or any discourse verging that way, that can tend to give him the smallest satisfaction. Grant even the proposition in general,—what are we the nearer? Grant that there are certain bounds to the authority of the legislature :—Of what use is it to say so, when these bounds are what nobody has ever attempted to mark out to any useful purpose ; that is, in any such manner whereby it might be known beforehand what description a law must be of to fall within, and what to fall beyond, them? Grant

that

that there are things which the legiflature cannot
do; grant that there are laws which exceed the
power of the legiflature to eftablifh :—What rule
does this fort of difcourfe furnifh us for determining whether any one that is in queftion, is
not of the number? As far as I can difcover,
none. Either the difcourfe goes on in the confufion it began; either all refts in vague affertions,
and no intelligible argument at all is offered; or
if any, fuch arguments as are drawn from the
principle of utility; arguments which, in whatever variety of words expreffed, come at laft to
neither more nor lefs than this, That the tendency
of the law is, to a greater or lefs degree, pernicious. If this, then, be the refult of the argument, why not come home to it at once? why
turn afide into a wildernefs of fophiftry, when the
path of plain reafon is ftraight before us? What
practical inferences thofe who maintain this language mean fhould be deduced from it, is not altogether clear; nor perhaps does every one mean
the fame. Some, who fpeak of a law as being
void, would perfuade us to look upon the authors
of it as having thereby forfeited, as the phrafe is,
their whole power, as well that of giving force to
the particular law in queftion as to any other.—
Thefe are they who, had they arrived at the fame
practical conclufion through the principle of utility, would have fpoken of the law as being to

I 2 fuch

such a degree pernicious; as that, were the
bulk of the community to fee it in its true light,
the probable mifchief of refifting it would be lefs
than the probable mifchief of fubmitting to it.
Thefe point, in the firft inftance, at hoftile oppofition.——Thofe who fay nothing about for-
feiture are commonly lefs violent in their views.
Thefe are they who, were they to ground themfelves on the principle of utility, and to ufe our
language, would have fpoken of the law as being
mifchievous indeed, but without fpeaking of it
as being mifchievous to the degree that has been
juft mentioned. The mode of oppofition which
they point to is one which paffes under the appel-
lation of a legal one.—Admit, then, the law to
be void in their fenfe, and mark the confequences.
The idea annexed to the epithet *void* is obtained
from thofe inftances in which we fee it applied
to a private inftrument.—The confequence of a
private inftrument's being void is, that all perfons concerned are to act as if no fuch inftrument
had exifted. The confequence, accordingly, of
a law's being void muft be, that people fhall act
as if there was no fuch law about the matter;
and therefore, that if any perfon, in virtue of the
mandate of the law, fhould do any thing in coercion of another perfon, which without fuch law
he would be punifhable for doing, he would ftill
be punifhable, to wit, by appointment of the judicial

dicial power. Let the law, for inftance, be a law
impofing a tax: a man who fhould go about to
levy the tax by force would be punifhable as a
trefpaffer: fhould he chance to be killed in the
attempt, the perfon killing him fhould *not* be punifhable as for murder: fhould he kill, he himfelf would perhaps be punifhable as for murder.
To whofe office does it appertain to do thofe acts
in virtue of which fuch punifhment would be inflicted? To that of the judges. Applied to practice, then, the effect of this language is, by an
appeal made to the judges, to confer on thofe
magiftrates a controlling power over the acts of
the legiflature. By this management, a particular purpofe might perhaps by chance be anfwered: and let this be fuppofed a good one. Still
what benefit would, from the *general* tendency of
fuch a doctrine, and fuch a practice in conformity to it, accrue to the body of the people; is
more than I can conceive. A parliament, let it
be fuppofed, is too much under the influence of
the Crown, pays too little regard to the interefts
of the people and their fentiments. Be it fo.
The people at any rate, if not fo great a fhare as
they might and ought to have, have had at leaft
fome fhare in choofing it. Give to the judges a
power of annulling its acts, and you transfer a
portion of the fupreme power from an affembly
which the people have had fome fhare at leaft in

I 3

choofing,

choofing, to a fet of men, in the choice of whom
they have not the leaft imaginable fhare ; to a fet
of men appointed folely by the Crown ; appointed
folely and avowedly, and conftantly, by that very
magiftrate whofe partial and occafional influence
is the very grievance you feek to remedy.—In the
heat of debate, fome perhaps would be for faying
of this management, that it was transferring at
once the fupreme authority from the legiflative
power to the judicial. But this would be going
too far on the other fide. There is a wide difference between a pofitive and a negative part in
legiflation. There is a wide difference, again,
between a negative upon reafons given, and a negative without any. The power of repealing a
law, even for reafons given, is a great power;
too great indeed for judges, but ftill very diftinguifhable from, and much inferior to, that of making one. Notwithftanding what has been faid,
it would be in vain to diffemble, but that, upon
occafion, an appeal of this fort may very well anfwer, and has indeed in general a tendency to anfwer in fome fort the purpofes of thofe who
efpoufe the interefts of the people. A public and
authorifed debate on the propriety of the law is
by this means brought on: an opportunity is
gained of impreffing fentiments unfavourable to
it, upon a numerous and attentive audience ;
from fuch an appeal we muft expect no other effects

fects except a certainty of miscarriage. Let us now go back a little. In denying the existence of any assignable bounds to the supreme power, I added, unless where limited by express convention; for this exception I could not but subjoin, while there are such governments as the German empire, Dutch provinces, Swiss cantons, and hath been of old the Achæan league. In this mode of limitation I see not any thing to surprise us. By what is it that any degree of power (meaning political power) is established? It is neither more nor less, as we have already had occasion to observe, than a habit of and a disposition to obedience; habit, speaking with regard to past acts; disposition, with respect to future. This disposition it is as easy, or I am much mistaken, to conceive as being absent with regard to one sort of acts, as present with regard to another; for a body then, which is in other respects supreme, to be conceived as being, with respect to a certain sort of acts, limited, all that is necessary is, that this sort of act be in its description distinguishable from every other.

J. BENTHAM.

THE OMNIPOTENCE OF EVERY LEGISLATURE.

IN all states, great or small, the sentiments of that body of men in whose hands the supreme power

power of the fociety is lodged, muft be underftood to be the fentiments of the whole body.
Thefe deputies or reprefentatives of the people
will make a wrong judgment, and purfue wrong
meafures, if they confult not the good of the
whole fociety, whofe reprefentatives they are;
juft as the people themfelves would make a wrong
judgment, and purfue wrong meafures, if they
did not confult their own good, provided they
could be affembled for that purpofe. No maxims
or rules of policy can be binding upon them, but
fuch as they themfelves fhall judge to be conducive to the public good. Their own reafon and
confcience are their only guide; and the people,
in whofe name they act, their only judge.——In
large ftates, this ultimate feat of power, this tribunal, to which lies an appeal from every other,
and from which no appeal can even be imagined,
is too much hid, and kept out of fight by the
prefent complex forms of government, which derive their authority from it. Hence hath arifen a
want of clearnefs and confiftency in the language
of the friends of liberty. Hence the prepofterous
and flavifh maxim, That whatever is enacted by
that body of men in whom the fupreme power of
the ftate is vefted, muft in all cafes be implicitly
obeyed; and that no attempt to repeal an unjuft
law can be vindicated beyond a fimple remon-
ftrance addreffed to the legiflators. A cafe which

is

is very intelligible, but which can never happen,
will demonſtrate the abſurdity of ſuch a maxim.
Suppoſe the King of England and the two Houſes
of Parliament ſhould make a law, in all the uſual
forms, to exempt the members of either Houſe
from paying taxes to the government, or to take
to themſelves the property of their fellow-citizens.
A law like this would open the eyes of the whole
nation, and ſhow them the true principles of government and the power of governors. The nation would ſee that the moſt regular governments
may become tyrannical, and their governors op-
preſſive, by ſeparating their intereſt from that of
the people whom they govern. Such a law would
ſhow them to be but ſervants, and ſervants who
had ſhamefully abuſed their truſt. In ſuch a caſe,
every man for himſelf would lay his hand upon
his ſword; and the authority of the ſupreme power
of the ſtate would be annihilated. Where regular commiſſions from the abuſed public cannot be
had, every man who has power, and who is actuated with the ſentiments of the public, may aſ-
ſume a public character, and bravely redreſs public wrongs. In ſuch diſmal and critical circumſtances, the ſtifled voice of an oppreſſed country
is a loud call upon every man to exert himſelf;
and whenever that voice ſhall be at liberty, it will
ratify and applaud the action, which it could not
formally authoriſe. PRIESTLEY.

L I.

LIBERTY.

LIBERTY is the abfence of coercion. Coercion is diftinguifhable into conftraint and reftraint; and, again, thefe into phyfical and moral: hence the ideas of phyfical and moral liberty. A man is deprived of his phyfical liberty, when he is conftrained by phyfical force to do or to forbear certain acts: he is deprived of his moral liberty, when, by moral motives, that is, the threat of painful events, to happen in confequence of his doing or forbearing, he is conftrained to do or forbear. But thefe motives muft arife, thefe events muft be brought about by foreign caufes, by extraneous will, over which we have no power. The abfence of phyfical coercion is phyfical liberty. The abfence of moral coercion is moral liberty.—Liberty is nothing pofitive; it is only the abfence of conftraint as well as reftraint.— The well-known ftory of Tarquin and Lucretia will illuftrate this. Had Tarquin entered the chamber of Lucretia attended by the companions of his debaucheries; had they held the haplefs victim while the prince fatiated his luft, this would have been a phyfical coercion. Inftead of this, what did Tarquin? He threatened her with inftant death, and future infamy, if fhe refufed to comply with his folicitations. This was applying

not

not phyſical coercion, but moral.—It is this moral
coercion that the legiſlator applies to make the
ſubject obey the laws. He has not recourſe to
phyſical coercion, except when he means to compel a ſubject to undergo the penalty of having
diſobeyed the laws.——Thus, for inſtance, the
legiſlator publiſhes a law, addreſſed to all his ſubjects, and ſays, " Deprive not another of his
" life." To this he adds a penalty, " If thou
" doſt, thou ſhalt loſe thy own life." This is
moral coercion ; our moral liberty alone is ſuf-
pended.—But when a man has deprived another
of life, then phyſical coercion is applied to compel that individual to ſtay for a certain time at a
certain place ; to appear at a certain time before
certain perſons ; to go afterwards to another certain place, and there to ſubmit to a certain puniſhment. LIND.

ON THE SAME SUBJECT.

LIBERTY is the abſence of reſtraint. The liberty of ſpeaking, of petitioning, of remonſtra-
ting, is not underſtood to mean any thing more
than the not being reſtrained from ſpeaking, &c.
Mr Lind has defined liberty as the abſence of
conſtraint and reſtraint. But it ſeems to me that
conſtraint is underſtood to include ſomething more
than a mere deprivation of liberty. If a perſon
by

by violence puts a pen into my hand, and then constrains or forces me to write certain words or fentences, I am indeed deprived of the liberty of holding my hand ftill, or of moving it the way that I choofe. But that is not all. I am forced into one particular and determinate action; which is fomething more—there is a pofitive violence exerted upon me. The common notion of liberty feems therefore to be merely the abfence of reftraint. To be permitted to do any act is the fame as having liberty to do it. Permiffion in the perfon, or authority permitting, produces liberty in the perfon permitted. This may be thought by fome the beft way of coming at the conception.   HEY.

A GENERAL IDEA OF THE PERFECTION OF CIVIL LIBERTY.

THAT fome civil fociety is neceffary to peace and good order, that many of the reftraints impofed by civil laws are of ufe, is eafily underftood. It may be added, that thofe reftraints which do no good will probably do harm. Many of them, we know, are immediately hurtful, taken fingly; but there is alfo fomething pernicious to be obferved in the effect common to all reftraints. One mifchief attending them is, that they muft by their nature operate in the way of general rules.

Special

Special laws cannot be made to direct the actions of each individual; much less can the attention of the legislature be called out to every action of each. And it is found by experience, that at least such general rules as human foresight is able to invent, however useful in the main, are yet in many particular cases prejudicial. In the opinion of some, perhaps, we might go further, and say, that general rules, by their very essence, do harm, though formed in absolute perfection.——The mischief of restraints may be further seen by recollecting how nice a matter it is to bring the mind of man into such a frame that it will exert its faculties with the greatest energy. When it acts by rule, how dull and ineffective! When it goes out in pursuit of its own inclinations, how lively and forcible! There is—even in a state disturbed by licentiousness, there is an animation which is favourable to the human mind, and which puts it upon exerting its powers. The fear of punishment turns a man's attention upon himself and his own interests. If the restraints are very numerous, he is employed in watching himself in his intercourse with his fellow-citizens, that he may not be caught offending. This habit of caution and minute attention to his conduct damps or extinguishes those generous sentiments which might lead him out to promote the happiness of others, and prompt him to catch with eagerness every opportunity of advancing the public welfare. It is therefore by no means the part of a good and wise legislature to impose restraints where they are not necessary to the production of some good, which may counterbalance the evil of restraining.—If a law commands me to keep to my right hand in walking along the streets, it abridges my liberty. But if, by enjoining the same to every other passenger, it removes many obstructions that would retard me, I am upon the whole more at liberty in walking along than I should have been without the law. We may see also in this trifling instance the evil of laying a restraint where it is not wanting. If the number of passengers is so small as to cause no confusion, it would be a hardship upon people to be under the necessity of observing such a regulation. Nay, we may go still further with the same instance: it shows the imperfection of a general rule. When the streets are thin, the reason of the law ceases, and the advantages of it: the inconvenience remains, without any good to counterbalance it. But where restraints are the necessary means to increase happiness, the best part that human wisdom and human benevolence can act, is to impose them; and, when imposed, they may possibly promote the liberty of the peaceable citizen: not indeed his civil liberty, understood as the absence of civil restraints; for that

most

muſt certainly be diminiſhed by every additional
civil reſtraint: but a law may, by tying up the
hands of the violent and unprincipled, contribute
more to the liberty of the peaceable citizen, than
it takes away from his liberty by the new reſtraint
which it does itſelf impoſe. So that, upon the
whole, he becomes freer to follow his own will,
and is leſs controlled in his actions than he was
before. Not that we muſt expect this always to
be the effect of a law, even in theory: there are
other good purpoſes to be anſwered in legiſlation:
national ſtrength, commerce, the health of the
people, muſt be attended to. But it is plain that
an increaſe of liberty, upon the whole, may be
owing to an immediate diminution of it by the
laws of the community.

We ſeem, then, to be arrived at one uſeful
principle by which a legiſlature may guide itſelf
in the formation of laws: To avoid as much as
poſſible multiplying reſtraints upon the ſubject.
This principle leads to the point of perfection in
civil liberty. It is the nature of ſociety that each
member of it can only be allowed to purſue his
own happineſs in a manner conſiſtent with that
of the other members; or we may ſay, that he
ought to procure his private good through the
medium (as it were) of the public good. Where-
ever that does not require him to be curbed, our
principle would leave him as free as he himſelf

can

can wish or conceive. If he is ambitious of being more free than the public good will allow, he forgets surely that he is a member of civil society.—— But why should any civil restraints at all be imposed? For two reasons; the ignorance of men, and their moral depravity. Did every man perfectly understand his own interests and those of the persons with whom he lived in society, and were his passions and his faculties always under such regulation that he could exert himself with energy wherever his knowledge directed him, we should neither want chains to tie us up from being mischievous, nor a guide to keep us from missing our road.   HEY.

CIVIL LIBERTY AND POLITICAL SECURITY.

LIBERTY is the absence of coercion. Perfect liberty would be a total absence of coercion. Civil liberty means not this. It means only a partial absence of coercion; and that enjoyed by one or more of that class of persons in a state of civil or political society who are called subjects; and with respect only to others of that same class, civil or political liberty consists in this: That no individual or body of subjects have the power of constraining another subject to do, or restraining him from doing, what the laws have ordered him to do or to forbear. This, then, is created by
law

law, and is beftowed on one fubjeƈt, or number of fubjeƈts, upon whom the law does *not* operate; and not upon all other fubjeƈts upon whom the law does operate.

Suppofe, for inftance, there were but one religion eftablifhed, or even tolerated, in a country; and that the minifters of that religion were the only perfons permitted to fpeak in public on the fubjeƈt of religion. To this clafs of citizens, called minifters, the liberty of fpeaking in public on the fubjeƈt of religion would be then referved. But how? Not by any operation of the law on them, but by its operation on every other fubjeƈt, whom it would reftrain from troubling them in the free performanee of this aƈt. But the reftraint upon other fubjeƈts in this cafe would be twofold: they would be reftrained from troubling this particular clafs in the free performance of this particular aƈt; and they would be again reftrained from performing that aƈt themfelves. Suppofing this laft reftraint never to have beeen impofed, and all the fubjeƈts in this inftance would have been free: fuppofing the reftraint to be taken off, and they would again become free. This liberty is beftowed by the operation of the law, not on the individual who means to do the aƈt in queftion, but on every other perfon who may attempt to reftrain him from doing it.—It may be faid, that this idea of civil liberty is imperfeƈt; that civil

K 3   liberty

liberty includes an abfence of coercion, with refpect not only to all others of the clafs called fubjects, but likewife with refpect to that perfon or
affemblage of perfons who are called governors.
It does not appear practicable to eftablifh fuch liberty by law. Law is the expreffion of will.
That perfon or affemblage of perfons, the expreffion of whofe will conftitutes law, are governors.
Is it poffible that they fhould give liberty againft
themfelves? The very attempt to do it, directly
and openly, would be deftructive of civil liberty
properly fo called. For the truth of this I may
appeal to the hiftory of Rome in ancient days, to
that of Poland in our own. In both thefe ftates,
in proportion as the power of governors has been
openly and directly checked, the civil liberty of
the fubject has been checked with it. The governors, as fuch, could not indeed infringe the liberty
of the fubject; but then neither could they protect
the accufed againft the abufe of power on the
part of the magiftrate, nor the feeble againft the
oppreffion of the more powerful individual. Add
too, that when this impotence of the governors
has produced, as it naturally muft produce, a
ftate of anarchy and confufion, they have been
compelled to have recourfe to the moft violent
methods to protect the ftate againft either the attacks of foreign foes, or the cabals of factious and
overpowerful citizens. Such was, at Rome, the
appoint-

appointment of a Dictator, or of a Consul armed with the dictatorial power, conveyed by that
arbitrary and unlimited commission of—*Videat
Consul ne quid Respublica detrimenti capiat*. Such
is, in Poland, the more dreadful tyranny of a
confederation. No bounds can be set to the supreme power; the very term of supreme power
precludes the idea. In a state where the supreme
power is distributed among different ranks and
bodies of men, against each of these ranks, taken
separately, there may be liberty; bounds may be
prescribed to them; they as well as individuals
may be restrained by law: against the whole there
can be no liberty; united, they are omnipotent.
The coronation-oath is frequently urged as a proof
that the supreme power not only may be, but actually is, circumscribed within certain bounds.
The fact is, that this oath is not a convention between the supreme power and the people, but a
promise only from one of the constituent parts of
the supreme power;—a very different thing:—
each part may have certain limits; and yet the
whole, united, be illimited. Notwithstanding
this omnipotency of the supreme power in every
state, there is a wide difference between a free
and despotic state. In a free state, besides civil
or political liberty, the subject enjoys what is often confounded with it, though very different
from it, civil or political security. This security
arises

arifes not from any limitation of the fupreme
power, but from fuch a diftribution of the feveral
parts of it as fhall beft infure the greateft happinefs of the greateft number.

If this diftinction could fo be made as to render
the interefts of the governors and governed perfectly undiftinguifhable, this end would be completely
obtained, and the fubject would enjoy perfect political fecurity: this fecurity is more or lefs perfect
as thefe interefts are lefs or more diftinguifhable.
But it is at firft fight apparent, that political fecurity cannot be produced in the fame manner as
civil liberty. This latter is produced by a pofitive
operation of the law; that is, by a pofitive act of
thofe perfons in whofe hands is lodged the power
of making and executing laws: But political fecurity cannot be fo produced; for this plain reafon,
becaufe whatever produces it, is to operate againft
thofe very perfons in whofe hands the power is
lodged.

Political fecurity, or the affurance the people
may have that the powers of government will be
applied to the production of the greateft happinefs of the greateft number, muft be created by
the manner of diftributing the feveral portions of
power, which, when united, form the fupreme
power; of arranging the functions of the feveral
claffes of governors who, taken together, compofe what is meant by government. The happy

effects

effects arising from a proper arrangement of the functions and power of the several classes of governors are exemplified in the English constitution.   LIND.

THE DIFFERENT SORTS OF LIBERTY.

NATURAL liberty is that which the laws of nature allow, or the absence of restraints imposed by the laws of nature. Physical, moral, religious, and civil liberty, are the absence of physical restraints, of moral, of religious, of civil restraints. There is a liberty which is the result of natural and civil liberty, as it were, mixed together. Natural restraints bind a man in one action, civil restraints bind him in another: the liberty left him upon the whole, is less than either his natural or civil liberty taken singly. Many actions are forbidden by the laws of nature, as hurtful merely to the individual who commits them; such as drunkenness and acts of imprudence. About these we generally find civil laws to be silent. On the other hand, natural laws are silent about many particulars in which the laws of civil society prescribe to us; as about the modes of transferring property. Sometimes a civil law merely enforces a prohibition of nature. Again, it very frequently happens, that a civil law, though it has the same action for its object as some law of nature, does yet narrow our liberty, by being more minute
and

and circumstantial in its prohibition. And it
seems, that the name of civil liberty is sometimes
given to this compounded or resulting liberty, which
we enjoy upon the whole by the joint permission
of natural and civil laws.   HEY.

POLITICAL AND CIVIL LIBERTY IN BAR-
BAROUS AGES.

THE great body of the people, in barbarous and
licentious ages, enjoy much less true liberty, than
where the execution of the laws is the most
severe, and where subjects are reduced to the
strictest subordination and dependance on the
civil magistrate.—The reason is derived from the
excess itself of that liberty.—Men must guard
themselves at any price against insults and injuries; and where they receive no protection
from the laws and magistrate, they will seek it
by submission to superiors, and by herding in
some inferior confederacy, which acts under the
direction of a powerful chieftain.—And thus all
anarchy is the immediate cause of tyranny, if not
over the state, at least over many of the individuals.—A barbarous people may be pronounced
incapable of any true or regular liberty; which
requires such a refinement of laws and institutions, such a comprehension of views, such a
sentiment of honour, such a spirit of obedience,
and.

and fuch a facrifice of private intereft and connections to public order, as can only be the refult
of great reflection and experience, and muft grow
to perfection during feveral ages of a fettled and
eftablifhed government.   HUME.

LOVE ONLY A DESIRE OF ENJOYMENT.

WHEN a perfon imagines that he loves only
the foul of a woman, it is certainly her perfon
that he defires; and here, to fatisfy his wants,
and efpecially his curiofity, he is rendered capable
of every thing. This truth may be proved from
the little fenfibility moft fpectators fhow at the
theatre, for the affection of a man and his wife;
when the fame fpectators are fo warmly moved
by the love of a young man for a young woman.
What can produce thefe different fenfations, if it
be not the different fenfations which they themfelves have experienced in thefe two relations?
Moft of them have felt, that as they will do every
thing for the favours defired, they will do little
for the favours obtained; that in the cafe of love,
curiofity being once gratified, they eafily comfort
themfelves for the lofs of one who proves un-
faithful, and that then the misfortune of a lover
is very fupportable. Love, therefore, can never
be any thing but a difguifed defire of enjoyment.
                              HELVETIUS.
                                   THE

THE PHYSICAL CAUSE OF LOVE.

WHEN we have before us such objects as excite love and complacency, the body is affected in the following manner: The head reclines something on one fide; the eye-lids are more clofed than ufual, and the eyes roll gently with an inclination to the object; the mouth is a little opened, and the breath drawn flowly, with now and then a low figh; the whole body is composed, and the hands fall idly to the fides. All this is accompanied with an inward fenfe of melting and languor. Thefe appearances are always in proportion to the degree of beauty in the object and of fenfibility in the obferver. And this gradation, from the higheft pitch of beauty and fenfibility even to the loweft of mediocrity and indifference, and their correfpondent effects, ought to be kept in view; elfe this defcription will feem exaggerated, which it certainly is not. But from this defcription it is almoft impoffible not to conclude, that beauty acts by relaxing the folids of the whole fyftem. There are all the appearances of fuch a relaxation; and a relaxation fomewhat below the natural tone feems to me to be the caufe of all pofitive pleafure. Who is a ftranger to that manner of expreffion fo common in all times and in all countries, of being foftened, re-

laxed,

2

laxed, enervated, diffolved, melted away by pleafure? The univerfal voice of mankind, faithful
to their feelings, concurs in affirming this uniform and general effect: and although fome odd
and particular inftance may, perhaps, be found,
wherein there appears a confiderable degree of
pofitive pleafure, without all the characters of relaxation; we muft not, therefore, reject the conclufion we had drawn from a concurrence of
many experiments, but we muft ftill retain it,
fubjoining the exceptions which may occur, according to the judicious rule laid down by Sir
Ifaac Newton in the third book of his Optics. This
pofition is confirmed by the genuine conftituents
of beauty having each of them, feparately taken,
a natural tendency to relax the fibres; and by
the appearance of the human body, when all
thefe conftituents are united together before the
fenfory. So that we may venture to conclude,
that the paffion called love is produced by this
relaxation. We may alfo conclude, that as a
beautiful object prefented to the fenfe, by caufing
a relaxation in the body, produces the paffion of
love in the mind; fo if by any means the paffion
fhould firft have its origin in the mind, a relaxation of the outward organs will as certainly enfue
in a degree proportioned to the caufe.

BURKE.

L U X U R Y.

EVERY refinement of conveniency, of elegance, and of splendour, which soothe the pride, or gratify the sensuality of mankind, have been severely arranged by the moralists of every age; and it might perhaps be more conducive to the virtue, as well as happiness of mankind, if all possessed the necessaries, and none the superfluities, of life. But in the present imperfect condition of society, luxury, though it may proceed from vice or folly, seems to be the only means that can correct the unequal distribution of property. The diligent mechanic, and the skilful artist, who have obtained no share in the division of the earth, receive a voluntary tax from the possessors of the land; and the latter are prompted, by a sense of interest, to improve those estates, with whose produce they may purchase additional pleasures. These operations impress the political machine with new degrees of activity, and are productive of the happiest effects in every society.   GIBBON.

ON THE SAME SUBJECT.

LUXURY is a word of an uncertain signification, and may be taken in a good as well as in a
bad

bad fenfe. In general, it means great refinement
in the gratification of the fenfes ; and any degree
of it may be innocent or blameable, according to
the age, or country, or condition of the perfon.
The bounds between the virtue and the vice
cannot here be fixed exactly, more than in other
moral fubjects. To imagine that the gratifying
any of the fenfes, or indulging any delicacy in
meats, drinks, or apparel, is of itfelf a vice, can
never enter into any head that is not difordered
by the frenzies of enthufiafm. Thefe indulgencies
are only vices when they are purfued at the expence of fome virtue, as liberality or charity ; in
like manner, they are follies, when for them a
man ruins his fortune, and reduces himfelf to
want and beggary. Where they intrench upon
no virtue, but leave ample fubject whence to
provide for friends, family, and every proper
object of generofity or compaffion, they are entirely innocent, and have in every age been acknowledged as fuch by almoft all moralifts. To
be entirely occupied with the luxury of the table,
for inftance, without any relifh for the pleafure
of ambition, ftudy, or converfation, is a mark of
ftupidity, and is incompatible with any vigour of
temper or genius. To confine one's expence entirely to fuch a gratification, without regard to
friends or family, is an indication of a heart de-
void of humanity or benevolence. But if a man

reserve time sufficient for all laudable pursuits, and money sufficient for all generous purposes, he is free from every shadow of blame or reproach.   Hume.

On the same Subject.

IT is in vain to attempt a precise definition of luxury. The word luxury, like that of greatness, is one of those comparative expressions that do not offer to the mind any determinate idea; that only express the relation two or more objects have to each other. It has no fixed sense till the moment it is put, if I may use the expression, into an equation; and we compare the luxury of one nation, class of men, or private person, with that of others of the same rank. An English peasant, well cloathed and fed, is in a state of luxury compared with a French peasant. The man dressed in a coarse cloth, is in a state of luxury, compared to a savage covered with a bear's skin. All things, even to the feathers that adorn the cap of a wild Indian, may be regarded as luxury.

Helvetius.

LUXURY

LUXURY and REFINEMENT OF MANNERS FAVOURABLE TO LIBERTY.

IN rude unpolished ages, when the arts are neglected, all labour is bestowed on the cultivation
of the ground ; and the whole society is divided
into two classes, proprietors of land and their
vassals or tenants. The latter are necessarily de-
pendant, and fitted for flavery and fubjection ;
especially where they possess no riches, and are
not valued for their knowledge in agriculture ;
as must always be the case where the arts are neglected. The former naturally erect themselves
into petty tyrants; and must either submit to an
absolute master, for the sake of peace and order;
or if they will preferve their independency, like
the ancient barons, they must fall into feuds and
contests among themselves, and throw the whole
society into such confusion, as is perhaps worse
than the most despotic government. But where
luxury nourishes commerce and industry, the peasants, by proper cultivation of the land, become
rich and independent; while the tradesmen and
merchants acquire a share of the property, and
draw authority and consideration to that middling
rank of men, who are the best and firmest basis of
public liberty. These submit not to flavery like
the peasants, from poverty and meanness of spirit;

L 3   and

and having no hopes of tyrannizing over others, like the barons, they are not tempted, for the fake of that gratification, to countenance the tyranny of their fovereign. They covet equal laws, which may fecure their property, and preferve them from monarchical as well as ariftocratical tyrranny.

HUME.

THE EFFECTS OF LUXURY DISCOVERABLE BY A COMPARISON OF DIFFERENT COTEMPORARY NATIONS.

TO declaim againft prefent times, and magnify the virtue of remote anceftors, is a propenfity almoft inherent in human nature: And as the fentiments and opinions of civilized ages alone are tranfmitted to pofterity, hence it is that we meet with fo many fevere judgments pronounced againft luxury and even fcience ; and hence it is that at prefent we give fo ready an affent to them.   But the fallacy is eafily perceived by comparing different nations that are cotemporaries; where we both judge more impartially, and can better fet in oppofition thofe manners with which we are fufficiently acquainted. Treachery and cruelty, the moft pernicious and moft odious of all vices, feem peculiar to uncivilized ages; and by the refined Greeks and Romans were afcribed to all the barbarous nations

which

which furrounded them. They might juftly, therefore, have prefumed, that their own anceftors, fo highly celebrated, poffeffed no greater virtue, and were as much inferior to their pofterity in honour and humanity as in tafte and fcience. An ancient Frank or Saxon may be highly extolled: but I believe every man would think his life or fortune much lefs fecure in the hands of a Moor or Tartar, than in thofe of a French or Englifh gentleman; the rank of men the moft civilized in the moft civilized nations.

Hume.

LUXURIOUS Ages most happy.

Human happinefs, acording to the moft received notions, feems to confift in three ingredients; action, pleafure, and indolence: and though thefe ingredients ought to be mixed in different proportions, according to the difpofitions of the perfon; yet no ingredient can be entirely wanting, without deftroying, in fome meafure, the relifh of the whole compofition. Indolence or repofe, indeed, feems not of itfelf to contribute much to our enjoyment; but, like fleep, is requifite as an indulgence to the weaknefs of human nature, which cannot fupport an uninterrupted courfe of bufinefs or pleafure. That quick march of the fpirits, which takes a man from

himfelf,

himfelf, and chiefly gives fatisfaction, does in the
end exhauft the mind, and requires fome intervals of repofe, which, though agreeable for a
moment, yet, if prolonged, beget a languor and
lethargy that deftroys all enjoyment. Education,
cuftom, and example, have a mighty influence in
turning the mind to any of thefe purfuits; and
it muft be owned, that where they promote a relifh
for action and pleafure, they are fo far favourable
to human happinefs. In times when induftry
and the arts flourifh, men are kept in perpetual
occupation, and enjoy, as their reward, the occupation itfelf, as well as thofe pleafures which
are the fruit of their labour. The mind acquires
new vigour; enlarges its powers and faculties;
and by an affiduity in honeft induftry, both fatif-
fies its natural appetites, and prevents the growth
of unnatural ones, which commonly fpring up
when nourifhed by eafe and idlenefs. Banifh
thofe arts from fociety, you deprive men both of
action and pleafure; and leaving nothing but indolence in their place, you even deftroy the relifh
of indolence; which never is agreeable but when
it fucceeds to labour, and recruits the fpirits, exhaufted by too much application and fatigue.—
The fpirit of the age affects all the arts; and the
minds of men, being once roufed from their
lethargy, and put into a fermentation, turn themfelves on all fides, and carry improvements into
every

every art and science. Profound ignorance is
totally banished, and men enjoy the privilege of
rational creatures to think as well as to act, to
cultivate the pleasures of the mind as well as those
of the body.—The more these refined arts advance, the more sociable men become : nor is it
possible that, when enriched with science, and
possessed of a fund of conversation, they should
be contented to remain in solitude, or live with
their fellow-citizens in that distant manner which
is peculiar to ignorant and barbarous nations.
They flock into cities; love to receive and communicate knowledge, to show their wit or their
breeding, their taste in conversation or living,
in cloaths and furniture. Curiosity allures the
wise; vanity the foolish; and pleasure both. Particular clubs and societies are every where formed;
both sexes meet in an easy and sociable manner;
and the tempers of men as well as their behaviour
refine apace. So that, besides the improvements
which they receive from knowledge and the liberal arts, it is impossible but they must feel an
increase of humanity, from the very habit of
conversing together and contributing to each
other's pleasure and entertainment. Thus industry, knowledge, and humanity, are linked together by an indissoluble chain; and are found,
from experience as well as reason, to be peculiar
to the more polished, and what are commonly
de-

denominated the more luxurious ages.—Nor are
thefe advantages attended with difadvantages that
bear any proportion to them. The more men refine upon pleafure, the lefs will they indulge in
exceffes of any kind; becaufe nothing is more
deftructive to true pleafure than fuch exceffes.
One may fafely affirm, that the Tartars are
oftener guilty of beaftly gluttony, when they
feaft on their dead horfes, than European cour-
tiers with all their refinements of cookery. And
if libertine love, or even infidelity to the mar-
riage-bed be more frequent in polite ages, when
it is often regarded only as a piece of gallantry;
drunkennefs, on the other hand, is much lefs
common; a vice more odious, and more pernicious both to body and mind.   HUME.

LUXURY AND REFINEMENT OF MANNERS FAVOURABLE TO GOVERNMENT.

THE increafe and confumption of all commodities which ferve to the ornament and pleafure
of life, are advantageous to fociety; becaufe at
the fame time that they multiply thofe innocent
gratifications to individuals, they are a kind of
ftore-houfe of labour, which, in the exigencies
of a ftate, may be turned to the public fervice.
In a nation where there is no demand for fuch
fuperfluities, men fink into indolence, and lofe
                                              all

all enjoyment of life; and are ufelefs to the public, which cannot maintain nor fupport its fleets and armies from the induftry of fuch flothful members.—The bounds of all the European kingdoms are at prefent nearly the fame they were two hundred years ago: But what a difference is there in the power and grandeur of thofe kingdoms? which can be afcribed to nothing but the increafe of art and induftry.—This induftry is much promoted by the knowledge infeparable from ages of art and refinement; as on the other hand this knowledge enables the public to make the beft advantage of the induftry of its fubjects. Laws, order, police, difcipline; thefe can never be carried to any degree of perfection, before human reafon has refined itfelf by exercife, and by an application to the more vulgar arts, at leaft of commerce and manufactures. Not to mention, that all ignorant ages are infefted with fuperftition, which throws the government off its bias, and difturbs men in the purfuit of their intereft and happinefs.—Knowledge in the arts of government naturally begets mildnefs and moderation, by inftructing men in the advantages of humane maxims above rigour and feverity, which drive fubjects into rebellion, and render the return to fubmiffion impracticable by cutting off all hopes of pardon. When the tempers of men are foftened, as well as their knowledge improved, this humanity

manity appears ftill more confpicuous; and is the
chief characteriftic which diftinguifhes a civilized
age from times of barbarity and ignorance. Factions are then lefs inveterate, revolutions lefs
tragical, authority lefs fevere, and feditions lefs
frequent.   Even foreign wars abate of their
cruelty; and after the field of battle, where
honour and intereft fteel men againft compaffion
as well as fear, the combatants diveft themfelves
of the brute, and refume the man.—Luxury and
refinement of manners in deftroying ferocity do
not annihilate the martial fpirit.   If anger, which
is faid to be the whetftone of courage, lofes fomewhat of its afperity by politenefs and refinement;
a fenfe of honour, which is a ftronger, more
conftant, and more governable principle, acquires
frefh vigour by that elevation of genius which
arifes from knowledge and a good education.—
Refinement on the pleafures and conveniences of
life has no natural tendency to beget venality and
corruption.   The diforders in the Roman ftate,
which have been afcribed to luxury and refinement, really proceeded from an ill-modelled government, and the unlimited extent of conquefts.
The value which all men put upon any particular
pleafure depends on comparifon and experience;
nor is a porter lefs greedy of money which he
fpends on bacon and brandy, than a courtier
who purchafes champagne and ortolans.   Riches

2   are

are valuable at all times to all men, becaufe they always purchafe pleafures, fuch as men are accuftomed to and defire: nor can any thing reftrain or regulate the love of money, but a fenfe of honour and virtue; which, if it be not nearly equal at all times, will naturally abound moft in ages of knowledge and refinement.

HUME.

M.

***

Of MADMEN and IDIOTS.

THOSE who either perceive but dully, or retain the ideas that come into their minds
but ill, who cannot readily excite or compound
them, will have but little matter to think on.
Those who cannot distinguish, compare, and abstract, would hardly be able to understand and
make use of language, or judge or reason, to
any tolerable degree ; but only a little, and im-
perfectly, about things present, and very familiar
to their senses. And indeed any of the foremen-
tioned faculties, if wanting, or out of order, produce suitable defects in mens understandings and
knowledge.

The defect of *naturals* seems to proceed from
want of quickness, activity, and motion in the
intellectual faculties; whereby they are deprived
of reason: whereas *madmen*, on the other side,
seem

seem to suffer by the other extreme. For they do not appear to me to have lost the faculty of reasoning; but having joined together some ideas very wrongly, they mistake them for truths; and they err as men do that argue right from wrong principles: For by the violence of their imaginations, having taken their fancies for realities, they make right deductions from them. Thus you shall find a distracted man fancying himself a king, with a right inference, require suitable attendance, respect, and obedience: Others, who have thought themselves made of glass, have used the caution necessary to preserve such brittle bodies. Hence it comes to pass, that a man who is very sober, and of a right understanding in all other things, may in one particular be as frantic as any in *Bedlam;* if either by any very sudden strong impression, or long fixing his fancy upon one sort of thoughts, incoherent ideas have been cemented together so powerfully as to remain united. But there are degrees of madness as of folly; the disorderly jumbling ideas together is in some more and some less. In short, herein seems to be the difference between idiots and madmen, that madmen put wrong ideas together, and so make wrong propositions, but argue and reason right from them: but idiots make very few or no propositions, and reason scarce at all.

LOCKE.

M 2

MADNESS.

THE caufes of madnefs are of two kinds, bodily and mental. That which arifes from bodily
caufes is nearly related to drunkennefs, and to the
deliriums attending difeafes. That from mental
caufes is of the fame kind with temporary alie-
nations of the mind during violent paffions, and
with the prejudices and opinionativenefs which
much application to one fet of ideas only occafions.

We may thus diftinguifh the caufes for the
more eafy conception and analyfis of the fubject;
but in fact they are both united for the moft
part. The bodily caufe lays hold of that paffion
or affection which is moft difproportionate; and
the mental caufe, when that is primary, generally
waits till fome bodily diftemper gives it full fcope
to exert itfelf. Agreeably to this, the prevention
and cure of all kinds of madnefs require an attention both to the body and mind.

It is obferved, that mad perfons often fpeak ra-
tionally and confiftently upon the fubjects that
occur, provided that fingle one which moft affects
them be kept out of view. And the reafon of
this may be, that whether they firft become mad
becaufe a particular original mental uneafinefs
falls in with an accidental bodily diforder, or becaufe

cause an original bodily disorder falls in with an accidental mental one; it must follow, that a particular set of ideas shall be extremely magnified, and consequently an unnatural association of sameness or repugnancy between them generated; all other ideas and associations remaining nearly the same. When one false position of this kind is admitted, it begets more of course, the same bodily and mental causes also continuing; but then this process stops after a certain number of false positions are adopted from their mutual inconsistency, unless the whole nervous system is deranged. The memory is often much impaired in madness; which is both a sign of the greatness of the bodily disorder and a hindrance to mental rectification, and therefore a bad prognostic. If an opposite state of body and mind can be introduced early, before the unnatural associations are too much cemented, the madness is cured; if otherwise, it will remain though both the bodily and mental cause should be at last removed.

In dissections after madness, the brain is often found dry, and the blood-vessels much distended; which are arguments that violent vibrations took place in the internal parts of the brain, the peculiar residence of ideas and passions; and that it was much compressed, so as to obstruct the natural course of association.

As in mad persons the vibrations in the inter-

nal

nal parts of the brain are preternaturally increafed, fo they are defective in the external organs, in the glands, &c. Hence maniacs eat little, are coftive, make little water, and take fcarce any notice of external impreffions. The violence of the ideas and paffions may give them great mufcular ftrength upon particular occafions : But maniacs are often fluggifh as well as infenfible, from the great prevalence of the ideal vibrations; juft as perfons in a ftate of deep attention are. Bodily labour, with a variety of mental occupations, and a confiderable abftemioufnefs in the quantity and quality of diet, ought always to be prefcribed, and are the beft prefervatives in hereditary and other tendencies to madnefs.

HARTLEY.

ON THE SAME SUBJECT.

THERE are different kinds of madmen; fome who are fo very mad, that they lofe all ufe of their reafon, and are as little able to deduce confequences as to eftablifh principles. Others again deduce confequences, and argue very juftly, but are ftill mad; becaufe they reafon from principles that have no reality out of their own heated and difordered imaginations. Inftances of this kind of madnefs are to be found in every form of life; even among thofe who are reputed fober and wife,

and

and who are really fuch, except on fome particular fubject. All are in this predicament, whofe
imaginations are run away with by the prejudices
of education on religious and political fubjects.

BOLINGBROKE,

ON THE SAME SUBJECT.

BY madnefs, is meant the diftemper of the organs of the brain, which neceffarily hinders a man
from thinking and acting like others. An important obfervation here is, that this man is not
without ideas; he has them, whilft waking, like
all other men, and often in his fleep. It may be
afked, how his foul, being fpiritual and immortal,
and refiding in his brain, whither all the ideas
are conveyed to it by the fenfes very plain and diftinct, yet never forms a right judgment of them?
It fees objects equally as the fouls of Ariftotle,
Plato, Locke, and Newton; it hears the fame
founds, it has the fame fenfe of the touch: how
happens it, then, that with the fame perceptions
as the wifeft men, it makes a wild incoherent
jumble without being able to help itfelf? If this
fimple and eternal fubftance has the fame inftruments for acting as the fouls of the wifeft brains,
it fhould reafon like them; what can hinder it?
If this madman fees red, and the fenfible men
blue; if when this hears mufic, the madman hears
the

the braying of an afs; if when they hear yes, he hears no; I muft of neceffity conclude, that his foul muft think differently from the others. But this madman has the like perceptions as they; and there is no apparent reafon why his foul, having through the fenfes received all its tools, cannot make ufe of them. It is faid to be pure, to be of itfelf fubject to no infirmity, to be provided with all neceffary helps; and whatever happens in the body, its effence remains unalterable, yet it is carried in its cafe to bedlam. This reflection may give rife to an apprehenfion, that the faculty of thinking with which man is endued is liable to be difordered like the other fenfes. A madman is a patient whofe brain fuffers, as a gouty man is a patient whofe feet and hands fuffer: he thought by means of the brain as he walked with his feet, without knowing any thing of his incomprehen- fible power to walk, or of his no lefs incompre- henfible power to think.

VOLTAIRE.

MAHOMETANISM.

IT was an error, to fuppofe it was by allowing a free indulgence to the paffions that Mahomet gained fo many followers: His doctrine, however abfurd and ftupid it may feem when compared with Chriftianity, was fevere and rigorous, in

com-

comparifon to the extravagant and licentious manners that prevailed in Arabia.—Frequent prayers,
charities, fafting, the prohibition of that crime
which defeats the views of nature, by deceiving
her with refpect to the object of her defires, the
denying the ufe of wine, and the forgivenefs of
injuries, were all fo many yokes on a people, with
whom the paffions, inflamed by example, had ob-
literated every appearance of juftice. It was not
therefore, as is generally afferted, by favouring li-
centioufnefs, that Mahomet made fo many profe-
lytes to his opinions, but by propofing a more
noble and virtuous fyftem than that which they
before followed; which is the only method of per-
fuading any people whatever.——Men love the
practice of vice, but they are alfo fond of con-
templating virtue.—If we examine different fects,
we fhall find that they generally affected the appearance of aufterity; and if they at any time in-
dulged licentious manners, they carefully concealed it: the reafon is, virtue has fuch a natural
influence over our minds, that we cannot deftroy
it but by affuming her venerable drefs.

MEHEGAN.

MANUFACTURES.

MANUFACTURES are founded in poverty: It
is the multitude of poor without land in a country,

try, and who muſt work for others at low wages
or ſtarve, that enables undertakers to carry on a
manufacture, and afford it cheap enough to prevent the importation of the ſame kind from a-
broad, and to bear the expence of its own expor-
tation. But no man who can have a piece of land
of his own, ſufficient by his labour to ſubſiſt his
family in plenty, is poor enough to be a manu-
facturer and work for a maſter. Hence, while
there is land in a country ſufficient for the people
upon eaſy terms, there can be no manufactures
to any amount or value. It is an obſervation
founded upon facts, that the natural livelihood of
the thin inhabitants of a foreſt country is hunt-
ing; that of a greater number, paſturage; that of
a middling population, agriculture; and that of
the greateſt, manufactures; which laſt muſt ſubſiſt the bulk of the people in a full country, or
they muſt be ſubſiſted by charity, or periſh.

FRANKLIN.

MARRIAGE.

THAT the human, like every other ſpecies of
animals ſhould multiply by the copulation of the
two ſexes, and be propagated by their care to
nurſe and breed up their young, is undoubtedly
a law of nature. Self-love, the great ſpring of
human actions, prompts to both. But as it is
more immediately determined, and more ſtrongly

ſtimu-

ftimulated by inftinct and by nature, to the one
than to the other; it becomes neceffary to give
this principle, by reafon and by art, to let it lofe
none that it had. For this purpofe it was neceffary that parents fhould know certainly their own
refpective broods; and that as a woman cannot
doubt whether fhe is the mother of the child fhe
bears, fo a man fhould have all the affurance law
can give him that he is the father of the child he
begets. Thus matrimony forms families, which
could not be formed without it; and families form
ftates, which could not be formed without them.
It was the firft natural union which preceded, and
prepared mankind for political or civil union: and
the bonds of this fecond union were more effectually ftrengthened by thofe of paternal and filial
affection and of confanguinity, than they could
have been by thofe alone of accidental interefts
liable to vary, and of covenants liable to be broken.
On fuch principles, and for fuch purpofes, matrimony was inftituted. They are evidently derived from the law of nature. The inftitution
therefore is conformable to the law of nature, as
far as it is fubfervient to thefe ends. But when
it is carried further than thefe ends require, and
that which is confiftent with them, or even conducive to them, is forbid, it is, in every fuch
refpect, a mere arbitrary impofition.—Great attention has been had in every well-regulated government

vernment to promote the multiplication of mankind: and this attention muſt be alway neceſſary;
for if the human race is daily increaſing, it is
daily decreaſing likewiſe; and it would be trifling
to maintain that celibacy is leſs hurtful, or polygamy leſs neceſſary, than they were formerly.
Men who were advanced in years, and had never
been married, were ſtigmatiſed at Sparta; and as
well there as at Rome, and in many other places,
great immunities, prerogatives, and other en-
couragements, were granted to thoſe who had a
large legitimate iſſue.   The Talmudiſts carry the
obligation ſo far of getting children, that they declare the neglect of it to be a ſort of homicide.—
All the ends of matrimony are anſwered by polygamy; and the cuſtom for one man to have ſeveral wives has prevailed always, and it ſtill prevails generally, if not univerſally, either as a
reaſonable indulgence to mankind, or as a proper, and in the early ages a neceſſary, expedient
to increaſe their numbers.   Such it is, no doubt;
ſuch it muſt be in the order of nature: and
when we are told that it has not this effect among
the people who retain the cuſtom to this day,
either the fact aſſerted by men, who cannot be
competent judges of it, may be untrue; or So-
domy and abortions, in conjunction with other
cauſes as unnatural, may prevent the natural
effect of polygamy.   Polygamy was allowed by
the

the Mofaical law, and was authorifed by God himfelf. The zeal of the Jews to promote the obfervation of the precept, To increafe and multiply, was fo great, that befides the eftablifhment and regulation of polygamy, their doctors defcended into many particulars for the fame purpofe; and among the reft were careful to appoint ftated periods, beyond which it was not lawful to neglect the performance of conjugal duty in any form of life. The periods were marked even to the artificer, the countryman, and the feaman; and the wife had her remedy if the law was not obferved. Polygamy is quite conformable to the law of nature, and provides the moft effectual means for the generation and education of children. Monogamy, on the other hand, or the confinement of one hufband to one wife, whilft they both live, will unite the care of both parents in breeding up fubjects of the commonwealth; but will not ferve as effectually, nor in as great numbers, to the begetting them. The prohibition of polygamy, therefore, is not only a prohibition of what nature permits in the fulleft manner, but what fhe requires alfo in the fame manner, and often in a greater degree than ordinary, for the reparation of ftates exhaufted by wars, by plagues, and other calamities.—The reafons that determined the lawgivers of Greece and Rome, and of fome few other ftates, to forbid

a plurality of wives, which was permitted in almoſt all countries, may have been ſuch as theſe:
They ſaw that polygamy would create large families, and large families a greater expence than
could be borne by men who were reduced to live
in cities, and other fixed habitations, where property was diſtinguiſhed, and where no one could
afford to ſpend more than his legal poſſeſſions,
his labour, and his induſtry gave him. Monogamy was a ſort of ſumptuary law, and might be
thought the more reaſonable, becauſe even in
thoſe countries where polygamy was eſtabliſhed,
men were not permitted to marry more women
than they were able to maintain.—But of all the
reaſons by which we may account for the prevalence of ſingle marriages in oppoſition to polygamy, divorces conſtituted the principal and the moſt
effectual. With them, monogamy may be thought
a reaſonable inſtitution; without them, it is an abſurd, unnatural, and cruel impoſition. It croſſes
the intention of nature doubly, as it ſtands in
oppoſition to the moſt effectual means of multiplying the human ſpecies, and as it forbids the
ſole expedient by which this evil can be leſſened
in any degree, and the intention of Nature can
be, in many caſes, at all carried on.—The inſtitution of divorces was of ſuch abſolute neceſſity
where a plurality of wives was forbid, and of ſo
much convenience where this plurality was allowed,

ed, that it continued on the fame foot among the
Romans till Chriftianity was eftablifhed fully in
the empire; and that it continues ftill among the
Jews in the eaft; if not practifed, for prudential
reafons, in the fame manner, and as openly in
the weft. BOLINGBROKE.

ON THE SAME SUBJECT.

MARRIAGE has two objects: the one the prefervation of the fpecies; the other the pleafure and
happinefs of the two fexes. To what fhall we
refer the uniformity of its inftitution? I anfwer,
To the conformity between this mode of matrimony and the primitive ftate of the inhabitants
of Europe, that is, the ftate of peafants. In that
rank, the man and woman have one common object of defire, which is the improvement of the
land they occupy; this improvement refults from
their mutual labours. The man and wife conftantly occupied in their farm, and always ufeful
to each other, fupport, without difguft, and without inconvenience, their indiffoluble union.——
The law of indiffolubility in marriage is a cruel
and barbarous law, (fays Fontenelle.) The few
happy marriages prove the neceffity of a reformation in this matter.——There are countries where
the lover and his miftrefs do not marry till after
they have lived together three years. During that
N 2 time

time they try the sympathy of their characters.
If they do not agree, they part, and the girl goes
to another.

These African marriages are the most proper to
secure the happiness of the parties. But how
then must the children be provided for? By the
same laws that secure their maintenance in countries where divorces are permited. Let the sons
remain with the father, and the daughters go
with the mother; and let a certain sum be stipu-
lated in the marriage-articles for the education of
such children. The inconvenience of divorces
will then be insignificant, and the happiness of
the married parties secured. But it may be said,
that divorces will enormously increase under a
law so favourable to human inconstancy. Experience proves the contrary.—To conclude, if
the variable and ambulatory desires of men and
women urge them sometimes to change the object
of their tenderness, why should they be deprived
of the pleasure of variety, if their inconstancy, by
the regulation of wise laws, be not detrimental to
society.—In France, the women are too much
mistresses; in the East, too much slaves: they
are there a sacrifice to the pleasure of men. But
why should they be a sacrifice? If the two parties
cease to love, and begin to hate each other, why
should they be obliged to live together? Marriage
frequently represents nothing more than the pic-

ture

ture of two unfortunate people who are chained together, to be a reciprocal torment to each other. HELVETIUS.

DEGREES OF MARRIAGE.

THE natural reason why marriage in certain degrees is prohibited by the civil laws, and condemned by the moral sentiments of all nations, is derived from mens care to preserve purity of manners; while they reflect, that if a commerce of love were authorised between the nearest relations, the frequent opportunities of intimate conversation, especially during early youth, would introduce an universal diffoluteness and corruption.—But as the customs of countries vary confiderably, and open an intercourse, more or less reftrained, between different families, or between the several members of the fame family; so we find, that the moral precept varying with its caufe, is fufceptible, without any inconvenience, of very different latitude in the feveral ages and nations of the world.—The extreme delicacy of the Greeks permitted no converfe between perfons of two fexes, except where they lived under the fame roof; and even the apartments of a ftepmother and her daughters were almoft as much fhut up againft vifits from the hufband's fons, as againft thofe from any ftrangers or more remote

N 3 rela-

relations: Hence, in that nation, it was lawful
for a man to marry, not only his niece, but his
half sister by the father. A liberty unknown to
the Romans, and other nations, where a more
open intercourse was authorised between the
sexes.   HUME.

MARRIAGE BETWEEN RELATIONS.

WITH regard to marriages between relations,
it is a thing extremely delicate to fix exactly the
point at which the laws of nature stop, and
where the civil laws begin. For this purpose we
must establish some principles.—The marriage of
the son with the mother confounds the state of
things: the son ought to have an unlimited respect to his mother, the wife an unlimited respect to her husband; therefore the marriage of
the mother to the son would subvert the natural
state of both. Besides, Nature has forwarded in
women the time in which they are able to have
children, but has retarded it in men; and for
the same reason, women sooner lose the ability
and men later. If the marriage between the
mother and the son were permitted, it would
almost always be the case, that when the husband
was capable of entering into the views of nature,
the wife would be incapable. The marriage between the father and the daughter is contrary to
                                              nature

nature as well as the other; but it is lefs contrary becaufe it has not thofe two obftacles. Thus
the Tartars, who may marry their daughters,
never marry their mothers, as we fee in accounts
of that nation. This law is very ancient among
them. Attila, (fays Prifcus) in his embaffy, ftopt
in a certain place to marry Efca his daughter. A
thing permitted, he adds, by the laws of the
Scythians.

It has ever been the natural duty of fathers to
watch over the chaftity of their children. In-
trufted with the care of their education, they are
obliged to preferve the body in the greateft perfection, and the mind from the leaft corruption;
to encourage whatever has a tendency to infpire
them with virtuous defires, and to nourifh a becoming tendernefs.

As children dwell, or are fuppofed to dwell, in
their father's houfe, marriages between fathers
and children, between brothers and fifters, are
prohibited, in order to preferve natural modefty
in families. On the fame principle, marriages
between the fon-in-law with the mother-in-law,
the father-in-law with the daughter-in-law, are
prohibited by the law of nature. In this cafe,
the refemblance has the fame effect as the reality,
becaufe it fprings from the fame caufe. There
are nations among whom coufin-germans are confidered as brothers, becaufe they commonly dwell
in

in the same house; there are others where this custom is not known. Among the first, the marriage of cousin-germans ought to be regarded as contrary to nature; not so among the others. But the laws of nature cannot be local; therefore, when these marriages are forbidden, or permitted, it must be done according to the circumstances by a civil law.

It is not a necessary custom for the brother-in-law and the sister-in-law to dwell together in the same house. The marriage between them is not then prohibited to preserve chastity in the family; and the law which forbids or permits it, is not a law of nature, but a civil law, regulated by circumstances, and dependent on the custom of each country.

The prohibitions of the law of nature are invariable; the father, the mother, and the children, necessarily dwell in the same house. The prohibitions of the civil laws are accidental, because they depend on accidental circumstances; cousin-germans and others dwelling in the house by accident. This explains why the law of Moses, those of the Egyptians, and of many other nations, permitted the marriage of the brother-in-law with the sister-in-law, whilst these very marriages were disallowed by other nations.

In India they have a very natural reason for admitting this sort of marriages. The uncle is
there

there confidered as the father, and is obliged to maintain and educate his nephew, as if he were his own child. This proceeds from the difpofition of thefe people, which is good-natured and full of humanity. This law or the cuftom has produced another: If a hufband has loft his wife, he does not fail to marry her fifter; which is extremely natural, for his new confort becomes the mother of her fifter's children, and not a cruel ftepmother. MONTESQUIEU.

MARRIAGE with a Brother's Widow.

MARRIAGE, in this degree of affinity, is indeed prohibited in Leviticus; but it is natural to interpret that prohibition as a part of the Jewifh ceremonial or municipal law: And though it is there faid in the conclufion, that the Gentile nations, by violating thefe degrees of confanguinity, had incurred the Divine difpleafure, the extenfion of this maxim to every precife cafe before fpecified, is fuppofing the Scriptures to be compofed with a minute accuracy and precifion, to which, we know with certainty, the facred penmen did not think proper to confine themfelves.—The defcent of mankind from one common father, obliged them, in the firft generation, to marry in the neareft degrees of confanguinity: inftances of a like nature occur among the patriarchs: and the

marriage

marriage of a brother's widow was, in certain
cafes, not only permitted, but even enjoined as
a pofitive precept by the Mofaical law.—It is in
vain to fay, that this precept was an exception
to the rule, and an exception confined merely to
the Jewifh nation.—The inference is ftill juft,
that it can contain no natural or moral turpitude;
otherwife God, who is the author of all purity,
would never in any cafe have enjoined it.

HUME.

MATTER.

WISE men, on being afked, What the foul is?
anfwer, They are entirely ignorant of it: And if
afked what matter is, give the like anfwer. This
almoft unknown being, is it eternal? So all antiquity believed. Has it of itfelf an active force?
This is the opinion of feveral philofophers. Have
they who deny it any fuperior reafon for their
opinion? You do not conceive that matter can,
intrinfically, have any property; but how can you
affirm that it has not, intrinfically, fuch properties as are neceffary to it? You know nothing of
its nature, and yet deny it to have modes which
refide in its nature: for, after all, as matter exifts,
it muft have a form and figure; and being neceffarily figured, is it impoffible that there are other
modes annexed to its configuration? Matter exifts,
this

this you know; but you know it no further than by your fenfations. We weigh, we meafure, we analyfe, we decompound matter; but on offering to go a ftep beyond thefe operations, we find ourfelves bewildered, and an abyfs opens before us. How can we conceive that what is without fucceffion has not always been? Were the exiftence of matter not neceffary, why exifts it? And if it was to exift, why fhould it not always have exifted? Never was an axiom more univerfally received than this: Nothing produces nothing. The contrary, indeed, is incomprehenfible: all nations have held their chaos anterior to the divine difpofition of the world. Matter, therefore, was looked on in the hands of God as clay under the potter's wheel; if fuch faint images may be ufed to exprefs the divine power. Matter being eternal, fhould have eternal properties; as configuration, the inert power, motion, and divifibility. But this divifibility is no more than the confequence of motion; as without motion there can be no divifion, feparation, and arrangement: therefore motion was looked on as effential to matter. The chaos had been a confufed motion; and the arrangement of the univerfe was a regular motion imprefled on all bodies by the Deity. But how fhould matter of itfelf have motion; as, according to all the ancients, it has extenfion and impenetrability? It cannot, however, be conceived without extenfion,

and

and it may without motion. To this the anſwer
was, It is impoſſible but matter muſt be permeable; and if permeable, ſomething muſt be continually paſſing into its pores: Where is the uſe of
paſſages, if nothing paſſes through them? The
ſyſtem of the eternity of matter has, like all other
ſyſtems, very great difficulties. That of matter
formed out of nothing is not leſs incomprehenſible. Happily, which ever ſyſtem is eſpouſed,
morality is hurt by neither; for what ſigniſies it
whether matter be made, or only arranged? God
is equally our abſolute maſter. Whether the chaos
was only put in order, or whether it was created
of nothing, ſtill it behoves us to be virtuous:
Scarce any of theſe metaphyſical queſtions have
a relation to the conduct of life. Diſputes are like
table-talk; every one forgets after dinner what he
has ſaid, and goes away where his intereſt or inclination leads him.   VOLTAIRE.

ON THE SAME SUBJECT.

IT has at all times been alternately aſſerted,
That matter felt, or did not feel. If a preciſe idea
had been affixed to the word matter, it would
have been perceived, if I may uſe the expreſſion,
that men were the creators of matter; that matter was not a being; that in nature there were
only individuals to which the name of body had

3   been

been given; and that this word *matter* could im-
port no more than the collection of properties
common to all bodies. The meaning of this word
being determined, all that remained was to know,
whether extent, folidity, and impenetrability were
the only properties common to all bodies; and
whether the difcovery of a power, fuch, for inftance, as attraction, might not give rife to a conjecture that bodies had fome properties hitherto
unknown, fuch as that of fenfation, which though
evident only in the organized members of animals, might yet be common to all individuals?—
The queftion being reduced to this, it would have
appeared, that if, ftrictly fpeaking, it is impoffible
to demonftrate that all bodies are abfolutely infenfible, no man, unlefs inftructed by a particular revelation, can decide the queftion otherwife
than by calculating and comparing the probabi-
lity of this opinion with that of the contrary.

HELVETIUS.

DEMONSTRATIONS OF MATTERS OF FACT.

THERE is an evident abfurdity in pretending
to demonftrate a matter of fact, or to prove it by
any arguments *à priori;* becaufe nothing is demonftrable, unlefs the contrary implies a contradiction.—Nothing that is diftinctly conceivable
implies a contradiction.—Whatever we conceive

as exiftent, we can alfo conceive as non-exiftent.
—There is therefore no being whofe non-exiftence implies a contradiction; confequently there
is no being whofe exiftence is demonftrable.

HUME.

ON THE SAME SUBJECT.

WHEN we once affume the exiftence of any
thing as a fact, the non-exiftence of the caufe implies the non-exiftence of the effect, or of the
thing affumed as a fact.—Nothing, it is faid by Mr
Hume, that is diftinctly conceivable implies a contradiction.—Is it diftinctly conceivable, that there
fhould be a firft caufe of all things? If it be not,
the neceffary exiftence of the Deity is eftablifhed.
—Whatever we conceive as exiftent, we can, according to that Philofopher, conceive alfo as non-
exiftent.—Not fo; we conceive fpace as exiftent:
Can we conceive it as non-exiftent? The utmoft
ftretch of the imagination cannot annihilate fpace;
therefore its exiftence is neceffary, and its non-
exiftence implies a contradiction.—So it is with
the firft caufe, or the Deity.—Allow the exiftence
of one thing, and of but a fingle atom, and the
non-exiftence of its primary caufe, or the Deity,
involves an abfurdity.   * *

MELAN-

MELANCHOLY.

VAPOURS, hypochondriacal and hyſterical diſ-orders, are comprehended under this claſs. The cauſes of it are ſelf-indulgence in eating and drinking, and particularly in fermented liquors, want of due bodily exerciſe, injuries done to the brain by fevers, concuſſions, &c. too much ap-plication of the mind, eſpecially to the ſame ob-jects and ideas, violent and long continued paſ-ſions, profuſe evacuations, and an hereditary diſ-poſition; which laſt we may ſuppoſe to conſiſt chiefly in an undue make of the brain. In wo-men, the uneaſy ſtates of the uterus are propaga-ted to the brain, both immediately and medi-ately; *i. e.* by firſt affecting the ſtomach, and thence the brain. In men, the original diſorder often begins, and continues a long time, chiefly in the organs of digeſtion.

The *cauſa proxima* of melancholy, is an irrita-bility of the medullary ſubſtance of the brain, diſ-poſing it upon ſlight occoſions to ſuch vibrations as enter the limits of pain; and particularly to ſuch kinds and degrees as belong to the paſſions of fear, ſorrow, anger, jealouſy, &c. And as theſe vibrations, when the paſſions are not in great exceſs, do not much tranſgreſs the limits of plea-ſure, it will often happen that hypochondriac and

O 2   hyſteric

hyfteric perfons fhall be tranfported with joy from trifling caufes, and be at times difpofed to mirth and laughter. They are alfo very fickle and changeable, as having their defires, hopes, and fears, increafed far beyond their natural ftate, when they fall in with fuch a ftate of the brain as favours them.

It often happens to thefe perfons to have very abfurd defires, hopes, and fears, and yet at the fame time to know them to be abfurd; and in confequence thereof to refift them. While they do this, we may reckon the difeafe within the bounds of melancholy; but when they endeavour to gratify very abfurd defires, or are permanently perfuaded of the reality of very groundlefs hopes and fears, and efpecially if they lofe the connecting confcioufnefs in any great degree, we may reckon the difeafe to have paffed into madnefs ftrictly fo called. HARTLEY.

THE DIFFERENT RACES OF MEN.

NONE but the blind can doubt that the Whites, the Negroes, the Albinoes, the Hottentots, the Laplanders, the Chinefe, the Americans, are races entirely different.

No curious traveller ever paffed through Leyden, without feeing part of the reticulum mucofum of a Negro diffected by the celebrated Ruyfch. This

This membrane is black; and communicates to Negroes that inherent blacknefs, which they do not lofe but in fuch diforders as may deftroy this texture, and allow the greafe to iffue from its cells and form white fpots under the fkin.

Their round eyes, fquat nofes, and invariable thick lips, the different configurations of their ears, their woolly heads, and the meafure of their intellects, make a prodigious difference between them and other fpecies of men; and what demon-ftrates that they are not indebted for this differ-ence to their climates is, that Negro men and women being tranfported into the coldeft coun-tries, conftantly produce animals of their own fpe-cies; and that Mulattoes are only a baftard race of black men and white women. The Albinoes are, indeed, a very fmall and fcarce nation; they inhabit the centre of Africa. Their weaknefs does not allow them to make excurfions far from the caverns which they inhabit; the Negroes, never-thelefs, catch fome of them at times, and thefe we purchafe of them as curiofities. To fay that they are dwarf Negroes, whofe fkin has been blanched by a kind of leprofy, is like faying that the Blacks themfelves are Whites blackened by the leprofy. An Albino no more refembles a Guinea Negro than he does an Englifhman or a Spaniard. Their whitenefs is not like ours; it does not appear like flefh, it has no mixture of white and brown; it

is

is the colour of linen, or rather of bleached wax; their hair and eye-brows are like the fineſt and ſofteſt ſilk; their eyes have no ſort of ſimilitude with thoſe of other men, but they come very near partridges eyes. Their ſhape reſembles that of the Laplanders, but their head that of no other nation whatever; as their hair, their eyes, their ears, are all different; and they have nothing that ſeems to belong to man but the ſtature of their bodies, with the faculty of ſpeaking and think-ing, but in a degree very different from ours.

The apron, which nature has given to the Caf-fres, and whoſe flabby and lank ſkin falls from their navel half way down their thighs; the black breaſts of the Samoides women, the beard of the males of our continent, and the beardleſs chins of the Americans, are ſuch ſtriking diſtinctions, that it is ſcarce poſſible to imagine that they are not each of them of different races.

But now if it ſhould be aſked, From whence came the Americans? it ſhould be aſked, From whence came the inhabitants of the Terra Au-ſtralis? And it has been already anſwered, That the ſame Providence which placed men in Nor-way, planted ſome alſo in America and under the antarctic circle, in the ſame manner as it planted trees and made graſs to grow there.

Several of the learned have ſurmiſed, that ſome races of men, or animals approximating to men,

have

have perifhed: The Albinoes are fo few in number, fo weak, and fo ill-ufed by the Negroes, that
there is reafon to apprehend this fpecies will not
long exift.

With refpect to the duration of the life of man
(if you abftract that line of Adam's defcendants
confecrated by the Jewifh books), it is probable
that all the races of man have enjoyed a life nearly
as fhort as our own; as animals, trees, and all
productions of nature, have ever had the fame duration.

But it fhould be obferved, that commerce, not
having always introduced among mankind the
productions and diforders of other climates, and
men being more robuft and laborious in the fimplicity of a country life, for which they are born,
they muft have enjoyed a more equal health, and
a life fomewhat longer, than in effeminacy, or in
the unhealthy works of great cities; that is to fay,
that if in Paris or London one man in 20,000
attains the age of a hundred years, it is probable
that 20 men in 20 years arrived formerly at that
age. This is feen in feveral parts of America,
where mankind have preferved a pure ftate of nature.—The plague and the fmall-pox, which Ara-
bian caravans communicated in a courfe of years
to the people of Afia and Europe, were for a long
time unknown. Thus mankind in Afia and the
fine climates of Europe multiplied more eafily
than

than elsewhere. Accidental diforders, and fomé wounds, were not indeed cured as they are at prefent; but the advantage of never being afflicted with the plague or fmall-pox, compenfated all the dangers attendant on our nature; fo that, every thing confidered, it is to be believed, that human kind formerly enjoyed, in the favourable climates, a more healthy and happy life than fince the foundation of great empires.

VOLTAIRE.

AN ORIGINAL INFERIORITY IN THE INTELLECTUAL ABILITIES OF MEN BEYOND THE POLAR CIRCLES AND BETWEEN THE TROPICS.

THERE is fome reafon to think, that all the nations which live beyond the polar circles, or between the tropics, are inferior to the reft of the fpecies, and are incapable of all the higher attainments of the human mind. The poverty and mifery of the northern inhabitants of the globe, and the indolence of the fouthern from their few neceffities, may perhaps account for this remarkable difference, without having recourfe to phyfical caufes. Though it may be fufpected, that the Negroes, and in general all the other fpecies of men (for there are four or five different kinds), are naturally inferior to the Whites, there fcarcely ever

ever was a civilized nation of any other complec-
tion than White, nor even any individual, eminent either in action or fpeculation. No ingenious manufactures among them, no arts, no fciences. On the other hand, the moft rude and
barbarous of the Whites, fuch as the ancient Ger-
mans and prefent Tartars, have ftill fomething
eminent about them, in their valour, form of government, or fome other particular. Such a uniform and conftant difference could not happen,
in fo many countries and ages, if Nature had not
made an original diftinction between thefe breeds
of men. Not to mention our colonies, there are
Negro flaves difperfed all over Europe, of whom
none ever difcovered any fymptoms of ingenuity;
though low people, without education, will ftart
up amongft us, and diftinguifh themfelves in every
profeffion. In Jamaica, indeed, they talk of one
Negro as a man of parts and learning; but it is
likely he is admired for flender accomplifhments,
like a parrot who fpeaks a few words plainly.

HUME.

No ORIGINAL DISTINCTION IN THE IN-TELLECTUAL ABILITIES OF MEN IN ANY PART OF THE GLOBE.

DAVID HUME, in a note to his Effay on National Characters, fays, " I am apt to fufpect that
" the

" the Negroes, and in general all the other spe-
" cies of men (for there are four or five different
" kinds), are inferior to the Whites. There ne-
" ver was a civilized nation of any other com-
" plection than White, nor even any individual,
" eminent either in action or speculation: No in-
" genious manufactures among them, no arts, no
" sciences; not to mention our colonies, there are
" Negro slaves dispersed all over Europe, of which
" none have ever discovered any symptoms of in-
" genuity."

This suspicion (for it seems scarcely to have
matured into an opinion) concerning an original
distinction in the breeds of men, has unaccount-
ably given occasion to some writers to quote Hume
as an advocate for the slavery of the Negroes;
which, if his facts were admitted, is foreign to
his argument.—But his assertions are doubtless
too general. Were the Carthaginians, a civilized
African nation, white? Were Hannibal or Ju-
gurtha, both Africans of great merit and emi-
nence, white? No instances, it is true, can be
produced among the Negroes; but examples taken
under the disadvantages of that oppression in
which they are usually seen by Europeans, will be
reasonably objected to. The bad qualities of slaves
may with more justice be attributed, not to their
complexion or climate, but to the abject servility
of their condition, which represses emulation, and

extin-

extinguishes whatever is great and noble in the
mind. Many instances, however, prove, that when
opportunities have occurred of relief from the severity of their bondage, the Negroes are capable
of instruction both in arts and sciences.—With
respect to their disposition in their own country,
Adanson, in his history of Senegal, says, that
they are good-natured, civil, and obliging; and
that he was convinced a considerable abatement
ought to be made in the accounts he had heard
and read of the savage character of the Africans.
Bosman, a Dutch governor, who resided some
years in Africa, relates, that they are friendly to
strangers; that they discover in conversation a
great quickness of parts and understanding; and
that they have a variety of mechanical arts, and
some curious manufactures, among them; particularly that of gold and silver hat-bands, in which he
doubts if they can be rivalled by the most polished
nations. Barbet, Brue, and Holben, who also resided in the country, unite in the favourable repre-
sentation which they give of their capacity for civil
government and the administration of justice.

These testimonials, extracted from writers who
had resided on the spot, evidently overthrow the
fallacious foundation on which Hume had hazard-
ed his speculation.

Strength

STRENGTH OF MIND.

ALL men are equally defirous of happiness; but few are fuccefsful in the pursuit. One chief caufe is the want of *ftrength of mind*, which might enable them to refift the temptation of prefent eafe or pleafure, and carry them forward in the fearch of more diftant profit and enjoyment. Our affections, on a general profpect of their objects, form certain rules of conduct, and certain meafures of preference of one above another. And thefe decifions, though really the refult of our calm paffions and propenfities, (for what elfe can pronounce any object eligible or the contrary?) are yet faid, by a natural abufe of terms, to be the determinations of pure reafon and reflection. But when fome of thefe objects approach nearer us, or acquire the advantages of favourable lights and pofitions, which catch the heart or imagination, our general refolutions are frequently confounded, a fmall enjoyment preferred, and lafting fhame and forrow entailed upon us. And however poets may employ their wit and eloquence in celebrating prefent pleafure, and rejecting all diftant views to fame, health, or fortune; it is obvious, that this practice is the fource of all diffolutenefs and diforder, repentance and mifery. A man of a ftrong determined temper

2   adheres

adheres tenaciously to his general resolutions; and is neither seduced by the allurements of pleasure, nor terrified by the menaces of pain; but keeps still in view those distant pursuits, by which he at once ensures his happiness and his honour.

HUME.

MIRACLES.

A MIRACLE, in the energetic sense of the word, means something wonderful; and thus every thing is a miracle. The order of nature, the activity of light, the life of animals, are perpetual miracles. According to the received notion, however, a miracle is a violation of the divine and eternal laws. A dead man walking two leagues with his head in his hands, is what we call a miracle. Several naturalists affirm, that, in this sense, there are no miracles; and their arguments are these: A miracle is a breach of the mathematical, divine, immutable, eternal laws; now this definition alone makes a miracle a contradiction in terms. A law cannot be both immutable and broken. But it is answered, Cannot a law of God's making be suspended by its Author? They boldly answer, No; and it cannot be that the infinitely wise Being should have made laws, and afterwards break them. If, say they, he made any alteration in his machine, it would be to

VOL. II.   P   †   make

make it go the better. Now it is clear that God has
framed this immense machine as good as it possibly could be : if he saw that any imperfection hereafter would be occasioned by the nature of the
materials, he at first provided against any such
future defect; so that there would be no cause
for any after-change. Besides, God can do nothing without reason: now, what reason could induce him to disfigure his own work for any time?
It is for man's sake, say their opponents. It is
to be hoped then, answer they, that it is for the
sake of all men; it being impossible to conceive
that the Divine Nature should work for some particular men, and not for all mankind. But supposing that God had been pleased to distinguish a
small number of men by particular favours, must
he therefore alter what he has settled for all times
and all places? Must he suspend or alter the eternal play of those immense springs on which depends the motion of the universe? He certainly
can favour his creatures without any such inconstancy and change: his favours are comprised in
his very laws: every thing has been wisely con-
trived and arranged for their good; and they all
irrevocably obey the force which he has originally
implanted in nature.—Wherefore is God to work
a miracle? to accomplish a design he has for
some living beings? That is making God to say,
I have not been able, by the fabric of the universe,

verſe, by my divine decrees, by my eternal laws,
to compaſs ſuch a deſign : I ſee I muſt make an
alteration in my eternal ideas, my immutable laws,
as what I intended cannot be executed by thoſe
means. This would be an acknowledgment of
weakneſs, not a declaration of power : it would
be the moſt inconceivable contradiction. So that
to ſuppoſe God works any miracles, is, if men
can inſult God, a downright inſult to him : it is
no leſs than ſaying to him, You are a weak and
and inconſiſtent Being.——A further reply to theſe
philoſophers is, Your crying up the immutability
of the Supreme Being, the eternity of his laws,
with the regularity of his infinite worlds, ſignifies
nothing : our ſmall heap of dirt has been covered
with miracles : in hiſtory, prodigies are as frequent as natural events. Name me one nation
where incredible prodigies have not been performed, eſpecially in times when reading and writing
were little known.——A philoſopher was one day
aſked, What he would ſay if the ſun ſtood ſtill ;
that is, if the motion of the earth round that body
ceaſed ? if all the dead aroſe ? and if all the moun-
tains went and threw themſelves into the ſea ?
and all this to prove ſome important truth. What
I ſhould ſay ! anſwered the philoſopher : I would
turn Manichean ; and ſay, that there is a principle which undoes what the other has done.

VOLTAIRE.

On the same Subject.

I HAVE seen the birth of many miracles of my time, which, although they were still-born, yet have we not failed to foresee what they would have come to had they lived. It is but finding the end of the clue, and a man may wind off as much as he will; and there is a greater distance betwixt nothing and the minutest thing in the world, than there is betwixt that and the greatest. Now, the first that are tinctured with the beginning of novelty, when they set out their history, find, by the opposition they meet with, where the difficulty of persuasion lies, and caulk that place with some false piece. Besides that, *Insita hominibus libidine alendi de industria rumores*, " men " having a natural lust to propagate reports," we naturally make a conscience of restoring what has been lent us, without some usury and addition of our own invention. Private error first creates public error; and afterwards, in turn, public error causes a particular one. Thus all this fabric rises by patch-work from hand to hand; so that the remotest witness knows more than the nearest, and the last informed is more certain than the first. It is a natural progress; for whoever believes any thing, thinks it a work of charity to persuade another into the same opinion; which
the

the better to do, he will make no difficulty of
adding as much of his own invention as he con-
ceives neceſſary to obviate the reſiſtance or want
of conception he ſuppoſes in others. There is nothing to which men commonly are more inclined
than to give way to their own opinions. Where
the ordinary means fail us, we add command and
force, fire and ſword. It is a misfortune to be at
that paſs, that the beſt touchſtone of the truth
muſt be the multitude of believers, in a crowd
where the number of fools ſo much exceed the
wiſe. *Quaſi vero quidquam ſit tam valde, quam
nihil ſapere, vulgare. Sanitatis patrocinium eſt
inſanientium turba.* " As if any thing were ſo
" common as ignorance." " The mob of fools
" is a protection to the wiſe." It is hard for a
man to form his judgment againſt the common
opinions. The firſt perſuaſion taken of the very
ſubject itſelf poſſeſſes the ſimple; and from that it
ſpreads to the wiſe, by the authority of the number and antiquity of the witneſſes. For my part,
what I would not believe from one, I would not believe from a hundred; and I do not judge of opinions by the years. It is not long ſince one of our
princes, in whom the gout has ſpoiled an excellent
natural genius and ſprightly diſpoſition, ſuffered
himſelf to be ſo far perſuaded with the report of
the wonderful operations of a certain prieſt, who
by words and geſtures cured all ſorts of diſeaſes, as

to

to go a long journey to feek him out; and, by the force of his apprehenfion, for fome time fo perfuaded and laid his legs afleep for feveral hours, as to obtain that fervice from them which they had a long time left off. Had fortune packed together five or fix fuch accidents, it had been enough to have brought this miracle into nature. There was after this difcovered fo much fimplicity, and fo little art, in the architect of fuch operations, that he was thought too contemptible to be punifhed; as would be the cafe of moft fuch things, were they examined to the bottom. *Miramur ex intervallo fallentia,* " We admire at things that de-" ceive by their diftance." So does our fight often reprefent to us ftrange things at a diftance, that vanifh in approaching them near. *Nunquam ad liquidum fama perducitur,* " Fame never reports " things in their true light." It is to be wondered at from how many idle beginnings and frivolous caufes fuch famous impreffions commonly proceed. This it is that obftructs the information; for whilft we feek out the caufes, and the great and weighty ends worthy of fo great a name, we lofe the true ones. They efcape our fight by their littlenefs: and, in truth, a prudent, diligent, and fubtle inquirer is neceffary in fuch refearches; one who is indifferent, and not prepoffeffed.

MONTAIGNE.

On

ON THE SAME SUBJECT.

A MIRACLE is a violation of the laws of nature; and as a firm and unalterable experience has eſtabliſhed theſe laws, the proof againſt a miracle, from the very nature of the fact, is as entire as any argument from experience can poſſibly be imagined. Why is it more than probable that all men muſt die; that lead cannot of itſelf remain ſuſpended in the air; that fire conſumes wood, and is extinguiſhed by water; unleſs it be, that theſe events are found agreeable to the laws of nature, and there is required a violation of theſe laws, or a miracle, to prevent them? Nothing is a miracle if it happen in the common courſe of nature. Sometimes an event may not in *itſelf ſeem* to be contrary to the laws of nature; and yet, if it were real, it might, by reaſon of ſome circumſtances, be denominated a miracle, becauſe in fact it is contrary to theſe laws. Thus, if a perſon claiming a divine authority ſhould command a ſick perſon to be well, the clouds to pour rain; in ſhort, ſhould order many natural events, which immediately follow upon his command; theſe might juſtly be eſteemed miracles, becauſe they are really, in this caſe, contrary to the laws of nature. For if any ſuſpicion remain, that the event and command concurred by accident, there

is

is no miracle and no tranfgreffion of the laws of nature. If this fufpicion be removed, there is evidently a miracle, and a tranfgreffion of thefe laws; becaufe nothing can be more contrary to nature, than that the voice or command of a man fhould have fuch an influence. A miracle may be accurately defined, *A tranfgreffion of a law of na-ture by a particular volition of the Deity, or by the interpofition of fome invifible agent.* A miracle may either be difcoverable by men or not. This alters not its nature and effence. The raifing of a houfe or fhip into the air is a vifible miracle. The raifing of a feather, when the wind wants ever fo little of a force for that purpofe, is a real miracle, though not fo fenfible with regard to us. —No event can be miraculous unlefs contrary to uniform experience. Uniform experience amounts to a proof; there is therefore a direct and a full proof, from the nature of the fact, againft every miracle; nor can fuch proof be deftroyed but by an oppofite fuperior proof.

HUME.

A MIRACLE DESTROYS THE TESTIMONY FOR IT, AND THE TESTIMONY DESTROYS ITSELF.

IN matters of religion, whatever is different is contrary; and it is impoffible the religions of
ancient

ancient Rome, of Turkey, of Siam, and of China,
fhould all of them be true. Every miracle, therefore, pretended to have been wrought in any of thefe
religions (and all of them abound in miracles), as
its direct fcope is to eftablifh the particular fyftem to which it is attributed; fo has it the fame
force, though more indirectly, to overthrow every
other fyftem. In deftroying a rival fyftem, it
likewife deftroys the credit of thofe miracles on
which that fyftem was eftablifhed: So that all
the prodigies of different religions are to be regarded as contrary facts; and the evidence to
thefe prodigies, whether weak or ftrong, as oppofite to each other. When we believe any miracle of Mahomet, &c. we have for our warrant
the teftimony of a few barbarous Arabians; and,
on the other hand, we are to regard the teftimony
of all the witneffes, Grecians, Chinefe, and Roman Catholic, in the fame light as if they had
mentioned that Mahometan miracle, and had in
exprefs terms contradicted it, with the fame certainty as they have for the miracle they relate.
This argument is not different from the reafoning
of a judge, who fuppofes, that the credit of two
witneffes, maintaining a crime againft any one,
is deftroyed by the teftimony of two others, who
affirm him to have been 200 miles diftant at the
fame inftant when the crime is faid to have been
committed.   * *

SOME

SOME MIRACLES OR VIOLATIONS OF THE USUAL COURSE OF NATURE MAY ADMIT OF PROOF FROM HUMAN TESTIMONY.

SUPPOSE all authors, in all languages, agree, that from the firſt of January 1600 there was a total darkneſs over the whole earth for eight days; ſuppoſe that the tradition of this extraordinary event is ſtill ſtrong and lively among the people; that all travellers, who return from foreign coun- tries, bringing us accounts of the ſome tradition, without the leaſt variation or contradiction: it is evident, that our philoſophers, inſtead of doubt- ing that fact, ought to receive it for certain, and ought to ſearch for the cauſes whence it might be derived. The decay, corruption, and diſſolu- tion of nature, is an event rendered probable by ſo many analogies, that any phenomenon which ſeems to have a tendency towards that cata- ſtrophe, comes within the reach of human teſti- mony, if that teſtimony be very extenſive and uni- form.   HUME.

ON THE SAME SUBJECT.

A MIRACLE is, in a particular fact, an imme- diate act of Divine power, a ſenſible change in the order of nature, a real and viſible exception
to

to its laws. Such is the idea, from which we muſt not wander, if we would be underſtood in reaſoning on this ſubject. Now this idea preſents two queries, which it is neceſſary for us to reſolve. The firſt is, Can the Deity work miracles? that is to ſay, Can he break through thoſe laws which he hath eſtabliſhed? To treat this queſtion ſeriouſly, would be impious, if not abſurd : to puniſh the man who ſhould reſolve it in the negative, would be doing him too much honour; he ſhould be confined to ſtraw and a dark chamber. But then who hath ever denied the power of the Deity to work miracles? A man muſt be a very Jew, to aſk if God Almighty could ſpread a table in the wilderneſs?—The ſecond queſtion is, Would the Deity work miracles? This is another thing. This queſtion, conſidered merely in itſelf, is perfectly indifferent. It by no means intereſts the glory of God, whoſe deſigns we cannot penetrate. I will go ſtill further, and ſay, if there were any difference with regard to faith, in the manner of anſwering it, the higheſt ideas we can entertain of the wiſdom and majeſty of the Divine Being would induce us to reply in the negative. It is nothing but human vanity that could object to it. Thus far can reaſon go, and no further. As for any thing elſe, this queſtion is futile and frivolous; as, in order to reſolve it, we ought to be able to read the eternal

decrees

decrees of Heaven; for, as we shall see presently, it is impossible to determine it by facts. These are mysteries; and so much respect is due to the Infinite Essence, as not to come to any determination about an object of which we know nothing but its immensity.—And yet when a mere mortal comes to us, and boldly affirms that he hath seen a miracle, he determines this great question at once. Judge, then, if he ought to be believed merely on his word.

It is gross sophistry to employ moral proofs to ascertain facts that are physically impossible; as in that case the very principle of credibility, founded on natural possibility, is in fault. Though men are willing, in such a cause, to admit of this proof in matters of mere speculation, or in regard to facts that are in nowise interesting, we may be assured they would be more difficult with respect to any thing that in the least affected their temporal interest. Let us suppose that a dead man should return to demand his estate and effects of his heirs, affirming that he is restored again to life, and requiring to be admitted to prove it. Is there a tribunal upon earth would grant him leave? But, not to enter into this controversy, we will admit the facts to have all the certitude ascribed to them, and content ourselves with distinguishing between what is apparent to the sense, and what is deducible from reason.

2   As

As a miracle is an exception to the laws of nature, it is neceffary, in order to enable us to judge of it, that we fhould be fully acquainted with thofe laws; and in order to judge of it with certainty, that we fhould be acquainted with them all. For if there fhould be but one we are ignorant of, it may, in fome circumftances unknown to the fpectators, alter the effect of thofe which may be known. Hence every one who takes upon him to fay, that fuch or fuch an act is a miracle, declares himfelf to be perfectly acquainted with all the laws of nature, and that he knows this act to be an exception.

But where is the man who knows all the laws of nature ? Newton himfelf never pretended to fuch knowledge. A fenfible man, being witnefs to an unheard of act, may affirm that he faw fuch a fact, and we may believe him. But neither that fenfible man, nor any other fenfible man upon earth, will take upon him to affirm, that fuch fact, how new and aftonifhing foever, is a miracle; for how can he know it ?

The moft that can be faid in favour of a perfon who boafts his working miracles is, that he does things very extraordinary. But who will deny the poffibility or reality of things very extraordinary?

New difcoveries are daily made in the operations of nature, while human induftry is hourly proceeding towards perfection. The curious art

of chemiftry alone hath its tranfmutations, preci-
pitations, detonations, explofions, its phofphorus,
its earthquakes, and a thoufand other wonders, to
operate on the beholders —With fuch inftruments, as cannon, the loadftone, the barometer,
and optical inftruments, what prodigies might
not be worked among ignorant people ? The
Europeans have, in confequence of their arts,
always paffed for Gods among the Barbarians.
And yet if, in the midft even of thefe arts, of
fciences, colleges, and academies ; if, in the midft
of Europe, in France, or in England, a perfon
had ftarted up, in the laft century, armed with
all thofe miracles of electricity, which are now
common to the meaneft of our experimentalifts,
it is probable he would have been burnt for a
forcerer, or followed as a prophet.—The fpectators of marvellous things are naturally led to
cry them up with exaggeration. In deceiving
others on this head, therefore, men may frequently, without ill intention, deceive themfelves.
When things are ever fo little above our knowledge or comprehenfion, we are apt to think them
above that of human reafon in general ; and the
mind is at length induced to fee a prodigy, where
the heart is fo ftrongly inclined to find one.

From what is here advanced, I conclude, that
mere facts, though ever fo well attefted and ad-
miffible in all their circumftances, ferve to prove
nothing;

nothing; and that we may fufpect an exaggeration of their circumftances, without fufpecting
the fincerity of thofe who have related them.
The difcoveries which are daily making in the
laws of nature, thofe which probably will be made
hereafter, and thofe which may ever remain to be
made; the paft and prefent progrefs of human
induftry; the different bounds which people fet
to the impoffible, according as they have more or
lefs knowledge; all thefe things ferve to prove
that we are unacquainted with thofe bounds.
And yet, in order to a miracle's being really fuch,
it muft furpafs them. Whether there be truly
any miracles or not, therefore, it is impoffible for
a wife man to be affured that any fact whatever
is truly fuch.   ROUSSEAU.

MIRACLES ESTABLISHED ONLY BY HU- MAN TESTIMONY, NO PROOF OF THE DI- VINE ORIGINAL OF ANY RELIGION.

IF we extend our theology beyond the profpect
of the univerfe and the proper ufe of our faculties, we muft have recourfe to extraordinary
means. Thefe means cannot depend on the authority of men: for all men being of the fame
fpecies, they have all the fame natural means of
knowledge, and one man is as likely to be deceived as another. Faith, therefore, muft depend

not

not on hearfay, but on proofs. The teftimony, therefore, of mankind is, at the bottom, that of reafon, and adds nothing to the natural means God hath given us for the difcovery of truth.— What can even the apoftle of truth have to tell us, of which we are not ftill to judge? *But God himfelf* hath fpoken; liften to the voice of revelation. But *to whom hath he fpoken?* and how comes it that he hath appointed others to teach his word? There would have been much lefs rifk of deception, if every individual had heard him fpeak; and this would have been no difficult matter to Omnipotence. It may be faid, we are fecure from deception by his manifefting the miffion of his meffengers by miracles. Where are thefe miracles to be feen? Are they related only in books? Who wrote thefe books? Men. Who were witneffes of thefe miracles? Men. Always human teftimony! It is always men that tell us what other men have told them. What a number of thefe are conftantly between us and the Deity! We are always reduced to the neceffity of examining, comparing, and verifying fuch evidence.

This occafions a very intricate difcuffion, for which we ftand in need of immenfe erudition. We muft recur back to the earlieft antiquity; we muft examine, weigh, confront prophecies, revelations, facts, with all the monuments of faith that have made their appearance in all the
countries

countries of the world, to ascertain their time, place, authors, and occasions. There is great sagacity requisite to enable us to distinguish between pieces that are supposititious and those which are authentic; to compare objections with their replies, translations with their originals; to judge of the impartiality of witnesses, of their good sense, of their capacity; to know if nothing be suppressed or added to their testimony, if nothing be changed, transposed or falsified; to obviate the contradictions that remain; to judge what weight we ought to ascribe to the silence of our opponents, in regard to facts alleged against them; whether they did not disdain them too much to make any reply; whether books were common enough for ours to reach them; or if we were honest enough to let theirs have a free circulation among us, and to leave their strongest objections in full force.

Again, supposing all these monuments acknowledged to be incontestable, we must proceed to examine the proofs of the mission of their authors. It would be necessary for us to be perfectly acquainted with the laws of chance, and the doctrine of probabilities, to judge what prediction could not be accomplished without a miracle; to know the genius of the original language, in order to distinguish what is predictive in these languages, and what is only figurative. It would

Q 3 be

be requifite for us to know what facts are agreeable to the eftablished order of nature, and what
are not fo; to be able to fay how far an artful
man may not fafcinate the eyes of the fimple,
and even aftonifh the moft enlightened fpectators;
to know of what kind a miracle fhould be, and
the authenticity it ought to bear, not only to
claim our belief, but to make it criminal to doubt
it; to compare the proofs of falfe and true miracles, and difcover the certain means of diftinguifhing them; and, after all, to tell why the Deity
fhould choofe, in order to confirm the truth of
his word, to make ufe of means which themfelves
require fo much confirmation, as if he took delight in playing upon the credulity of mankind,
and had purpofely avoided the direct means to
perfuade them.

Suppofe that the Divine Majefty hath really
condefcended to make man the organ of promul-
gating its facred will; is it reafonable, is it juft,
to require all mankind to obey the voice of fuch
a minifter, without his making himfelf known to
be fuch? Where is the equity or propriety of
furnifhing him, for univerfal credentials, with
only a few particular tokens difplayed before a
handful of obfcure perfons, and of which all the
reft of mankind know nothing but hearfay? In
every country in the world, if we fhould believe
all the prodigies to be true which the common
people,

people, and the ignorant, affirm to have feen, every fect would be in the right; there would be more miraculous events than natural ones; and the greateft miracle of all would be to find that no miracles had happened where fanaticifm had been perfecuted. The Supreme Being is beft difplayed by the fixed and unalterable order of nature. Who is there will venture to determine how many eye-witneffes are neceffary to render a miracle worthy of credit? If the miracles intended to prove the truth of a doctrine, ftand themfelves in need of proof, of what ufe are they? There might as well be none performed at all.

The moft important examination, after all, remains to be made into the truth of the doctrines delivered; for as thofe who fay that God is pleafed to work thefe miracles, pretend that the devil fometimes imitates them, we are not a jot nearer than before, though fuch miracles fhould be ever fo well attefted. As the magicians of Pharaoh worked the fame miracles, even in the prefence of Mofes, as he himfelf performed by the exprefs command of God, why might not they, in his abfence, from the fame proofs, pretend to the fame authority? Thus, after proving the truth of the doctrine by the miracle, we are reduced to prove the truth of the miracle by that of the doctrine, left the works of the devil fhould be miftaken for thofe of the Lord.—The doctrines

coming

coming from God ought to bear the sacred characters of the Divinity; and should not only clear
up those confused ideas which unenlightened reason excits in the mind, but should also furnish
us with a system of religion and morals agreeable
to those attributes by which only we form a conception of his essence.

ROUSSEAU.

THE PASSION OF SURPRISE AND WONDER FAVOURABLE TO MIRACLES.

THE passion of surprise and wonder arising
from miracles, being an agreeable emotion, gives
a sensible tendency towards the belief of those
events from which it is derived.——With what
greediness are the miraculous accounts of travellers received; their descriptions of sea and land
monsters, &c.? But if the spirit of religion join
itself to the love of wonder, there is an end of
common sense; human testimony, in these circumstances, loses all pretensions to authority. A
religionist may be an enthusiast, and imagine he
sees what has no reality. What greater temptation than to appear a missionary, a prophet, an
ambassador from heaven? If, by the help of vanity
and a heated imagination, a man has first made a
convert of himself, and entered seriously into the
delusion; who ever scruples to make use of pious
frauds

frauds in fupport of fo holy and meritorious a caufe? The fmalleft fpark may here kindle into the greateft flame. The gazing multitude receive greedily, without examination, whatever foothes fuperftition, and promotes wonder. His auditors may not have, and commonly have not, fufficient judgment to canvafs his evidence: what judgment they have, they renounce by principle; or if they were ever fo willing to employ it, paffion and a heated imagination difturb the regularity of its operations. Their credulity increafes his impudence; and his impudence overpowers their credulity. The many inftances of forged miracles, and prophecies, and fupernatural events, which, in all ages, have either been detected by contrary evidence, or which detect themfelves by their abfurdity, prove the ftrong propenfity of mankind to the extraordinary and the marvellous; and ought reafonably to beget a fufpicion againft all relations of this kind. We judge, therefore, in conformity to experience and obfervation, when we account for them by the known and natural principles of credulity and delufion. And fhall we, rather than have recourfe to fo natural a folution, allow of a miraculous violation of all the laws of nature?

HUME.

MIRACLES ABOUND IN IGNORANT AND BARBAROUS AGES.

IT forms a very ftrong prefumption againft all miraculous relations, that they are obferved to abound chiefly among ignorant and barbarous nations; or if a civilized people has ever given admiffion to any of them, that people will be found to have received them from ignorant and barbarous anceftors, who tranfmitted them with that inviolable fanction and authority which always attend received opinions. When we perufe the firft hiftories of all nations, we are apt to imagine ourfelves tranfported into a new world. Peftilences, famines, death, &c. are never the effects of thofe natural caufes which we experience. Prophecies, omens, oracles, judgments, quite obfcure the few natural events that are intermingled with them. But as the former grow thinner every page, in proportion as we advance nearer the enlightened ages, we foon learn that there is nothing myfterious or fupernatural in the cafe, but that all proceeds from the ufual propenfity of mankind towards the marvellous; and that though this inclination may at intervals receive a check from fenfe and learning, it can never be thoroughly extirpated from human nature.

The advantages are fo great of ftarting an impofture

posture among an ignorant people, that, even though the delusion should be too gross to impose on the generality of them (which, though seldom, is sometimes the case), it has a much better chance for succeeding in remote countries, than if the first scene had been laid in a city renowned for arts and knowledge. The most ignorant and barbarous of these barbarians carry the report abroad. None of their countrymen have large enough correspondence, or sufficient credit and authority, to contradict and beat down the delusion. Mens inclination to the marvellous has full opportunity to display itself. And thus a story, which is universally exploded in the place where it was first started, shall pass for certain at a thousand miles distance.   HUME.

MIRACLES CAN NEVER BE PROVED BY HUMAN TESTIMONY, SO AS TO BE THE FOUNDATION OF A SYSTEM OF RELIGION.

IF a miracle be ascribed to any new system of religion, men, in all ages, have been so much imposed on by ridiculous stories of that kind, that this very circumstance would be a full proof of a cheat; and sufficient with all men of sense, not only to make them reject the fact, but even reject it without further examination. Though the Being to whom the miracle is ascribed be Almighty,

mighty, it does not, upon that account, become a whit more probable; since it is impossible for us to know the attributes or actions of such a Being, otherwise than from the experience which we have of his productions in the usual course of nature. This still reduces us to past observation; and obliges us to compare the instances of the violations of truth in the testimony of men, with those of the violations of the laws of nature by miracles, in order to judge which of them is most likely or probable. As the violations of truth are more common in the testimony concerning religious miracles than in that concerning any other matter of fact, this must diminish very much the authority of the former testimony, and make us form a resolution, never to lend any attention to it, with whatever specious pretext it may be covered.

HUME.

PRINCIPLES OF THE MONKS, NOT A PROPER STANDARD OF RIGHT AND WRONG.

AMONG the different principles adopted as a standard of right and wrong, is the principle of the Monks; or, as it is more frequently called, the *ascetic* principle, or *asceticism;* a term from a Greek word which signifies *exercise*. The practices by which the Monks sought to distinguish

them-

themselves from other men, were called their exercises. These exercises consisted in so many contrivances they had for tormenting themselves. By this they thought to ingratiate themselves with the Deity. For the Deity, said they, is a Being of infinite benevolence: now a Being of the most ordinary benevolence is pleased to see others make themselves as happy as they can; therefore to make ourselves as unhappy as we can is the way to please the Deity. If any body asked them, What motive they could find for doing all this? Oh! said they, you are not to imagine that we are punishing ourselves for nothing: we know very well what we are about. You are to know, that for every grain of pain it costs us now, we are to have a hundred grains of pleasure by and by. The case is, that God loves to see us torment ourselves at present: indeed he has as good as told us so. But this is done only to try us, in order just to see how we should behave; which it is plain he could not know, without making the experiment. Now, then, from the satisfaction it gives him to see us make ourselves as unhappy as we can make ourselves in this present life, we have a sure proof of the satisfaction it will give him to see us as happy as he can make us in a life to come.

By the principle of *asceticism* therefore is meant, that principle which, like the principle of *utility*, approves or disapproves of any action, according to

the tendency which it appears to have to augment
or diminish the happiness of the party whose interest is in question; but in an inverse manner: ap-
proving of actions in as far as they tend to diminish
his happiness; disapproving of them in as far as
they tend to augment it. It is evident that any
one who reprobates any the least particle of pleasure, as such, from whatever source derived, is
pro tanto a partizan of the principle of asceticism.
It is only upon that principle, and not from the
principle of utility, that the most abominable pleasure which the vilest of malefactors ever reaped
from his crime would be to be reprobated, if it
stood alone. The case is, that it never does stand
alone; but is necessarily followed by such a quantity of pain (or, what comes to the same thing,
such a chance for a certain quantity of pain), that
the pleasure, in comparison of it, is as nothing:
and this is the true and sole, but perfectly sufficient, reason for making it a ground for punishment.

There are two classes of men of very different
complexions, by whom the principle of asceticism appears to have been embraced: the one a
set of moralists; the other a set of religionists.
Different accordingly have been the motives which
appear to have recommended it to the notice of
these different parties. Hope, that is, the prospect
of pleasure, seems to have animated the former:

                                        hope,

hope, the aliment of philosophic pride; the hope
of honour and reputation at the hands of men.
Fear, that is, the prospect of pain, the latter: fear,
the offspring of superstitious fancy; the fear of
future punishment at the hands of a splenetic and
revengeful Deity. I say in this case, fear; for of
the invisible future, fear is more powerful than
hope. These circumstances characterize the two
different parties among the partizans of the principle of asceticism; the parties and their motives
different, the principle the same.

The religious party, however, appear to have
carried it further than the philosophical: they
have acted more consistently and less wisely. The
philosophical party have scarcely gone further than
to reprobate pleasure: the religious party have
frequently gone so far as to make it a matter of
merit and of duty to court pain. The philosophical party have hardly gone further than the making pain a matter of indifference. It is no evil,
they have said: they have not said, It is a good.
They have not so much as reprobated all pleasure
in the lump. They have discarded only what
they have called the gross; that is, such as are
organical, or of which the origin is easily traced
up to such as are organical: they have even che-
rished and magnified the refined. Yet this, however, not under the name of pleasure: to cleanse
itself from the sordes of its impure original, it was

necef-

neceffary it fhould change its name: the honourable, the glorious, the reputable, the becoming,
the *honeſtum*, the *decorum*, it was to be called; in
fhort, any thing but pleafure.

From thefe two fources have flowed the doctrines
from which the fentiments of the bulk of mankind
have all along received a tincture of this principle;
fome from the philofophical, fome from the religious, fome from both. Men of education more
frequently from the philofophical, as more fuited to
the elevation of their fentiments: the vulgar more
frequently from the fuperftitious, as more fuited
to the narrownefs of their intellect, undilated by
knowledge; and to the abjectnefs of their condition, continually open to the attacks of fear. The
tinctures, however, derived from the two fources,
would naturally intermingle, infomuch that a man
would not always know by which of them he was
moft influenced; and they would often ferve to
corroborate and enliven one another. It was this
conformity that made a kind of alliance between
parties of a complexion otherwife fo diffimilar;
and difpofed them to unite upon various occafions
againft the common enemy, the partizan of the
principle of utility, whom they joined in brand-
ing with the odious name of Epicurean.

The principle of afceticifm, however, with whatever warmth it may have been embraced by its
partizans as a rule of private conduct, feems not
to

to have been carried to any confiderable length when applied to the bufinefs of government. In a few inftances it has been carried a little way by the philofophical party: witnefs the Spartan regimen. Though then, perhaps, it may be confidered as having been a meafure of fecurity; and an application, though a precipitate and perverfe application, of the principle of utility. Scarcely in any inftances, to any confiderable length, by the religious: for the various monaftic orders, and the focieties of the Quakers, Dumplers, Moravians, and other religionifts, have been free focieties, whofe regimen no man has been aftricted to without the intervention of his own confent. Whatever merit a man may have thought there would be in making himfelf miferable, no fuch notion feems ever to have occurred to any of them, that it may be a merit, much lefs a duty, to make others miferable; although it fhould feem, that if a certain quantity of mifery were a thing fo defirable, it would not matter much whether it were brought by each man upon himfelf, or by one man upon another. It is true, that from the fame fource from whence, among the religionifts, the attachment to the principle of afceticifm took its rife, flowed other doctrines and practices, from which mifery in abundance was produced in one man by the inftrumentality of another: witnefs the holy wars, and the perfecutions for religion.

But the paſſion for producing miſery in theſe caſes
proceeded upon ſome ſpecial ground: the exerciſe
of it was confined to perſons of particular de-
ſcriptions; they were tormented, not as men, but
as heretics and infidels. To have inflicted the
ſame miſeries on their fellow-believers and fellow-
ſectaries, would have been as blameable in the
eyes even of theſe religioniſts, as in thoſe of a partizan of the principle of utility. For a man to
give himſelf a certain number of ſtripes was indeed meritorious; but to give the ſame number
of ſtripes to another man, not conſenting, would
have been a ſin. We read of ſaints, who for the
good of their ſouls, and the mortification of their
bodies, have voluntarily yielded themſelves a prey
to vermin: but though many perſons of this claſs
have wielded the reins of empire, we read of none
who have ſet themſelves to work, and made laws
on purpoſe, with a view of ſtocking the body po-
litic with the breed of highwaymen, houſebreak-
ers, or incendiaries. If at any time they have ſuffered the nation to be preyed upon by ſwarms of
idle penſioners, or uſeleſs placemen, it has rather
been from negligence and imbecillity, than from
any ſettled plan for oppreſſing and plundering of
the people. If at any time they have ſapped the
ſources of national wealth, by cramping commerce, and driving the inhabitants into emigra-
tion, it has been with other views, and in purſuit
of

of other ends. If they have declaimed againſt the
purſuit of pleaſure, and the uſe of wealth, they
have commonly ſtopt at declamation; they have
not, like Lycurgus, made expreſs ordinances for
the purpoſe of baniſhing the precious metals. If
they have eſtabliſhed idleneſs by law, it has been,
not becauſe idleneſs, the mother of vice and miſery, is itſelf a virtue, but becauſe idleneſs (ſay
they) is the road to holineſs. If under the notion
of faſting, they have joined in the plan of confi-
ning their ſubjects to a diet, thought by ſome to be
of the moſt nouriſhing and prolific nature, it has
been not for the ſake of making them tributaries
to the nations by whom that diet was to be ſupplied, but for the ſake of manifeſting their own
power, and exerciſing the obedience of the people.
If they have eſtabliſhed, or ſuffered to be eſtabliſhed, puniſhments for the breach of celibacy,
they have done no more than comply with the
petitions of thoſe deluded rigoriſts, who, dupes to
the ambitious and deep-laid policy of their rulers,
firſt laid themſelves under that idle obligation by
a vow.

The principle of aſceticiſm ſeems originally to
have been the reverie of certain haſty ſpeculators,
who having perceived, or fancied, that certain pleaſures, when reaped in certain circumſtances, have,
at the long run, been attended with pains more
than equivalent to them, took occaſion to quarrel
with

with every thing that offered itself under the name
of pleasure. Having then got thus far, and having forgot the point which they set out from,
they pushed on, and went so much further as to
think it meritorious to fall in love with pain.
Even this, we see, is at bottom but the principle
of utility misapplied.

The principle of utility is capable of being consistently pursued; and it is but tautology to say,
that the more consistently it is pursued, the better
it must ever be for human-kind. The principle
of asceticism never was, nor ever can be, consistently pursued by any living creature. Let but one
tenth part of the inhabitants of this earth pursue
it consistently, and in a day's time they will have
turned it into a hell. *See the article* RIGHT and
WRONG.   J. BENTHAM.

MORALITY.

THE truths of morality, like all other truths,
are discovered only by trials and experiments.
The principles of moral conduct would be totally
insignificant if they did not lead to some ends;
and if a certain manner of exercising our faculties, a certain manner of acting, had not been
found, by repeated experiments, to have made us
happy, and a different manner to have made us
unhappy, we should never have had any principles
of

of morals. This fcience, therefore, which, under
its own name, but more efpecially under that of
religion, has been confidered as a matter of mere
fpeculation, and abounding with doubts and un-
certainties and difficulties, is as plain and as clear
as geometry; it depends on facts, which cannot
eafily be miftaken, becaufe the whole world is
collecting and obferving them: and it has this advantage over other fciences, that all men have an
equal intereft in the fuccefs of their inquiries.

WILLIAMS.

THE ORIGIN OF MORAL RULES.

THE rules of morality are ultimately founded
on experience of what, in particular inftances,
our moral faculties, our natural fenfe of merit and
propriety, approve or difapprove of. We do not
originally approve or condemn particular actions,
becaufe, upon examination, they appear to be
agreeable or inconfiftent with a certain general
rule. The general rule, on the contrary, is formed, by finding from experience, that all actions
of a certain kind, or circumftanced in a certain
manner, are approved or difapproved of. To the
man who firft faw an inhuman murder, committed from avarice, envy, or unjuft refentment,
and upon one too who loved and trufted the mur-
derer; who beheld the laft agonies of the dying
perfon;

perſon; who heard him with his expiring breath complain more of the perfidy and ingratitude of his falſe friend, than of the violence which had been done to him; there could be no occaſion, in order to conceive how horrible ſuch an action was, that he ſhould reflect that one of the moſt ſacred rules of conduct was what prohibited the taking away the life of an innocent perſon; that this was a plain violation of that rule, and conſequently a very blameable action. His deteſtation of this crime, it is evident, would ariſe inſtantaneouſly, and antecedent to his having formed to himſelf any ſuch general rule. The general rule, on the contrary, which he might afterwards form, would be founded upon the deteſtation which he felt neceſſarily ariſe in his own breaſt at the thought of this and every other particular action of the ſame kind. When we read in hiſtory or romance the account of actions either of generoſity or of baſeneſs, the admiration which we conceive for the one, and the contempt which we feel for the other, neither of them ariſe from reflecting that there are certain general rules which declare all actions of the one kind admirable, and all actions of the other contemptible. Thoſe general rules, on the contrary, are all formed from the experience we have had of the effects which actions of all different kinds naturally produce upon us. An amiable action, a reſpectable action
tion

tion, an horrid action, are all of them actions which naturally excite the love, the respect, or the horror of the spectator, for the person who performs them. The general rules which determine what actions are, and what are not, the objects of each of those sentiments, can be formed no other way than by observing what actions actually and in fact excite them. When these general rules indeed have been formed, and when they are universally acknowledged and established by the concurring sentiments of mankind, we frequently appeal to them, as to the standards of judgment, in debating concerning the degree of praise or blame that is due to certain actions of a complicated and dubious nature. They are upon these occasions commonly cited as the ultimate foundations of what is just or unjust in human conduct: and this circumstance seems to have misled several eminent authors to draw up their systems in such a manner, as if they had supposed that the original judgments of mankind, with regard to right or wrong, were formed, like the decisions of a court of judicatory, by considering, first, the general rule; and then, secondly, whether the particular action under consideration fell properly within its comprehension. *See the article* RIGHT *and* WRONG.

A. SMITH.

GE-

GENERAL STATE OF MORALS IN DIFFERENT CLIMATES.

IN point of morality in general, it is agreed, that the manners of cold climates far exceed those of warm; in the latter, the paffions are naturally very ftrong, and likewife kept in a perpetual ftate of irritation from the high degree of fenfibility that prevails, which caufes a great multiplication of crimes, by multiplying the objects of temptation. Many defires and paffions arife there, from caufes that would either never occur in a cold climate, or be eafily refifted; but in a warm one the paffion or inclination is ftronger, and the power of reftraint lefs. In cold climates, the defires are but few in comparifon, and not often of a very immoral kind; and thofe repreffed with lefs difficulty, as they are feldom very violent. In temperate climates, the paffions are in a middle ftate, and generally inconftant in their nature; fufficiently ftrong, however, to furnifh motives for action, though not fo powerful as to admit of no reftraints from confiderations of prudence, juftice, or religion.   FALCONER.

THE

THE ORIGIN OF THE IDEAS OF MORAL OBLIGATION.

EVERY person feels a gleam of pleasure the moment that light is introduced into a dark room; and disagreeable sensations, tending to melancholy, and sometimes verging towards the borders of terror, upon passing suddenly from a light into a perfectly dark place. These feelings are instantaneous and constant, and to appearance *simple;* yet they are unquestionably the offspring of association, but formed by a thousand sensations and ideas, which it is impossible to analyse or separate; and they vary exceedingly in different persons, especially according to the circumstances of their early lives.

The ideas annexed to the words *moral right* and *wrong* are likewise far from being simple in reality; though the association of their parts has become so intimate and perfect in a long course of time, that, upon first naming them, they present that appearance. So the motion of the head, and of any particular limb, may seem to be a very simple thing, though a great number of muscles are employed to perform it.

The first rudiments of the ideas of *right, wrong,* and *obligation,* seem to be acquired by a child when he finds himself checked and controuled by a fuperior power. At firſt, he feels nothing but mere *force*; and confequently he has no idea of any kind of reſtraint but that of mere *neceſſity*. He finds he cannot have his will, and therefore he ſubmits. Afterwards, he attends to many circumſtances, which diſtinguiſh the authority of a *father* or of a *maſter*, from that of other perfons. Ideas of reverence, love, eſteem, dependence, accompany thoſe commands; and by degrees he experiences the peculiar advantages of filial ſubjection. He ſees alfo, that all his companions, who are noticed and admired by others, obey their parents, and that thoſe who are of a refractory difpofition are univerfally difliked.

Theſe and other circumſtances now begin to alter and modify the idea of mere neceſſity, till by degrees he confiders the commands of a parent as fomething that *muſt not* be refifted or difputed, even though he has a power of doing it; and all theſe ideas coalefcing, form the ideas of moral right and moral obligation, which are eafily transferred from the commands of a parent to thoſe of a magiftrate, of God, and of confcience. It is plainly apparent to every perfon who has attended to the ideas of children, that their ideas of moral right and moral obligation are formed very gradually and flowly, from a long train of circumſtances, and that it is a confiderable time before they become at all diſtinct and perfect.

This

This opinion of the gradual formation of the ideas of moral right and wrong from a great variety of elements, eafily accounts for that prodigious diverfity in the fentiments of mankind refpecting the objects of moral obligation; and they feem unaccountable on any other hypothefis. If the idea of moral obligation was a fimple idea, arifing from the view of certain actions or fentiments, why fhould it not be as invariable as the perception of colours and founds? But though the fhape and colour of a flower appear the fame to every human eye, one man practifes as a moral duty what another looks upon with abhorrence, and reflects upon with remorfe. Now a thing that varies with education and inftruction, as moral fentiments are known to do, certainly has the appearance of being generated by a feries of different impreffions, in the manner here defcribed.

The moft fhocking crimes that men can commit are thofe of *injuftice* and *murder*; and yet it is hardly poffible to define any circumftances in which fome part of mankind have not, without the leaft fcruple or remorfe, feized the property or taken away the lives of others: fo that the definition of thefe crimes muft vary in almoft every country. Now an idea or feeling, that depends upon arbitrary definition, cannot be, properly fpeaking, natural, but muft be factitious.

A crime the leaft liable to variation in its defi-

nition,

nition, is that of a lie; and yet a child will, upon the flighteft temptation, tell an untruth as readily as the truth; that is, as foon as he can fufpect that it will be to his advantage; and the dread that he afterwards has of telling a lie is acquired principally by his being threatened, punifhed, and terrified by thofe who detect him in it; till at length a number of painful impreffions are annexed to the telling of an untruth, and he comes even to fhudder at the thought of it. But where this care has not been taken, fuch a facility in telling lies, and fuch an indifference to truth, are acquired, as is hardly credible to perfons who have been differently educated.

But whether the feelings which accompany the ideas of virtue and vice be inftinctive or acquired, their operation is the very fame; fo that the interefts of virtue may be equally fecured on this fcheme as on any other. There is a fufficient provifion in the courfe of our lives to generate moral principles, fentiments, and feelings, in the degree in which they are wanted in life; and with thofe variations, with refpect to modes and other circumftances, which we fee in different ages and countries; and which the different circumftances of mankind, in different ages and countries, feem to require. PRIESTLEY.

MORAL

MORAL RULES, AND SENSE OF DUTY.

THE regard to the general rules of morality is
what is properly called a fenfe of duty; a principle of the greateft confequence in human life,
and the only principle by which the bulk of mankind are capable of directing their actions. There
is fcarce any man who, by difcipline, education,
and example, may not be fo impreffed with a regard to thefe general rules of conduct, as to act
upon almoft every occafion with tolerable decency,
and through the whole of his life avoid any tolerable degree of blame.   Without this facred regard to the general rules of morality, there is no
man whofe conduct can be much depended upon.
It is this which conftitutes the moft effential difference between a man of principle and honour,
and a worthlefs fellow.   The one adheres, on all
occafions, fteadily and refolutely to his maxims,
and preferves through the whole of his life one
even tenor of conduct.   The other acts varioufly
and accidentally, as humour, inclination, or intereft, chance to be uppermoft.   Nay, fuch are the
inequalities of humour to which all men are fubject, that without this principle, the man who,
in all his cool hours, had the moft delicate fenfibility to the propriety of conduct, might often be
                    S 3   led

led to act abfurdly upon the moft frivolous occafions, and when it was fcarcely poffible to affign any
ferious motive for his behaving in this manner. Upon the tolerable obfervance of thefe rules depends
the very exiftence of human fociety, which would
crumble into nothing if mankind were not generally impreffed with a reverence for thofe important rules of conduct. Falfe notions of religion are
almoft the only caufes which can occafion any very
grofs perverfion of the general rules of morality;
and that principle, which ought to give the greateft
authority to the rules of duty, is alone capable of
diftorting our ideas of them in any confiderable
degree. In all other cafes, common fenfe is fufficient to direct us, if not to the moft exquifite
propriety of conduct, yet to fomething which is
not very far from it; and provided we are in earneft defirous to do well, our behaviour will always, upon the whole, be praife-worthy. But
wherever the natural principles of religion are
not corrupted by the factious and party zeal of
fome worthlefs cabal; wherever the firft duty
which it requires is to fulfil all the obligations of
morality; wherever men are not taught to regard
frivolous obfervances as more immediate duties
of religion than acts of juftice and beneficence;
and to imagine, that by facrifices and ceremonies,
and vain fupplications, they can bargain with
the Deity for fraud and perfidy and violence; it

efta-eſtabliſhes and confirms the general rules of morality. A. SMITH.

THE MORAL SENSE.

THE moral ſenſe is formed by time and experience, and not born with us. So are all the natural ſenſes, not one of which is born with us: they are all created; ſome inſtantaneouſly, ſome in a little time, ſome in a long time; but all by experience. The moral ſenſe differs from a natural one, as much as the effect of reflection differs from ſimple feeling. But the conformation given by nature and education may be ſo exquiſitely juſt in ſome men, that they may be ſaid to judge of actions and principles by a kind of inſtantaneous ſenſation; which may be very properly called a moral ſenſe. The eye, as a ſenſe, is formed by the experience of many years: but when it is formed, it judges of diſtances and magnitude, of beauty and deformity, apparently by an immediate ſenſation; but in fact by a proceſs which is the effect of experience. The mind is in the ſame ſtate as to morals: it has judged of cauſes by effects, on all material occaſions; it has ſo aſſociated virtue with pleaſure, and vice with pain, that when the actions and principles under thoſe denominations preſent themſelves, they ſeem to act on the mere ſenſe, not as virtues or vices,

but

but as pleasures or pains. The present fashionable affectation of sentiment arises from the same cause. Persons whose organization is just, perfect, and delicate, are susceptible of very lively impressions, from those principles and actions which experience has taught them to be good or bad. When they present themselves again, the associated ideas of pleasure or pain immediately present themselves; and before any judgment can be made, that is, before those circumstances, which have been often and sufficiently examined, can undergo a second examination. In time, they forget that experience and reason had any share in classing the virtues and vices; and finding this moral intelligent sensibility seldom err, they refer every thing to it: so that we very commonly hear people say, We act from our feelings; or, We judge of men and things according as they excite our sensibility.

WILLIAMS.

MORAL Systems.

IF there is a universal system of morality, it cannot be the effect of a particular cause. It has been the same in past ages, and it will continue the same in future times; it cannot then be grounded on religious opinions, which, ever since the beginning of the world, and from one pole to the other, have continually varied. Greece had

vicious

vicious deities, the Romans had them likewise : the senseless worshipper of the Fetiche adores rather a devil than a God. Every people made gods for themselves, and gave them such attributes as they pleased : to some they ascribed goodness, to others cruelty; to some immorality, to others the greatest sanctity and severity of manners. One would imagine that every nation intended to deify its own passions and opinions. Notwithstanding that diversity in religious systems and modes of worship, all nations have perceived that men ought to be just : they have all honoured as virtues, goodness, pity, friendship, fidelity, paternal tenderness, filial respect, sincerity, gratitude, patriotism ; in short, all those sentiments that can be considered as so many ties adapted to unite men more closely to one another. The origin of that uniformity of judgment, so constant, so general, ought not then to be looked for in the midst of contradictory and fluctuating opinions. If the ministers of religion have appeared to think otherwise, it is because by their system they were enabled to regulate all the actions of mankind; to dispose of their fortunes, and command their wills; and to secure to themselves, in the name of heaven, the arbitrary government of the world.—The veil is now removed. At the tribunal of philosophy and reason, morality is a science whose object is the preservation and common happiness of the human species.

species. To this double end all its rules ought
to tend. Their natural, constant, eternal principle is in man himself, and in a resemblance there
is in the general organization of man; which includes a similarity of wants, of pleasures and
pains, of force and weakness; a resemblance from
whence arises the necessity of society, or of a
common opposition against such dangers as are
equally incident to each individual, which proceed
from nature herself, and threaten man on all sides.
Such is the origin of particular duties and of do-
mestic virtues; such is the origin of general duties
and public virtues; such is the source of the notion of personal and public utility; the source of all
compacts between individuals, and of all laws of
government.—Several writers have endeavoured
to trace the first principles of morality in the sentiments of friendship, tenderness, compassion, honour, and benevolence; because they found them
engraved on the human heart: But did they not
also find there hatred, jealousy, revenge, pride,
and the love of dominion? For what reason therefore have they founded morality on the former
principles rather than on the latter? It is because
they found that the former were of general advantage to society, and the others fatal to it. The
very sentiments which these philosophers adopted
as the ground-work of morality, because they
appear to be serviceable to the common good, if
                                        left

left to themselves would be very prejudicial to it.
How can we determine to punish the guilty, if
we listen only to the pleas of compassion?—How
shall we guard against partiality, if we consult only the dictates of friendship?—How shall
we avoid being favourable to idleness, if we attend only to the sentiments of benevolence? All
these virtues have their limits, beyond which they
degenerate into vices: and those limits are settled
by the invariable rules of essential justice; or,
which is the same thing, by the common interests
of men united together in society, and the constant
object of that union.

These limits, it is true, have not yet been ascer-
tained; nor indeed could they, since it has not
been possible to fix what the common interest itself was. And this is the reason why among all
people, and at all times, men have formed such
different ideas of virtue and vice; why hitherto
morality has appeared to be but a matter of mere
convention among men. That so many ages
should have passed away in an entire ignorance of
the first principles of a science so important to our
happiness, is a certain fact; but so extraordinary,
that it should appear incredible. We cannot imagine how it has not been sooner discovered, that
the uniting of men in society has not, and indeed could not have, any other design but the general happiness of individuals; and therefore, that
there

there is not, and cannot be, any other social tie between them than that of their common interest;
and that nothing can be confiftent with the order
of focieties, unlefs it be confiftent with the common utility of the members that compofe them:
that it is this principle which neceffarily determines virtue and vice; and that our actions are
confequently more or lefs virtuous, according as
they tend more or lefs to the common advantage
of fociety; that they are more or lefs vicious,
according as the prejudice, fociety receives from
them, is greater or lefs.

Is it on its own account that valour is ranked
among the number of virtues? No; it is on account of the fervice it is of to fociety. This is
evident from hence, that it is punifhed as a crime
in a man whom it caufes to difturb the public
peace. Why then is drunkennefs a vice? Becaufe every man is bound to contribute to the
common good; and, to fulfil that obligation, he
has occafion for the free exercife of his faculties.
Why are certain vices more blameable in a magiftrate than in a private man? Becaufe greater
inconveniences refult from them to fociety.

As fociety ought to be beneficial to every one
of its members, it is but juft that each of its
members fhould contribute to the advantage of
fociety. To be virtuous, therefore, is to be ufeful; to be vicious, is to be ufelefs or hurtful.

This

This is morality. This, indeed, is univerfal morality.—That morality which, being connected
with the nature of man, is connected with the
nature of fociety; that morality which can vary
only in its application, but never in its effence:
that morality, in fhort, to which all law fhould
refer, and to which they fhould be fubordinate.

Raynal.

The different Systems of MORALITY,
and their Influence.

IN every civilized fociety, in every fociety
where the diftinction of ranks has once been completely eftablifhed, there have been always two
different fchemes or fyftems of morality current
at the fame time; of which the one may be called
the *ftrict* or *auftere*; the other the *liberal*, or, if
you will, the *loofe* fyftem. The former is generally admired and revered by the common people:
The latter is commonly more efteemed and adopted by what are called people of fafhion. The
degree of difapprobation with which we ought to
mark the vices of levity, the vices which are apt
to arife from great profperity, and from the ex-
cefs of gaiety and good-humour, feems to conftitute the principal diftinction between thofe two
oppofite fchemes or fyftems. In the liberal or
loofe fyftem, luxury, wanton and even diforderly
mirth, the purfuit of pleafure to fome degree of

intemperance, the breach of chastity, at least in
one of the two sexes, &c. provided they are not
accompanied with grofs indecency, and do not
lead to falsehood or injustice, are generally treated
with a good deal of indulgence, and are easily
either excused or pardoned altogether. In the
austere system, on the contrary, those excesses are
regarded with the utmost abhorrence and detestation. The vices of levity are always ruinous to
the common people; and a single week's thought-
lessness and dissipation is often sufficient to undo
a poor workman for ever, and to drive him,
through despair, upon committing the most enor-
mous crimes. The wiser and better sort of the
common people, therefore, have always the utmost abhorrence and detestation of such excesses,
which their experience tells them are so immediately fatal to people of their condition. The diforder and extravagance of several years, on the
contrary, will not always ruin a man of fashion;
and people of that rank are very apt to consider
the power of indulging in some degree of excess
as one of the advantages of their fortune; and the
liberty of doing so without censure or reproach,
as one of the privileges which belong to their station. In people of their own station, therefore,
they regard such excesses with but a small degree
of disapprobation, and censure them either very
slightly or not at all.

                                        Almost

Almoſt all religious ſects have begun among the common people, from whom they have generally drawn their earlieſt, as well as their moſt numerous proſelytes. The auſtere ſyſtem of morality has, accordingly, been adopted by thoſe ſects almoſt conſtantly, or with very few exceptions; for there have been ſome. It was the ſyſtem by which they could beſt recommend themſelves to that order of people to whom they firſt propoſed their plan of reformation upon what had been before eſtabliſhed. Many of them, perhaps the greater part of them, have even endeavoured to gain credit by refining upon this auſtere ſyſtem, and by carrying it to ſome degree of folly and extravagance; and this exceſſive rigour has frequently recommended them more than any thing elſe to the reſpect and veneration of the common people.

A man of rank and fortune is by his ſtation a diſtinguiſhed member of a great ſociety, who attend to every part of his conduct, and who thereby oblige him to attend to every part of it himſelf. His authority and conſideration depend very much upon the reſpect which this ſociety bears to him. He dare not do any thing which would diſgrace or diſcredit him in it; and he is obliged to a very ſtrict obſervation of that ſpecies of morals, whether liberal or auſtere, which the general conſent of this ſociety preſcribes to per-

ſons

fons of his rank and fortune. A man of low condition, on the contrary, is far from being a diftinguifhed member of any great fociety. While he remains in a country village, his conduct may be attended to, and he may be obliged to attend to it himfelf. In this fituation, and in this fituation only, he may have what is called a character to lofe. But as foon as he comes into a great city, he is funk in obfcurity and darknefs. His conduct is obferved and attended to by nobody; and he is therefore very likely to neglect it himfelf, and to abandon himfelf to every fort of low profligacy and vice. He never emerges fo effectually from this obfcurity, his conduct never excites fo much the attention of any refpectable fociety, as by his becoming the member of a fmall religious fect. He from that moment acquires a degree of confideration which he never had before. All his brother fectaries are, for the credit of the fect, interefted to obferve his conduct; and if he gives occafion to any fcandal, if he deviates very much from thofe auftere morals which they almoft always require of one another, they punifh him by what is always a very fevere punifhment, even where no civil effects attend it, expulfion or excommunication from the fect. In little religious fects, accordingly, the morals of the common people have been almoft always remarkably regular and orderly; generally much

more

more so than in the established church. The morals of those little sects, indeed, have frequently been rather disagreeably rigorous and unsocial.

There are two very easy and effectual remedies, however, by whose joint operation the state might, without violence, correct whatever was unsocial or disagreeably rigorous in the morals of all the little sects into which the country was divided.

The first of those remedies is the study of science and philosophy, which the state might render almost universal among all people of middling or more than middling rank and fortune; not by giving salaries to teachers in order to make them negligent and idle, but by instituting some sort of probation, even in the higher and more difficult sciences, to be undergone by every person before he was permitted to exercise any liberal profession, or before he could be received as a candidate for any honourable office of trust or profit. If the state imposed upon this order of men the necessity of learning, it would have no occasion to give itself any trouble about providing them with proper teachers. They would soon find better teachers for themselves than any whom the state could provide for them. Science is the great antidote to the poison of enthusiasm and superstition; and where all the superior ranks

T 3 of

of people were fecured from it, the inferior ranks could not be much expofed to it.

The fecond of thofe remedies is the frequency and gaiety of public diverfions. The ftate, by encouraging, that is, by giving entire liberty to all thofe who for their own intereft would attempt, without fcandal or indecency, to amufe and divert the people by painting, poetry, mufic, dancing, by all forts of dramatic reprefentations and exhibitions, would eafily diffipate, in the greater part of them, that melancholy and gloomy humour which is almoft always the nurfe of popular fuperftition and enthufiafm. Public diverfions have always been the objects of dread and hatred, to all the fanatical promoters of thofe popular frenzies. The gaiety and good-humour which thofe diverfions infpire were altogether inconfiftent with that temper of mind, which was fitteft for their purpofe, or which they could beft work upon. Dramatic reprefentations befides, frequently expofing their artifices to public ridicule, and fometimes even to public execration, were upon that account, more than all other diverfions, the objects of their peculiar abhorrence.

In a country where the law favoured the teachers of no one religion more than thofe of another, it would not be neceffary that any of them fhould have any particular or immediate dependency upon

on the fovereign or executive power; or that he
fhould have any thing to do, either in appointing,
or in difmiffing them from their offices. In fuch
a fituation he would have no occafion to give himfelf any concern about them, further than to keep
the peace among them, in the fame manner as
among the reft of his fubjects; that is, to hinder
them from perfecuting, abufing, or oppreffing
one another. But it is quite otherwife in countries where there is an eftablifhed or governing
religion. The fovereign can in this cafe never
be fecure, unlefs he has the means of influencing
in a confiderable degree the greater part of the
teachers of that religion.

The clergy of every eftablifhed church conftitute
a great incorporation. They can act in concert,
and purfue their intereft upon one plan and with
one fpirit, as much as if they were under the direction of one man; and they are frequently too
under fuch direction. Their intereft as an incor-
porated body is never the fame with that of the
fovereign, and is fometimes directly oppofite to it.
Their great intereft is to maintain their authority
with the people; and this authority depends upon the fuppofed certainty and importance of the
whole doctrine which they inculcate, and upon
the fuppofed neceffity of adopting every part of it
with the moft implicit faith, in order to avoid
eternal mifery. Should the fovereign have the
im-

imprudence to appear either to deride or doubt himself of the moft trifling part of their doctrine, or from humanity attempt to protect thofe who did either the one or the other, the punctilious honour of a clergy, who have no fort of dependency upon him, is immediately provoked to profcribe him as a profane perfon, and to employ all the terrors of religion, in order to oblige the people to transfer their allegiance to fome more orthodox and obedient prince. Should he oppofe any of their pretenfions or ufurpations, the danger is equally great. The princes who have dared in this manner to rebel againft the church, over and above this crime of rebellion, have generally been charged too with the additional crime of herefy, notwithftanding their folemn proteftations of their faith and humble fubmiffion to every tenet which fhe thought proper to prefcribe to them. But the authority of religion is fuperior to every other authority. The fears which it fuggefts conquer all other fears. When the authorifed teachers of religion propagate through the great body of the people doctrines fubverfive of the authority of the fovereign, it is by violence only, or by the force of a ftanding army, that he can maintain his authority. Even a ftanding army cannot in this cafe give him any lafting fecurity; becaufe if the foldiers are not foreigners, which can feldom be the cafe, but drawn from the
great

great body of the people, which muft almoft always be the cafe, they are likely to be foon corrupted by thofe very doctrines. The revolutions which the turbulence of the Greek clergy was continually occafioning at Conftantinople, as long as the eaftern empire fubfifted; the convulfions which, during the courfe of feveral centuries, the turbulence of the Roman clergy was continually occafioning in every part of Europe; fufficiently demonftrate how precarious and infecure muft always be the fituation of the fovereign who has no proper means of influencing the clergy of the eftablifhed and governing religion of his country.

Articles of faith, as well as all other fpiritual matters, it is evident enough, are not within the proper department of a temporal fovereign, who, though he may be very well qualified for protecting, is feldom fuppofed to be fo for inftructing the people. With regard to fuch matters, therefore, his authority can feldom be fufficient to counterbalance the united authority of the clergy of the eftablifhed church. The public tranquillity, however, and his own fecurity, may frequently depend upon the doctrines which they may think proper to propagate concerning fuch matters. As he can feldom directly oppofe their decifion, therefore, with proper weight and authority, it is neceffary that he fhould be able to influence it; and he can influence it only by the fears and ex-

pectations

pectations which he may excite in the greater part of the individuals of the order. Those fears and expectations may confist in the fear of deprivation or other punifhment, and in the expectation of further preferment.

A. SMITH.

THE PRINCIPLE OF MORAL VIRTUE.

MEN are no more to be told what they muft believe, and how they muft act, than an inftrument is to be told what harmony it is to afford. The thoughts and actions of a man refult from his conftruction, as harmony does from that of an inftrument. That conftruction is good or evil, and will lead to virtue or vice, according as he has been originally formed by nature; according as he has been attempered in his childhood; according as he has been educated in his youth; and according to the company and friends he has been connected with. This organization of the mind, or this moral conftitution, is the true principle of human actions. When this is right, truly or nobly, or delicately harmonized; virtues of a noble or of an amiable afpect, and every fpecies of genuine happinefs, will be the effects. When this is wrong, when it is defective or difarranged, the effect is vice; and no precepts, no inftructions, no doctrines from heaven or hell, will make

diffo-

diffonance harmony, darkness light, or vice to be
virtue. If a god had defcended, and told the
world, in a language to be underftood from pole
to pole, This you are to believe, and thus you are
to act :—What would have been the confequence?
Exactly what we fee to be the confequence in
the Chriftian world, where every true believer
is thoroughly perfuaded that God Almighty came
from heaven; laid down in his gofpel every thing
neceffary to be believed and practifed, in order
to bear things patiently here, and to be everlaft-
ingly happy hereafter. And are men the wifer,
or the better? We muft be thoroughly blinded
by prejudice, and extremely ignorant of hiftory,
to fay they are.   WILLIAMS.

N.

N.

NATIONAL Characters.

DIFFERENT reasons are assigned for national characters: some account for them from *moral*, and others from *physical* causes. By moral causes we may understand all circumstances which are fitted to work on the mind as motives or reasons, and which render a peculiar set of manners habitual to us. Of this kind are the nature of government, the revolutions of public affairs, the plenty or penury in which the people live, the situation of the nation with regard to its neighbours, and such like circumstances. By physical causes we may understand those qualities of the air and climate which are supposed to work insensibly on the temper, by altering the tone and habit of the body, and giving a particular com-

2 plexion;

plexion; which though reflection and reason may sometimes overcome it, yet it will prevail among the generality of mankind, and have an influence on their manners. That the character of a nation will depend much on moral causes, is evident to every observer; since a nation is nothing but a collection of individuals; and the manners of individuals are frequently determined by these causes. As poverty and hard labour debase the minds of the common people, and render them unfit for any science or ingenious profession; so where any government becomes very oppressive to all its subjects, it has a proportional effect on their temper and genius, and banishes all the liberal arts from among them.

As to *physical causes*, their operation is doubtful: in this particular, men seem to owe nothing of their temper or genius to the air, food, or climate. The contrary opinion seems, at first sight, probable; since we find those circumstances have an influence over every other animal. The human mind is of a very imitative nature; nor is it possible for any set of men to converse often together, without acquiring a similitude of manners, and communicating to each other their vices as well as virtues. Where a number of men are united into one political body, the occasions of their intercourse must be so frequent, for defence, commerce, and government, that, together with

the fame fpeech or language, they muft acquire a
refemblance in their manners, and have a common and national character, as well as a perfonal
one, peculiar to each individual. Now, though
nature produces all kinds of temper and underftanding in great abundance, it follows not that
fhe always produces them in like proporti ns, and
that in every fociety the ingredients of induftry
and indolence, valour and cowardice, humanity
and brutality, wifdom and folly, will be mixed
after the fame manner. In the infancy of fociety,
if any of thefe difpofitions be found in greater
abundance than the reft, it will naturally prevail
in the compofition, and give a tincture to the national character. If, on the firft eftablifhment of
a republic, a Brutus fhould be placed in authority,
and be tranfported with fuch an enthufiafm for
liberty, as to overlook all the ties of nature as well
as private intereft, fuch an example will naturally
have an effect on the whole fociety, and kindle
the fame paffion in every bofom. Whatever it be
that forms the manners of one generation, the next
muft imbibe a deeper tincture of the fame die;
men being more fufceptible of all impreffions during infancy, and retaining thefe impreffions as
long as they remain in the world. All national
characters, where they depend not on fixed moral
caufes, proceed from fuch accidents as thefe; and
phyfical caufes appear not to have any difcernible
opera-

operation on the human mind. It is a maxim in
all philosophy, That causes which do not appear
are to be considered as not exifting. The Chinese
have the greatest uniformity of character imaginable; though the air and climate, in different
parts of those vast dominions, admit of very confiderable variations. Athens and Thebes were
but a short day's journey from each other; though
the Athenians were as remarkable for ingenuity,
politeness, and gaiety, as the Thebans for dul-
nefs, rufticity, and a phlegmatic temper. Strabo
(*lib.* ii.) rejects, in a great measure, the influence of climate upon men. " All is custom and
" education," says he: " It is not from nature
" that the Athenians are learned, the Lacedæmo-
" nians ignorant, and the Thebans too, who are
" ftill nearer neighbours to the former. Even the
" difference of animals," he adds, " depends not
" on climate."

The fame national character commonly follows
the authority of government to a precife boun-
dary; and upon crofling a river, or paffing a
mountain, one finds a new fet of manners, with a
new government. Is it conceivable, that the qualities of the air fhould change exactly with the
limits of an empire? Any fet of men, fcattered
over diftant nations, who have a clofe communication together, acquire a fimilitude of manners,
and have but little in common with the nations

U 2

amongſt

amongst whom they live. Thus the Jews in Europe, and the Armenians in the East, have a peculiar character.

Where a difference of language or religion keeps two nations, inhabiting the same country, from mixing with each other, their manners will be very distinct, and even opposite. The Turks and modern Greeks have very different characters.

The same set of manners will follow a nation, and adhere to them, over the whole globe, as well as the same language and laws.—The manners of a people change very considerably from one age to another. The ingenuity, industry, and activity of the ancient Greeks, have nothing in common with the stupidity and indolence of the present inhabitants of those regions. Candour, bravery, and love of liberty, formed the character of the ancient Romans; as subtlety, cowardice, and a slavish disposition, do that of the modern.

Where the government of a nation is altogether republican, it is apt to beget a particular set of manners. Where it is altogether monarchical, it is more apt to have the same effect; the imitation of superiors spreading the national manners faster among the people. If the governing part of a state consists altogether of merchants, as in Holland, their uniform way of life will fix their character. If it consist chiefly of nobles and landed gentry, like Germany, France, and Spain, the

same

fame effect follows. The genius of a particular
fect of religion is alfo apt to mould the manners
of a people.. If the characters of men depended
on the air, the degrees of heat and cold would
naturally be expected to have a mighty influence,
fince nothing has a greater effect on all plants and
animals. And indeed there is fome reafon to
think, that all the nations that live beyond the
polar circles, or between the tropics, are inferior
to the reft of the fpecies. The poverty of the
northern inhabitants, and the indolence of the
fouthern from their few neceffities, may perhaps
account for this difference without phyfical caufes.
This, however, is certain, that the character of
nations is very promifcuous in the temperate climates; and that almoft all the general obfervations which have been formed of the more fouthern or more northern nations in thefe climates,
are found to be uncertain and fallacious.

HUME.

THE CHARACTER OF NATIONS, AND THE CAUSES OF THEIR ALTERATIONS.

EACH nation has its particular manner of feeing and feeling, which forms its character: and
in every nation its character either changes on a
fudden, or alters by degrees, according to the
fudden or infenfible alterations in the form of its

government, and consequently of its public education; for the form of government under which
we live always makes a part of our education.
That of the French, which has been for a long time
gay, was not always so. The Emperor Julian says
of the Parisians, " I like them, because their character, like mine, is austere and serious."

The characters of nations, therefore, change:
but at what period is the alteration most percep-
tible? At the moment of revolution, when a
people pass on a sudden from liberty to slavery.
Then from bold and haughty they become weak
and pusillanimous: they dare not look on the man
in office: they are enthralled. This dejected
people say, like the ass in the fable, *Whoever be
my master, I cannot carry a heavier load*. As
much as a free citizen is zealous for the honour
of his nation, so much is a slave indifferent to the
public welfare. His heart is deprived of activity
and energy; is without virtue, without spirit,
and without talents; he becomes indifferent to
the arts, commerce, agriculture, &c. It is not for
servile hands, say the English, to till and fertilize
the lands. Simonides entered the empire of a
despotic sovereign, and found there no traces of
men. A free people are courageous, open, humane, and loyal. A nation of slaves are base,
perfidious, malicious, and barbarous: they push
their cruelty to the greatest excess. If the severe

officer

officer has all to fear from the resentment of the injured soldier on the day of battle, that of sedition is in like manner, for the slave oppressed, the long-expected day of vengeance; and he is the more enraged in proportion as fear has held his fury the longer restrained.

What a striking picture of a sudden change in the character of a nation does the Roman history present us with! What people, before the elevation of the Cæsars, showed more force, more virtue, more love of liberty, and horror for slavery? And what people, when the throne of the Cæsars was established, showed more weakness or depravity? Their baseness disgusted Tiberius.

Indifferent to liberty, when Trajan offered it, they refused it: they disdained that liberty their ancestors had purchased with so much blood. All things were then changed in Rome; and that determined and grave character, which distinguished its first inhabitants, was succeeded by that light and frivolous disposition with which Juvenal reproaches them in his tenth Satire.—Let us exemplify this matter by a more recent change. Compare the English of the present day with those under Henry VIII. Edward VI. Mary and Elizabeth. This people, now so humane, indulgent, learned, free, and industrious, such lovers of the arts and philosophy, were then nothing more than a nation of slaves; inhuman and superstitious; with-

out

out arts, and without industry.—When a prince usurps over his people a boundless authority, he is sure to change their character; to enervate their souls; to render them timid and base. From that moment, indifferent to glory, his subjects lose that character of boldness and constancy proper to support all labours, and brave all dangers. The weight of arbitrary power destroys the spring of their emulation. Does a prince, impatient of contradiction, give the name of factious to the man of veracity? he substitutes in his nation the character of falsity for that of frankness. If, in those critical moments, the prince, giving himself up to flatterers, finds that he is surrounded by men void of all merit, whom should he blame? Himself; for it is he that has made them such. Who could believe, when he considers the evils of servitude, that there were still princes mean enough to wish to reign over slaves; and stupid enough to be ignorant of the fatal changes that despotism produces in the character of their subjects? What is arbitrary power? The seed of calamities, that, sown in the bosom of a state, springs up to bear the fruit of misery and devastation. Let us hear the King of Prussia: *Nothing is better*, said he, in a discourse pronounced to the Academy of Berlin, *than an arbitrary government, under princes just, humane, and virtuous; nothing worse under the common race of kings.* Now, how many kings are

are there of the latter fort? and how many
fuch as Titus, Trajan, and Antoninus? Thefe
are the thoughts of a great man. What elevation
of mind, what knowledge, does not fuch a declaration fuppofe in a monarch?—What, in fact, does
a defpotic power announce? Often ruin to the
defpot, and always to his pofterity. The founder
of fuch power fets his kingdom on a fandy foundation. It is only a tranfient ill-judged notion of
royalty, that is, of pride, idlenefs, or fome fimilar paffion, which prefers the exercife of an unjuft and cruel defpotifm over wretched flaves, to
that of a legitimate and friendly power over a
free and happy people. Arbitrary power is a
thoughtlefs child, who continually facrifices the
future to the prefent.—The moft formidable enemy of the public welfare is not riot and fedition,
but defpotifm: it changes the character of a nation, and always for the worfe: it produces nothing but vices. Whatever might be the power
of an Indian Sultan, he could never form mag-
nanimous fubjects; he would never find among
his flaves the virtues of free men. Chemiftry can
extract no more gold from a mixed body than it
includes; and the moft arbitrary power can draw
nothing from a flave but the bafenefs he contains.
Experience, then, proves, that the character and
fpirit of a people change with the form of government; and that a different government gives by
turns,

turns, to the same nation, a character noble or base, firm or fickle, courageous or cowardly. If the Persian have no idea of liberty, and the savage no idea of servitude, it is the effect of their different instruction.   HELVETIUS.

NATIONAL FAITH.

WHEN a number of political societies are erected, and maintain a great intercourse together, a new set of rules are immediately discovered to be useful in that particular situation; and accordingly take place under the title of the *laws of nations*. The rules of justice, such as prevail among individuals, are not entirely suspended among political societies. All princes pretend a regard to the rights of other princes; and some, no doubt, without hypocrisy. Alliances and treaties are every day made between independent states, which would be only so much waste of parchment, if they were not found by experience to have *some* influence and authority. But here is the difference between kingdoms and individuals. Human nature cannot by any means subsist without the association of individuals; and that association never could have place, were no regard paid to the laws of equity and justice. Disorder, confusion, the war of all against all, are the necessary consequences of such a licentious conduct. But nations

nations can fubfift without intercourfe. They
may even fubfift, in fome degree, under a general
war. The obfervance of juftice, though ufeful
among them, is not guarded by fo ftrong a neceffity as among individuals; and the moral obligation holds proportion with the ufefulnefs. All
politicians will allow, and moft philofophers, that
reafons of ftate may, in particular emergencies,
difpenfe with the rules of juftice, and invalidate
any treaty or alliance, where the ftrict obfervance
of it would be prejudicial in a confiderable degree
to either of the contracting parties. But nothing
lefs than the extremeft neceffity, it is confeffed,
can juftify individuals in a breach of promife or
an invafion of the properties of others. In a con-
federated commonwealth, fuch as the Achæan republic of old, or the Swifs Cantons and the United Provinces in modern times; as the league has
here a peculiar utility, the conditions of union
have a peculiar facrednefs and authority; and a
violation of them would be regarded as equally
criminal, or even as more criminal than any private injury or injuftice.

HUME.

ON THE SAME SUBJECT.

WHEN two nations conclude a treaty between
them, they have, like private perfons, no other
objec̄t

object than their reciprocal advantage and happiness; when this reciprocal advantage no longer subsists, the treaty becomes void: one of the two nations may break it. Ought they to do it? No, if there result but a small damage to them from observing it: for then it would be better to suffer that damage, than be regarded as too easy violators of their engagements. Now, in the motives themselves that make those two people observe their treaty, we see the right that every people have to disannul a treaty when it is evidently destructive to their happiness.

HELVETIUS.

ON THE SAME SUBJECT.

IF treaties between nations were as sacred as promises between individuals, nations would be perpetually sacrificed to the folly and inattention of their rulers; who ought always to consult the interest of the community, and not their own reputation for integrity when it must be injurious to the people.   HELVETIUS.

THE PUPIL OF NATURE.

WAS it possible that a human creature could grow up to manhood in some solitary place without any communication with his own species, he

could no more think of his own character, of the
propriety or demerit of his own fentiments and
conduct, of the beauty and deformity of his own
mind, than of the beauty or deformity of his own
face. All thefe are objects which he cannot eafily
fee, which naturally he does not look at, and with
regard to which he is provided with no mirror
which can prefent them to his view. Bring him
into fociety, and he is immediately provided with
the mirror which he wanted before. It is placed
in the countenance and behaviour of thofe he lives
with, which always mark when they enter into,
and when they difapprove of his fentiments; and
it is here he firft views the propriety and impro-
priety of his own paffions, the beauty and deformity of his own mind. To a man who from his
birth was a ftranger to fociety, the objects of his
paffions, the external bodies which either pleafed
or hurt him, would occupy his whole attention.
The paffions themfelves, the defires or averfions,
the joys or forrows, which thofe objects excited,
though of all things the moft immediately prefent
to him, would fcarce ever be the objects of his
thoughts. The idea of them could never intereft
him fo much as to call upon his attentive confideration. The confideration of his joy could in
him excite no new joy, nor that of his forrow any
new forrow, though the confideration of the caufes
of thofe paffions might often excite both. Bring

him into fociety, and all his own paffions will immediately become the caufes of new paffions. He
will obferve that mankind approve of fome of
them, and are difgufted by others. He will be
elevated in the one cafe, and caft down in the
other; his defires and averfions, his joys and forrows, will now become the caufes of new defires
and new averfions, new joys and new forrows:
they will now therefore intereft him deeply, and
often call upon his moft attentive confideration.

A. SMITH.

LIBERTY AND NECESSITY.

IS not the will neceffarily determined by what
appears to be the beft reafon?—It no doubt is fo;
nor is it poffible to conceive any creature willing
what he does not think beft. But this is improperly called neceffity: for neceffity is always from
without, and cannot be without two things; an
agent who applies force and violence, and a patient who fuffers it. Nothing therefore can force
itfelf: fo that when we fay the intellect is neceffarily determined by the ftrongeft reafon, we can
mean nothing, but that neceffity which is in the
nature of every thing, and is the fame by which
a triangle, or any other geometrical figure, has all
the properties belonging to its nature.

L. MONBODDO.

ON

ON THE SAME SUBJECT.

IF moral motives are certain in their operation, is not man as much a machine as if he were
impelled by a mechanical force? If the Deity pro-
poses a motive which I cannot resist, am I in that
case a free agent? Are not my elective powers
absolutely over-ruled and determined to one particular choice? On the contrary, if moral motives
are not certain in their effects, there will be a difficulty in reconciling divine fore-knowledge and
man's free-will. In reply to this it may be answered, That even admitting the certain operation of moral motives, man is not so much a machine as if he were impelled by mere mechanical
force. The very asking, If he be not as much a
machine as some others? necessarily implies a
comparative gradation in machinery: so that a
man may even be admitted to be a machine, and
yet possess a capacity of being actuated by moral
motives, which none but rational machines are.
For distinction sake, he may be called a moral
machine; possessed of a principle of self-determi-
nation or volition, in which he is infinitely superior to inanimate machines. In the operation,
however, of the moral motives by which he is actuated, and the actions subsequent thereto, he is
as very a mechanical machine as a piece of clock-

work.

work. How should it be otherwise, when the operations of the Deity himself in the government of the world are mechanical? The universe itself is one great machine, moved by the power of its great Creator. It is pride, therefore, alone which makes man ashamed to be thought a microcosm, subject to similar laws of motion: he is ambitious of being thought a god, capable of willing and moving solely of himself.

KENRICK.

THE ORIGIN OF OBJECTIONS TO THE DOCTRINE OF PHILOSOPHICAL NECESSITY.

IF we examine the operations of bodies, and the production of effects from their causes, we shall find, that all our faculties can never carry us further in our knowledge of this relation, than barely to observe, that particular objects are constantly conjoined together, and that the mind is carried, by a customary transition, from the appearance of one to the belief of the other. But though this conclusion concerning human ignorance be the result of the strictest scrutiny of this subject, men still entertain a strong propensity to believe, that they penetrate further into the powers of nature, and perceive something like a necessary connection between the cause and effect. When, again, they turn their reflections towards the operation
ration

ration of their own minds, and feel no such connection of the motive and the action, they are apt from thence to suppose, that there is a difference between the effects resulting from material force, and those which arise from thought and intelligence. But being once convinced, that we know nothing further of causation of any kind, than merely the *constant conjunction* of objects, and the consequent *inference* of the mind from one to another; and finding that these two circumstances are universally allowed to have place in voluntary actions, we may thence be more easily led to own the same necessity common to all causes.

The prevalence of the doctrine of liberty may be accounted for from another cause, viz. a false sensation or seeming experience which we have, or may have, of liberty or indifference in many of our actions. The necessity of any action, whether of matter or mind, is not, properly speaking, a quality in the agent, but in any thinking intelligent being, who may consider the action; and it consists chiefly in the determination of his thoughts to infer the existence of that action from some preceding objects; as liberty, when opposed to necessity, is nothing but the want of that determination, and a certain looseness or indifference, which we feel in passing, or not passing, from the idea of one object to that of any succeeding one. Now we may observe, that, though,

X 3

in *reflecting* on human actions, we feldom feel
such a loofenefs and indifference, but are commonly able to infer them with confiderable certainty from their motives, and from the difpofitions of the agent; yet it frequently happens, that
in *performing* the actions themfelves, we are fenfible of fomething like it: and as all refembling
objects are readily taken for each other, this has
been employed as a demonftrative, and even intuitive proof of human liberty. We feel that our
actions are fubject to our will on moft occafions;
and imagine we feel, that the will itfelf is fubject
to nothing, becaufe, when by a denial of it we are
provoked to try, we feel that it moves eafily every
way, and produces an image of itfelf (or a vel-
leity, as it is called in fchools), even on that fide
on which it did not fettle. This image, or faint
motion, we perfuade ourfelves, could at that time
have been completed into the thing itfelf; becaufe fhould that be denied, we find, upon a fecond trial, that at prefent it can. We confider
not, that the fantaftical defire of fhowing liberty
is here the motive of our actions. And it feems
certain, that, however we imagine we feel a liberty within ourfelves, a fpectator can commonly
infer our actions from our motives and character;
and even where he cannot, he concludes in general, that he might, were he perfectly acquainted
with every circumftance of our fituation and temper,

per, and the moſt ſecret ſprings of our complec-
tion and diſpoſition. Now this is the very eſſence
of neceſſity, according to the foregoing doctrine.

HOME.

PHILOSOPHICAL NECESSITY.

IT is univerſally allowed, that matter in all its
operations, is actuated by a neceſſary force; and
that every natural effect is ſo preciſely determined by the energy of its cauſe, that no other effect, in ſuch particular circumſtance, could poſſibly have reſulted from the operation of that cauſe.
Would we, therefore, form a juſt and preciſe idea
of *neceſſity*, we muſt conſider whence that idea
ariſes, when we apply it to the operation of bodies. It ſeems evident, that if all the ſcenes of
nature were ſhifted continually in ſuch a manner,
that no two events bore any reſemblance to each
other, but every object was entirely new, without any ſimilitude to whatever had been ſeen before, we ſhould never, in that caſe, have attained
the leaſt idea of neceſſity, or of a connection a-
mong thoſe objects, or of cauſe and effect. Inference and reaſoning concerning the operations
of nature would, from that moment, be at an end.
Our idea, therefore, of neceſſity and cauſation
ariſes entirely from the uniformity in the operations of nature; where ſimilar objects are conſtantly

ftantly conjoined together, and the mind is, by
cuftom, determined to infer the one from the
other. Thefe two circumftances form the whole
of that neceffity we afcribe to matter. And thefe
two circumftances take place in the voluntary actions of men, and in the operations of the mind.
The conftant conjunction of fimilar events in voluntary actions, appears from their uniformity in
all nations and ages. The fame motives produce
always the fame actions. The fame events follow
from the fame caufes. Ambition, avarice, felf-
love, vanity, friendfhip, generofity, public fpirit;
thefe paffions, mixed in various degrees, and diftributed through fociety, have been from the beginning of the world, and ftill are, the fource of
all the actions and enterprizes which have ever
been obferved among mankind. Mankind are fo
much the fame, in all times and places, that hiftory informs us of nothing new or ftrange in this
particular. The records of wars, intrigues, and
factions, are collections of experiments, by which
the politician or moral philofopher fixes the principles of his fcience; in the fame manner as the
phyfician or natural philofopher is acquainted
with the nature of plants, minerals, &c. by experiments. Nor are the earth, water, or other
elements, examined by Ariftotle and Hippocrates,
more like to thofe which at prefent lie under our
obfervation, than the men defcribed by Polybius
                                              and

and Tacitus are to thofe who now govern the
world. The veracity of Quintus Curtius is as
much to be fufpected, when he defcribes the fupernatural courage of Alexander, by which he
was hurried on fingly to attack multitudes, as
when he defcribes his fupernatural force and activity, by which he was able to refift them. So
readily and univerfally do we acknowledge an uniformity in human motives and actions as well as
in the operations of body. Hence likewife the
benefit of that experience, acquired by long life
and a variety of bufinefs and company, in order
to inftruct us in the principles of human nature,
and regulate our future conduct, as well as fpeculation. By means of this guide we mount up
to the knowledge of mens inclinations and motives, from their actions, expreffions, and even
geftures; and again defcend to the interpretation
of their actions from our knowledge of their motives and inclinations. But were there no uniformity in human actions, and were every experiment we could form of this kind irregular and
anomalous, it were impoffible to collect any general obfervations concerning mankind. We muft
not, however, expect, that this uniformity of actions fhould be carried to fuch a length, as that
all men, in the fame circumftances, will always
act precifely in the fame manner, without making any allowance for the diverfity of characters,

prejudices,

prejudices, and opinions. Such an uniformity in every particular is found in no part of nature. An artificer who handles only dead matter, may be difappointed of his aim as well as the politician, who directs the conduct of fenfible and intelligent beings. It is from the variety of conduct in different men we form a greater variety of maxims, which still fupport a degree of regularity. Are the manners of men different in different ages and countries? We learn thence the great force of cuftom and education. Even the characters which are peculiar to each individual have an uniformity in their influence; otherwife our acquaintance with the perfons, and our obfervation of their conduct, could never teach us their difpofitions, nor ferve to direct our behaviour with regard to them. The irregular and unexpected refolutions of men may frequently be accounted for by thofe who know every particular circumftance of their character and fituation. Even when an action, as fometimes happens, cannot be particularly accounted for, either by the perfon himfelf or by others; we know, in general, that the characters of men are, to a certain degree, inconftant and irregular. This is in a manner the conftant character of human nature; though it be applicable, in a more particular manner, to fome perfons, who have no fixed rule for their conduct, but proceed in a continued courfe of ca-

                                              price

price and inconftancy. The internal principles and motives, however, may operate uniformly, notwithftanding thefe feeming irregularities.

HUME.

LIBERTY AND NECESSITY, A DISPUTE OF WORDS.

MEN begin at the wrong end of the queftion concerning liberty and neceffity, when they enter upon it by examining the faculties of the foul, the influence of the underftanding, and the operations of the will. Let them firft difcufs a more fimple queftion, viz. the operations of body, and of brute unintelligent matter; and try whether they can there form any idea of caufation and neceffity, except that of a conftant conjunction of objects, and fubfequent inference of the mind from one to another. If thefe circumftances form, in reality, the whole of that neceffity which we conceive in matter, and if thefe circumftances be alfo univerfally acknowledged to take place in the operations of the mind, the difpute is merely verbal.

HUME.

PHILOSOPHICAL NECESSITY.

WHOEVER defires to injure himfelf, fay the Stoics, and without motives fhould throw himfelf

into

into the fire, the sea, or out of a window, would
be justly thought a madman: for in his natural
state man pursues pleasure and flies pain; and in
all his actions is necessarily determined by a desire of happiness, real or apparent. Man, therefore, is not free. His will is as necessarily the effect of his ideas, and consequently of his sensations, as pain is the effect of a blow. Beside,
add the Stoics, is there a single instant when the
liberty of man can be referred to the different
operations of the same mind? If, for example, the
same thing cannot, at the same instant, be and
not be, it is not therefore possible, that at the moment the mind acts, it could act otherwise; that
at the moment it chooses, it could choose otherwise; that at the moment it deliberates, it could
deliberate otherwise; that at the moment it wills,
it could will otherwise. Now if it be my will,
such as it is, that makes me deliberate; if my deliberation, such as it is, makes me choose; if my
choice, such as it is, makes me act; and if, when I
deliberated, it was not possible for me (considering
the love I have for myself) not to deliberate; it is
evident that that liberty does not consist in the actual volition, nor in the actual deliberation, nor
in the actual choice, nor in the actual action; and,
in short, that liberty does not relate to any of the
operations of the mind. If that were the case,
the same thing must be and not be at the same

inftant.

inftant. Now, add the Stoics, this is the queftion we afk the philofophers, Can the mind be
free, if when it wills, when it deliberates, and
when it choofes, it is not free?

HELVETIUS.

THE LIBERTY OF THE WILL IS NECES-
SITY.

WHEN the word liberty is applied to the will,
nothing more can be underftood by it than the
free power of willing or not willing a thing. But
this power would fuppofe that there could be wills
without a motive, and confequently effects without a caufe. And it would follow, that we could
equally wifh ourfelves good and evil; a fuppofi-
tion abfolutely impoffible. In fact, if the defire
of happinefs be the true principle of all our
thoughts and of all our actions; if all men really
tend towards their true or apparent happinefs; it
will follow, that all our wills are no more than
the effect of this tendency. In this fenfe, therefore, no adequate idea can be annexed to the word
liberty. But it will be faid, if we are under a neceffity of purfuing happinefs wherever we difcern
it, we are at leaft at liberty in making choice of
the means for procuring our happinefs. Yes, it
may be anfwered; but then liberty is only a fy-
nonimous term for knowledge. The more or lefs

a perfon underftands of the law, or the more or
lefs able the counfellor is by whom he is directed
in his affairs, the more or lefs eligible will be his
meafures.   But whatever his conduct be, the defire of happinefs will always induce him to take
thofe meafures which appear to him the beft calculated to promote his intereft, his difpofition,
his paffions, and, in fine, whatever he accounts
his happinefs.   There are fome who confider the
fufpenfion of the mind as a proof of liberty.
They are not aware, that in volition, fufpenfion
is no lefs neceffary than precipitancy. When, for
want of confideration, we have drawn on ourfelves fome misfortune, felf-love renders fufpenfion abfolutely neceffary.   The word deliberation
is equally miftaken.   We conceive, for inftance,
that while we are choofing between two pleafures
nearly equal, that we are deliberating. But what
we confider as deliberation, is only the flownefs
with which the heavier of two weights, nearly
equal, makes one of the fcales of a balance fub-
fide.   How can the problem of liberty be philo-
fophically folved, if, as Mr Locke has proved, we
are difciples of friends, parents, books, and, in
fine, all the objects that furround us? All our
thoughts and wills muft then be either the immediate effects, or neceffary confequences, of the impreffions we have received.

HELVETIUS.

LI-

LIBERTY AND NECESSITY.

WHEN any paſt perception is brought into view again, whether by any conatus or exertion of the percipient, or *ab extra* only, or without any deſign of his, ſuch being in view is what we call memory. The perceptions of living beings may be related to each other two ways extremely different; the one, when a being exerts an internal power to make a paſt perception again preſent; the other, when the perception, or the reſemblance of it, is offered by ſome external cauſe, without any exertion on the part of the percipient. Hence it appears that there are two kinds of memory ſpecifically different, an active and a paſſive memory.—Reaſon implies or ſuppoſes memory in general; for without memory, whatever is in the mind would be a train of unconnected and unrelated perceptions, which is inconſiſtent with a power producing a chain of depending conſequences: and without active memory, whatever is in the mind, would be related by accident only with reſpect to us; which is inconſiſtent with a power, by which we bring together any two perceptions or ideas, that we may ſee their agreement and diverſity. In a word, reaſoning ſuppoſes our comparing, and comparing ſuppoſes our bringing together, preceptions, that

are

are in nature fucceffive, and confequently diftant;
that is, it fuppofes active memory. Since reafon
implies and fuppofes active memory, it follows
that it implies or fuppofes liberty; this kind of
memory being only the power of reflecting back,
and applying voluntarily our attention to any paft
perception, and confequently to any part of our
paft confcioufnefs within certain limits at leaft.
The power of reflecting and applying, is here
oppofed to the neceffity of doing it on the one
hand, and the neceffity of not doing it on the
other. But we are not free in feeing the iden-
tities, diverfities, agreements, or difagreements of
our ideas: we are not free in feeing the natures,
and habitudes, and relations of thofe perceptions,
upon which we have thus freely and voluntarily
reflected back our attention. For every percipient, if it fhall bring together and compare any
two perceptions, muft of neceffity, according to
its faculty of difcernment, fee whether they agree
or difagree, or how far they are the fame or
different. It muft by its original conftitution be
thus far purely paffive in its perception, being
active and free only in reflecting and applying its
attention to it. So that it is wonderful that there
fhould ever have been any difpute in the world,
whether a rational creature could be a free creature; fince the pronouncing a creature rational is
the fame thing as the pronouncing it free in other
words.

words. It happens to human liberty, as to motion, that it is eafier to feel it, and be certain of
the reality of it, than accurately to explain its
nature. The friends of common fenfe and found
philofophy fhould therefore deduce their inftances
of it from the firft and higheft kind of liberty,
that over the perceptions of the mind, which is
the caufe; rather than from the motions of the
body, which are but the confequence and effect
of the other. BAXTER.

PHILOSOPHICAL NECESSITY AND LIBERTY IN MAN.

ACCORDING to Newton and others, the infinitely free Being has communicated to man a limited portion of that liberty; and by liberty here, is
not underftood the fimple power of applying our
thoughts to fuch or fuch an object, and of beginning the motion: not only the faculty of willing
is meant, but that of willing in the moft free and
efficacious manner; and even of willing without
any other reafon than the will itfelf. There is
not a man on the earth who does not believe
that he fometimes feels himfelf poffeffed of this
liberty. Many philofophers however think the
contrary; and that all the liberty we enjoy, is
that of wearing fometimes freely the fetters of
fatality. Collins is of this opinion: he calls man

a neceffary agent. Clarke fays, if this be true,
man is no longer an agent. But who does not
fee that this is true chicanery? Whatever produces neceffary effects, Collins calls a neceffary
agent. Is it of any confequence whether he be
called agent or patient? The point is to know
whether he be neceffarily determined.

If only one fingle cafe can be found where
man is really free with a liberty of indifference,
that alone feems fufficient to decide the queftion.
Now what cafe fhall we find more proper than
that where our liberty is put to a trial? For inftance, it is propofed to me to turn to the right
or the left, or to do fome other action, to which
neither pleafure attracts, nor difguft diverts. I then
choofe, and do not follow the dictates of my underftanding which reprefents to me the beft; for in
this cafe there is neither better nor worfe. How
do I act? I exercife a right, God has given me of
willing and acting in certain cafes without any
other reafon than my own will. I enjoy a right
and power to begin the motion, and begin it on
which fide I pleafe. If in this cafe my will directs
me, why fhould any other caufe be fought than
my own will? It feems probable, therefore, that
in indifferent things we have the liberty of indifference. For who can fay that God has or has
not been able to confer on us this gift? And if
he is able, and we feel this power in ourfelves,

how

how can it be affirmed that we do not enjoy it?
—This liberty of indifference is, however, treated
as a chimera : it is faid, that to determine without a reafon, belongs only to madmen. But it
fhould be remembered, that madmen are diftem-
pered perfons, without any liberty. They are
neceffarily determined by the diforder of their
organs. They are not their own mafters; they
choofe nothing. He is free who determines for
himfelf. Now, why fhall we not in things indifferent determine ourfelves merely by our own
will ?

We enjoy, in all other cafes, the liberty called
fpontaniety; that is, our will is determined by
motives when there are any; and thefe motives
are always the laft refult of the underftanding or
inftinct. Thus, when my underftanding reprefents to itfelf, that it is better for me to obey
than break the law, I conform to the law with a
fpontaneous liberty; I perform voluntarily what
the laft dictamen of my underftanding leads me
to perform. This fpecies of liberty is never better perceived, than when our will oppofes our
defires. I have a violent paffion for fomething;
but my underftanding tells me, I muft refift this
paffion; it reprefents to me a greater good in
victory, than in a compliance with my appetite.
This laft motive preponderates, and I oppofe my
defires by my will. This command of my reafon

I

I neceſſarily and willingly obey. I do not what I deſire, but what I will; and in this caſe I am free, and enjoy all the liberty of which ſuch a circumſtance can make me ſuſceptible.

In fine, I am free in no reſpect, when my paſſion is too ſtrong, and my underſtanding too weak, or when my organs are diſordered; and this unfortunately is very often the caſe of men. So that ſpontaneous liberty is to the ſoul what health is to the body: ſome perſons enjoy it entirely and conſtantly; many are often deprived of it; and others are ſick during their whole life: all the other faculties of man are ſubject to the ſame variation. Sight, hearing, taſte, ſtrength, cogitation, are ſometimes ſtronger and ſometimes weaker: our liberty, like every thing elſe, is limited, variable: in a word, very trifling; becauſe man is himſelf inconſiderable.

The difficulty of reconciling human actions with God's eternal preſcience, was no obſtacle to Newton; he avoided that labyrinth. Liberty being once proved, it is not for us to determine how God foreſees what we ſhall freely do. We know not how God ſees what paſſes at preſent. We have no idea of his mode of ſeeing: why then ſhould we have any of his mode of foreſeeing? We ſhould conſider all his attributes as equally incomprehenſible.

It muſt be owned, that agaiſtn this idea of liberty

liberty there are objections which ftartle. It is immediately feen that this liberty of indifference would be but a trivial prefent, if it extended no further than fpitting to the right or left, or chuoo-fing either odd or even. The bufinefs is whether Cartouche and Shah Nadier have a liberty of not fhedding human blood ? Of what confequence is the liberty of putting the left or right foot firft ? This liberty of indifference is then found to be impoffible ; for how can we be faid to determine without reafon ? You will, but why will you ? You are afked even or odd ; you choofe even, without being aware of the motive ; which is, that even prefents itfelf to your mind at the in-ftant you make the choice.

Every thing has its caufe : confequently your will is not excepted. There is then no willing, but in confequence of the laft idea received. No perfon can know what idea he will have the next moment ; therefore, no perfon is mafter of his own ideas ; therefore no perfon is mafter of willing or not willing. Were he mafter of thefe, he might perform the contrary of what God has difpofed in the concatenation of the things of this world. Thus every perfon might and actu-ally would, change the Eternal order.

All the liberty the wife Locke knew, was the power of doing what one wills. Free-will feem-ed to him only a chimera. A patient during the

paroxifm

262 NECESSITY.

paroxifm of the gout has not the liberty of walking; nor the prifoner that of going abroad: the
one becomes free when cured; the other on
opening to him the gate.

To place thefe difficulties in a ftronger light,
I will fuppofe that Cicero is attempting to prove
to Catiline that he ought not to confpire againft
his country. Catiline tells him, it is out of his
power; that his conferences with Cethegus have
imprinted in his mind the idea of the confpiracy;
that this idea pleafes him beyond any other; and
that we only will in confequence of our laft
decifion. But you might, anfwers Cicero, adopt
other ideas as well as I, by liftening attentively
to me, and reflecting on the duty of confulting
the good of your country. It is of no confequence,
returns Catiline, your ideas offend me; and the
defire of affaffinating you prevails. I am forry
for your madnefs, fays Cicero; endeavour to take
fome of my medicines. If I am mad, replies
Catiline, I cannot command my endeavours to
be cured. But, urged the conful, men are endued
with reafon, which they may confult, and may
cure the diforder of the organs, which renders
you thus perverfe, thus hardened in fo horrid a
crime; efpecially if this diforder be not too
ftrong. Show me, fays Catiline, the point where
this diforder is curable. For my part, I own,
that from the firft moment I began the confpiracy,

all

all my reflections have tended to make me per-
fevere in the undertaking. When did you firft
take this fatal refolution? afks the conful. When
I had loft my money at play. And could not you
have abftained from play? No; for the idea of
play predominated at that time in my mind above
all other ideas: and had I not played, I fhould
have difcompofed the order of the univerfe, by
which Quartilla was to win 400000 fefterces of
me; with this money fhe was to purchafe a houfe
and a gallant; by this gallant fhe was to have a
fon; Cethegus and Lentulus were to come to my
houfe, and we were to confpire againft the republic. Deftiny has made me a wolf, and you a
fhepherd's dog: deftiny will decide which is to
cut the throat of the other. To this Cicero could
have anfwered only by an oration. It muft indeed be allowed, that the objections againft liberty
can hardly be anfwered but by a vague eloquence:
a fubject on which the wifer a perfon is, the
more he fears to confider it. But whichever
fyftem we embrace, by whatever fatality we fuppofe all our actions are governed, we fhall always
act as if we were free.

VOLTAIRE.

PHI-

PHILOSOPHICAL NECESSITY, AND THE LI-
BERTY OF INDIFFERENCE.

1. PLANTS are organised beings, in which
every thing is done neceffarily. Some plants belong to the animal-kingdom, and are, in effect,
animals attached to the earth.

2. Can thefe animal-plants, with roots, leaves,
and fenfations, be fuppofed to have liberty? No,
furely.

3. Have not animals a perception, an inftinct,
a reafon begun, a meafure of ideas and of memory? What, in reality, is inftinct? Is it not
one of thofe fecret fprings we can never know?
Nothing can be known but by analyfis, or a confequence of what are called the firft principles.
Now, what analyfis, or what fynthefis, can explain the nature of inftinct? We only perceive
that this inftinct is always neceffarily accompanied with ideas. A filk worm has a perception
of the leaf which nourifhes it; the partridge, of
the worm which it feeks and fwallows; the fox,
of the partridge which it eats; the wolf, of the fox
which it devours. Now it is not very likely that
thefe beings poffefs what we call liberty: may
we not, therefore, have ideas without being free?

4. Men receive and combine ideas in their
fleep; but they cannot be faid to be then free.

Is not this a fresh proof, that we may have ideas without being free?

5. Man has, above other animals, the gift of a more comprehensive memory: this memory is the sole source of all his thoughts. Can this source, common to animals and men, produce liberty? The ideas of reflection in one brain, can they be any other than ideas of reflection in another?

6. Are not all men determined by their instinct? And is not this the reason why they never change their character? Is not this instinct what we call the disposition?

7. Were we free, where is the man who would not change his disposition? But was ever a man seen on earth, who gave himself one single propensity? Was there ever a man born with an aversion to dancing, that gave himself a taste for dancing? A sluggish and sedentary man, that gave himself an inclination to seek motion? Do not age and regimen diminish the passions, which reason fancies it has subdued?

8. Is not the will the last consequence of the last ideas received? If these ideas are necessary, is not the will also necessary?

9. Is liberty any thing more than the power of acting or not acting? And was not Locke in the right to call liberty, Power?

10. A wolf has the perception of sheep feeding in a meadow; his instinct prompts him to de-

vour them, but is prevented by the dogs. A conqueror has the perception of a province, which his instinct leads him to invade; he finds fortresses and armies to obstruct his passage. Where is the great difference between the wolf and the conqueror?

11. Does not this universe appear in all its parts subjected to immutable laws? If a man might at his pleasure direct his will, is it not plain, that he might discompose these immutable laws?

12. By what privilege should man be exempted from the same necessity, to which the stars, animals, plants, and every thing else in nature are subjected?

13. Is it justly said, that in the system of this universal fatality, punishments and rewards would be useless and absurd? Is it not rather evident, that the inutility and absurdity of punishments and rewards appears in the system of liberty? In short, if a highwayman is possessed of a free will, determining itself solely by itself, the fear of punishment may very well fail of determining him to renounce robbery: but if the physical causes act alone; if the sight of the gibbet and wheel make a necessary and violent impression; they then necessarily correct the villain, while he is gazing at the execution of another.

14. To know if the soul be free, should we not first know what this soul is? Can any one

boast

boaft that his reafon alone demonftrates to him
the fpiritual nature, the immortality of the foul?
It is the general opinion of phyficians, that the
principle of fenfation refides in the place where
the nerves unite in the brain. But this place
is not a mathematical point. The origin of
every nerve is extended. There is in that place
a bell on which the fine organs of our fenfes
ftrike; but who can conceive that this bell oc-
cupies no point of fpace? Are we not automata;
born to will always, to do fometimes what we
will, and fometimes the contrary? Stars at the
centre of the earth, without us and within us,
every effence, every fubftance is to us unknown.
We fee only appearances. We are in a dream.

15. Whether in this dream we believe the will
free or fubject; the organifed earth of which we
are formed endued with an immortal or perifh-
able faculty; whether we think like Epicurus or
like Socrates, the wheels that move the machine
of the univerfe will be always the fame.

VOLTAIRE.

LIBERTY AND NECESSITY.

EVERY one finds in himfelf a power to begin
or forbear, continue or put an end to feveral
actions in himfelf. From the confideration of the
extent of this power of the mind over the actions

of

of the man, which every one finds in himself, arise
the ideas of liberty and necessity.

All the actions that we have any idea of, reducing themselves to these two, viz. thinking and
motion; so far as a man has power to think or
not to think, to move or not to move, according
to the preference or direction of his own mind,
so far is a man free. Wherever any performance
or forbearance are not equally in a man's power;
wherever doing or not doing will not equally
follow upon the preference of his mind directing
it; there he is not free, though perhaps the action
may be voluntary. So that the idea of liberty is
the idea of a power in any agent to do or forbear
any particular action, according to the determination or thought of the mind, whereby either of
them is preferred to the other; where either of
them is not in the power of the agent to be produced by him according to his volition, there he
is not at liberty; that agent is under necessity.
So that liberty cannot be where there is no
thought, no volition, no will; but there may be
thought, there may be will, there may be volition,
where there is no liberty. A little consideration
of an obvious instance or two may make this
clear.

A tennis-ball, whether in motion by the stroke
of a racket, or lying still at rest, is not by any one
taken to be a free agent. If we inquire into the
reason,

reafon, we fhall find it is becaufe we conceive not a tennis-ball to think, and confequently not to have any volition or preference of motion to reft, or *vice verſa*, and therefore has not liberty, is not a free agent; but both its motion and reft come under our idea of neceffary, and are fo called. Likewife a man falling into the water (a bridge breaking under him) has not herein liberty, is not a free agent. For though he has volition, though he prefers his not falling to falling; yet the forbearance of that motion not being in his power, the ftop or ceffation of that motion follows not upon his volition; and therefore therein he is not free. So a man ftriking himſelf, or his friend, by a convulfive motion of his arm which it is not in his power, by volition or the direction of his mind, to ftop or forbear; nobody thinks he has in this liberty; every one pities him, as acting by neceffity and conftraint.

Again, fuppofe a man to be carried, whilft faft afleep, into a room, where is a perfon he longs to fee and fpeak with; and to be there locked faft in, beyond his power to get out; he awakes, and is glad to find himſelf in fo defirable company, which he ftays willingly in, *i. e.* prefers his ftay to going away; I afk, Is not this ftay voluntary? I think nobody will doubt it: and yet being lock-ed faft in, it is evident he is not at liberty not to ftay; he has not freedom to be gone. So that

Z 3

liberty is not an idea belonging to volition or preferring; but to the person having the power of doing, or forbearing to do, according as the mind shall choose or direct. Our idea of liberty reaches as far as that power, and no further. For wherever restraint comes to check that power, or compulsion takes away that indifferency of ability on either side to act, or to forbear acting; there liberty and our notion of it presently ceases.

We have instances enough, and often more than enough, in our own bodies. A man's heart beats, and the blood circulates, which it is not in his power by any thought or volition to stop; and therefore, in respect of these motions, where rest depends not on his choice, nor would follow the determination of his mind, if it should prefer it, he is not a free agent. Convulsive motions agitate his legs, so that though he will it ever so much, he cannot by any power of his mind stop their motion (as in that odd disease called *chorea sancti Viti*), but he is perpetually dancing: he is not at liberty in this action, but under as much necessity of moving as a stone that falls, or a tennis-ball struck with a racket. On the other side, a palsy or the stocks hinder his legs from obeying the determination of his mind, if it would thereby transfer his body to another place. In all these there is want of freedom; though the sitting still even of a paralytic, whilst he prefers it

to

to a removal, is truly voluntary. Voluntary, then, is not oppofed to neceffary, but to involuntary. For a man may prefer what he can do to what he cannot do; the ftate he is in to its abfence or change, though neceffity has made it in itfelf unalterable.

As it is in the motions of the body, fo it is in the thoughts of our minds: where any one is fuch, that we have power to take it up, or lay it by, according to the preference of the mind, there we are at liberty. A waking man, being under the neceffity of having fome ideas conftantly in his mind, is not at liberty to think or not to think; no more than he is at liberty, whether his body fhall touch any other or no: but whether he will remove his contemplation from one idea to another, is many times in his choice; and then he is in refpect of his ideas as much at liberty as he is in refpect of bodies he refts on: he can at pleafure remove himfelf from one to another. But yet fome ideas to the mind, like fome motions to the body, are fuch as in certain circumftances it cannot avoid, nor obtain their abfence by the utmoft effort it can ufe. A man on the rack is not at liberty to lay by the idea of pain, and divert himfelf with other contemplations; and fometimes a boifterous paffion hurries our thoughts as a hurricane does our bodies, without leaving us the liberty of thinking on other things, which we would rather choofe. But as foon as the mind regains the power

power to ſtop or continue, begin or forbear, any of theſe motions of the body without, or thoughts within, according as it thinks fit to prefer either to the other, we then conſider the man as a free agent again.

Wherever thought is wholly wanting, or the power to act or forbear according to the direction of thought; there neceſſity takes place. This, in an agent capable of volition, when the beginning or continuation of any action is contrary to that preference of his mind, is called Compulſion; when the hindering or ſtopping any action is contrary to his volition, it is called Reſtraint. Agents that have no thought, no volition at all, are in every thing neceſſary agents.

If this be ſo (as I imagine it is), I leave it to be conſidered, whether it may not help to put an end to that long agitated, and I think unreaſonable, becauſe unintelligible, queſtion, viz. Whether man's will be free or no? For if I miſtake not, it follows from what I have ſaid, that the queſtion itſelf is altogether improper; and it is as inſignificant as to aſk whether his ſleep be ſwift, or his virtue ſquare; liberty being as little applicable to the will, as ſwiftneſs of motion is to ſleep or ſquareneſs to virtue. Every one would laugh at the abſurdity of ſuch a queſtion as either of theſe; becauſe it is obvious, that the modifications of motion belong not to ſleep, nor the difference of

figure

figure to virtue: and when any one well confiders it, I think he will as plainly perceive, that liberty, which is but a power, belongs only to agents, and cannot be an attribute or modification of the will, which is alfo but a power.

I think the queftion is not proper, Whether the will be free? but, Whether a man be free? Thus I think,

That fo far as any one can, by the direction or choice of his mind, preferring the exiftence of any action to the non-exiftence of that action, and *vice verfa*, make it to exift or not exift; fo far he is free. For if I can, by a thought directing the motion of my finger, make it move when it was at reft, or *vice verfa*, it is evident, that in refpect of that I am free: and if I can, by a like thought of my mind, preferring one to the other, produce either words or filence, I am at liberty to fpeak or hold my peace. And as far as this power reaches, of acting or not acting, by the determination of his own thought preferring either, fo far is a man free. For how can we think any one freer, than to have the power to do what he will? And fo far as any one can, by preferring any action to its not being, or reft to any action, produce that action or reft; fo far can he do what he will. For fuch a preferring of action to its abfence, is the willing of it; and we can fcarce tell how to imagine any being freer, than to be
able

able to do what he will. So that in refpect of actions within the reach of fuch a power in him, a man feems as free as it is poffible for freedom to make him.

But the inquifitive mind of man, willing to fhift off from himfelf, as far as he can, all thoughts of guilt, though it be by putting himfelf into a worfe ftate than that of fatal neceffity, is not content with this; freedom, unlefs it reaches further than this, will not ferve the turn: and it paffes for a good plea, that a man is not free at all, if he be not as free to will as he is to act what he wills. Concerning a man's liberty, there yet therefore is raifed this further queftion, Whether a man be free to will? Which I think is what is meant, when it is difputed whether the will be free. And as to that I imagine,

That willing or volition, being an action and freedom confifting in a power of acting or not acting, a man, in refpect of willing, or the act of volition, when any action in his power is once propofed to his thoughts as prefently to be done, cannot be free. The reafon whereof is very manifeft: for it being unavoidable that the action depending on his will fhould exift or not exift; and its exiftence or not exiftence following perfectly the determination and preference of his will; he cannot avoid willing the exiftence or not exiftence of that action: it is abfolutely ne-

ceffary

ceffary that he will the one or the other; *i. e.*
prefer the one to the other : fince one of them
muft neceffarily follow; and that which does
follow, follows by the choice and determination
of his mind, that is, by his willing it; for if he
did not will it, it would not be. So that in refpect of the act of willing, a man in fuch a cafe
is not free: liberty confifting in a power to act
or not to act; which, in regard of volition, a man,
upon fuch a propofal, has not. For it is unavoidably neceffary to prefer the doing or forbearance
of an action in a man's power which is once fo
propofed to his thoughts: a man muft neceffarliy
will the one or the other of them; upon which
preference or volition, the action, or its forbearance, certainly follows, and is truly voluntary.
But the act of volition, or preferring one of the
two, being that which he cannot avoid, a man, in
refpect of that act of willing, is under a neceffity,
and fo cannot be free; unlefs neceffity and freedom can confift together, and a man can be free
and bound at once.

This then is evident, that in all propofals of
prefent actions, a man is not at liberty to will
or not to will, becaufe he cannot forbear willing;
liberty confifting in a power to act or forbear acting, and in that only. For a man that fits ftill is
faid yet to be at liberty, becaufe he can walk if
he wills it : but if a man fitting ftill has not a
                                        power

power to remove himself, he is not at liberty. So likewise a man falling down a precipice, though in motion, is not at liberty, because he cannot stop that motion if he would. This being so, it is plain that a man that is walking, to whom it is proposed to give off walking, is not at liberty whether he will determine himself to walk or give off walking or no: he must necessarily prefer one or the other of them; walking or not walking. And so it is in regard of all other actions in our power so proposed; which are the far greater number. For considering the vast number of voluntary actions that succeed one another every moment that we are awake in the course of our lives, there are but few of them that are thought on or proposed to the will, till the time they are to be done; and in all such actions, as I have shown, the mind, in respect of willing, has not a power to act or not to act, wherein consists liberty. The mind in that case has not a power to forbear willing; it cannot avoid some determination concerning them, let the consideration be as short, the thought as quick, as it will; it either leaves the man in the state he was before thinking, or changes it; continues the action, or puts an end to it. Whereby it is manifest, that it orders and directs one, in preference to or with neglect to the other; and thereby either the continuation or change becomes unavoidably voluntary.

2

Since,

Since, then, it is plain, that, in moſt cafes, a man is not at liberty whether he will or no, the next thing demanded is, Whether a man be at liberty to will which of the two he pleaſes, motion or reſt? This queſtion carries the abſurdity of it ſo manifeſtly in itſelf, that one might thereby ſufficiently be convinced that liberty concerns not the will. For to aſk, Whether a man be at liberty to will either motion or reſt, ſpeaking or ſilence, which he pleaſes? is to aſk, Whether a man can will what he wills, or be pleaſed with what he is pleaſed with? A queſtion which, I think, needs no anſwer; and they who can make a queſtion of it, muſt ſuppoſe one will to determine the acts of another, and another to determine that, and ſo on *in infinitum*.

To avoid theſe and the like abſurdities, nothing can be of greater uſe than to eſtabliſh in our minds determined ideas of the things under conſideration. If the ideas of liberty and volition were well fixed in the underſtandings, and carried along with us in our minds, as they ought, through all the queſtions that are raiſed about them, I ſuppoſe a great part of the difficulties that perplex mens thoughts, and entangle their underſtandings, would be much eaſier reſolved; and we ſhould perceive where the confuſed ſignification of terms, or where the nature of the thing, cauſed the obſcurity.

It

It is carefully to be remembered, that freedom
confifts in the dependence of the exiftence or not
exiftence of any action upon our volition of it;
and not in the dependence of any action, or its contrary, on our preference. A man ftanding on a cliff
is at liberty to leap twenty yards downwards into
the fea; not becaufe he has a power to do the contrary action, which is to leap twenty yards up-
wards, for that he cannot do; but he is therefore
free, becaufe he has a power to leap or not to
leap. But if a greater force than his either holds
him faft, or tumbles him down, he is no longer
free in that cafe; becaufe the doing or forbearance of that particular action is no longer in his
power. He that is a clofe prifoner in a room
twenty feet fquare, being at the north fide of his
chamber, is at liberty to walk twenty feet fouth-
ward, becaufe he can walk or not walk it; but is
not at the fame time at liberty to do the contrary,
i. e. to walk twenty feet northward.

In this, then, confifts freedom; viz. in our being able to act or not to act, according as we fhall
choofe or will.

We muft remember, that volition, or willing,
is an act of the mind, directing its thought to the
production of any action, and thereby exerting its
power to produce it. To avoid multiplying of
words, I would crave leave here, under the word
action, to comprehend the forbearance too of any

action

action propofed; fitting ftill, or holding one's peace, when walking or fpeaking are propofed, though mere forbearances, requiring as much the determination of the will, and being as often weighty in their confequences, as the contrary actions, may, on that confideration, well enough pafs for actions too.

The will being nothing but a power in the mind to direct the operative faculties of a man to motion or reft, as far as they depend on fuch direction; to the queftion, What is it that determines the will? the true and proper anfwer is, The mind: for that which determines the general power of directing to this or that particular direction, is nothing but the agent itfelf exercifing the power it has that particular way. If this anfwer fatisfies not, it is plain the meaning of the queftion, What determines the will? is this, What moves the mind, in every particular inftance, to determine its general power of directing to this or that particular motion or reft? And to this I anfwer, The motive for continuing in the fame ftate or action is only the prefent fatisfaction in it: the motive to change is always fome uneafinefs; nothing fetting us upon the change of ftate, or upon any new action, but fome uneafinefs. This is the great motive that works on the mind to put it upon action; which, for fhortnefs fake, we will call determining of the will.

That

That which determines the will in regard to our actions, upon second thoughts, I am apt to imagine, is not, as is generally supposed, the greater good in view; but some (and for the most part the most pressing) uneasiness a man is at present under. This is that which successively determines the will, and sets us upon those actions we perform. This uneasiness we may call, as it is, *desire*; which is an uneasiness of the mind for want of some absent good. All pain of the body, of what sort soever, and disquiet of the mind, is uneasiness; and with this is always joined desire equal to the pain or uneasiness felt, and is scarce distinguishable from it. For desire being nothing but an uneasiness in the want of an absent good, in reference to any pain felt, ease is that absent good; and till that ease be attained, we may call it desire; nobody feeling pain that he wishes not to be eased of, with a desire equal to that pain, and inseparable from it. Besides this desire of ease from pain, there is another of absent positive good; and here also the desire and uneasiness are equal. As much as we desire any absent good, so much are we in pain for it. But here all absent good does not, according to the greatness it has, or is acknowledged to have, cause pain equal to that greatness, as all pain causes desire equal to itself; because the absence of good is not always a pain, as the presence of pain is. And therefore
absent

absent good may be looked on and considered without desire. But so much as there is any where of desire, so much there is of uneasiness.

That desire is a state of uneasiness, every one who reflects on himself will quickly find. Who is there that has not felt in desire what the wise man says of hope, (which is not much different from it), " that it being deferred makes the heart sick;" and that still proportionable to the greatness of the desire; which sometimes raises the uneasiness to that pitch, that it makes people cry out, Give me children, give me the thing desired, or I die? Life itself, and all its enjoyments, is a burden cannot be borne under the lasting and unremoved pressure of such an uneasiness.

Good and evil, present and absent, it is true, work upon the mind: but that which immediately determines the will, from time to time, to every voluntary action, is the uneasiness of desire fixed on some absent good; either negative, as indolence to one in pain; or positive, as enjoyment of pleasure. That it is this uneasiness that determines the will to the successive voluntary actions whereof the greatest part of our lives are made up, and by which we are conducted through different courses to different ends, I shall endeavour to show, both from experience and the reason of the thing.

When a man is perfectly content with the

A a 3   state

state he is in, which is when he is perfectly without any uneasiness, what industry, what action, what will is there left but to continue in it? Of this every man's observation will satisfy him. And thus we see our all-wise Maker, suitable to our constitution and frame, and knowing what it is that determines the will, has put into man the uneasiness of hunger and thirst, and other natural desires, that return at their seasons, to move and determine their wills, for the preservation of themselves and the continuation of their species. For I think we may conclude, that if the bare contemplation of these good ends, to which we are carried by these several uneasinesses, had been sufficient to determine the will, and set us on work, we should have had none of these natural pains, and perhaps, in this world, little or no pain at all. "It is better to marry than to burn," says St Paul; where we may see what it is that chiefly drives men into the enjoyments of a conjugal life. A little burning felt, pushes us more powerfully, than greater pleasures in prospect draw or allure.

We being in this world beset with sundry uneasinesses, distracted with different desires, the next inquiry naturally will be, Which of them has the precedency in determining the will to the next action? And to that the answer is, That, ordinarily, which is the most pressing of those

that

that are judged capable of being then removed. For the will being the power of directing our operative faculties to fome action for fome end, cannot at any time be moved towards what is judged at that time unattainable: that would be to fuppofe an intelligent being defignedly to act for an end, only to lofe its labour, for fo it is to act for what is judged not attainable; and therefore very great uneafineffes move not the will when they are judged not capable of a cure; they in that cafe put us not upon endeavours. But, thefe fet apart, the moft important and urgent uneafinefs we at that time feel, is that which ordinarily determines the will fucceffively in that train of voluntary actions which makes up our lives. The greateft prefent uneafinefs is the fpur to action, that is conftantly felt, and for the moft part determines the will in its choice of the next action. For this we muft carry along with us, that the proper and only object of the will is fome action of ours, and nothing elfe; for we producing nothing by our willing it but fome action in our power, it is there the will terminates, and reaches no further.

There being in us a great many uneafineffes always foliciting and ready to determine the will, it is natural that the greateft and moft preffing fhould determine the will to the next action: and fo it does for the moft part, but not always; for the mind having in moft cafes, as is evident in
expe-

experience, a power to fuspend the execution and fatisfaction of any of its defires, and fo all, one after another, is at liberty to confider the objects of them, examine them on all fides, and weigh them with others. In this lies the liberty man has: and from the not ufing of it right comes all that variety of miftakes, errors, and faults, which we run into in the conduct of our lives and our endeavours after happinefs; whilft we precipitate the determination of our wills, and engage too foon before due examination. To prevent this, we have a power to fufpend the profecution of this or that defire, as every one may experience in himfelf. This feems to me the fource of all liberty; in this feems to confift that which is (as I think, improperly) called free-will: For during this fufpenfion of any defire, before the will be determined to action, and the action (which follows that determination) done, we have opportunity to examine, view, and judge of the good or evil of what we are going to do; and when, upon due examination, we have judged we have done our duty, all that we can or ought to do in purfuit of our happinefs; and it is not a fault, but a perfection of our nature, to defire, will, and act, according to the laft refult of a fair examination.

This is fo far from being a reftraint or diminution of freedom, that it is the very improvement and benefit of it: it is not an abridgment, it is

the

the end and ufe of our liberty; and the further
we are removed from fuch a determination, the
nearer we are to mifery and flavery. A perfect
indifferency on the mind, not determinable by its
laft judgment of the good or evil that is thought
to attend its choice, would be fo far from being
an advantage and excellency of any intellectual
nature, that it would be as great an imperfection
as the want of indifferency to act or not to act till
determined by the will, would be an imperfection on the other fide. A man is at liberty to lift
up his hand to his head, or let it reft quiet: he
is perfectly indifferent in either; and it would be
an imperfection in him if he wanted that power,
if he were deprived of that indifferency. But it
would be as great an imperfection if he had the
fame indifferency whether he would prefer the
lifting up his hand, or its remaining in reft, when
it would fave his head or eyes from a blow he fees
coming: it is as much a perfection that defire, or
the power of preferring, fhould be determined by
good, as that the power of acting fhould be determined by the will; and the more certain fuch a determination is, the greater is the perfection. Nay,
were we determined by any thing but the laft
refult of our own minds, judging of the good or
evil of any action, we were not free; the very
end of our freedom being, that we may attain
the good we choofe. And therefore every man

is

is put under a neceſſity by his conſtitution, as an intelligent being, to be determined in willing by his own thought and judgment what is beſt for him to do; elſe he would be under the determination of ſome other than himſelf; which is want of liberty. And to deny that a man's will, in every determination, follows his own judgment, is to ſay, that a man wills and acts for an end that he would not have, at the time that he wills and acts for it: For if he prefers it in his preſent thoughts before any other, it is plain he then thinks better of it, and would have it before any other; unleſs he can have and not have it, will and not will, at the ſame time; a contradiction too manifeſt to be admitted.

If we look upon thoſe ſuperior beings above us, who enjoy perfect happineſs, we ſhall have reaſon to judge that they are more ſteadily determined in their choice of good than we; and yet we have no reaſon to think they are leſs happy or leſs free than we are. And if it were fit for ſuch poor finite creatures as we are to pronounce what infinite wiſdom and goodneſs could do, I think we might ſay, that God himſelf cannot chooſe what is not good: the freedom of the Almighty hinders not his being determined by what is beſt.

Locke.

Phi-

PHILOSOPHICAL NECESSITY ESSENTIAL TO BUSINESS AND SCIENCE.

THE mutual dependence of men is fo great in all focieties, that fcarce any human action is entirely complete in itfelf, or is performed without fome reference to the actions of others, which are requifite to make it anfwer fully the intention of the agent. The artificer expects, when he carries his goods to market and offers them at a reafonable price, he fhall find buyers, and fhall be able, by the money he acquires, to engage others to fupply him with thofe commodities which are requifite for his fubfiftence. In proportion as men extend their dealings, and render their intercourfe with others more complicated, they always comprehend a greater variety of voluntary actions, which they expect, from their proper motives, to co-operate with their own. In all thefe conclufions, they take their meafures from paft experience, in the fame manner as in their reafonings concerning external objects; and firmly believe that men, as well as all the elements, are to continue in their operations the fame which they have ever found them.—What would become of hiftory, had we not a dependence on the veracity of the hiftorian, according to the experience which we have had of mankind? How

could

could politics be a science, if laws and forms of
government had not an uniform influence upon
society? Where could be the foundation of morals, if particular characters had no certain nor
determinate power to produce particular sentiments, and if these sentiments had no constant
operation on actions? And with what pretence
could we employ our *criticism* upon any poet or
polite author, if we could not pronounce the conduct and sentiments of his actors either natural
or unnatural to such characters and in such circumstances? It seems almost impossible, therefore, to engage either in science or action of any
kind, without acknowledging the doctrine of necessity, and this *inference* from motives to voluntary actions, from characters to conduct.

HUME.

PHILOSOPHICAL NECESSITY ESSENTIAL TO MORALITY AND RELIGION.

NECESSITY may be defined two ways. It
consists either in the constant conjunction of like
objects, or in the inference of the understanding from one object to another. It has never
been denied, that we can draw inferences concerning human actions; and that those inferences
are founded in the experienced union of like actions, with like motives, inclinations, and circumstances.

cumftances.—All laws being founded on rewards and punifhments, it is fuppofed as a fundamental principle, that thefe motives have a regular and uniform influence on the mind, and both produce the good and prevent the evil actions. Actions are, by their very nature, temporary and perifhing; and where they proceed not from fome caufe in the character and difpofition of the perfon who performed them, they can neither redound to his honour if good, nor infamy if evil. The actions themfelves may be blameable; they may be contrary to all the rules of morality and religion: but the perfon is not anfwerable for them; and as they proceeded from nothing in him that is durable and conftant, and leave nothing of that nature behind them, it is impoffible he can upon their account become the object of punifhment or vengeance. According to the principle, therefore, which denies neceffity and, confequently, caufes, a man is as pure and untainted, after having committed the moft horrid crime, as at the firft moment of his birth: nor is his character any way concerned in his actions, fince they are not derived from it; and the wickednefs of the one can never be ufed as a proof of the depravity of the other.

Men are not blamed for fuch actions as they perform ignorantly and cafually, whatever may be the confequences. Why, but becaufe the

principles of thefe actions are only momentary,
and terminate in them alone? Men are blamed
lefs for fuch actions as they perform haftily and
unpremeditately, than for fuch as proceed from
deliberation.   For what reafon, but becaufe a
hafty temper, though a conftant caufe and principle in the mind, operates only by intervals, and
infects not the whole character? Again, repentance wipes off every crime, if attended with a reformation of life and manners.   How is this to
be accounted for, but by afferting, that actions
render a perfon criminal merely as they are proofs
of criminal principles in the mind; and when,
by any alteration of thefe principles, they ceafe
to be juft proofs, they likewife ceafe to be criminal? But, except upon the doctrine of neceffity,
they never were juft proofs, and confequently
never were criminal.   HUME.

THE ORIGIN OF THE LOVE OF NOVELTY.

THE continuance of the fame fenfations render
them at length infenfible to us: and from hence
that inconftancy and love of novelty common to
all men; for all would be affected in a ftrong
and lively manner.   Habit dulls the vivacity of
an impreffion.   I fee with indifference what I always fee; and even the beautiful ceafes to be fo
to me.   I have fo often regarded the fun, that
                                          fea,

sea, this landscape, and fine woman, that, to excite my attention or admiration, the sun must
paint the heavens with colours more lively than
common; the sea must be ravaged by storms;
the landscape must appear with uncommon lustre;
and the woman present herself to me under a
new form. The more forcibly we are affected,
the more happy we are; provided, however, the
sensations be not painful.

HELVETIUS.

Bb 2   O.

O.

OATHS.

OATHS are requisite in all courts of judicature; but it is a question whether their authority arises from any popular religion. It is the solemnity and importance of the occasion, the regard to reputation, and the reflecting on the general interests of society, together with the punishments annexed to perjury in all well-regulated governments, that are the chief restraints upon mankind. Custom-house oaths, and political oaths, are but little regarded, even by some who pretend to principles of honesty and religion; and a Quaker's affirmation is with us justly put upon the same footing with the oath of any other person. Polybius ascribes, indeed, the infamy of Greek faith to the prevalence of the Epicurean philosophy: but the Punic faith, it is well known, had as bad a reputation in ancient times, as Irish

evidence

evidence has in modern; though we cannot account for thefe vulgar obfervations by the fame reafon. Not to mention, that Greek faith was infamous before the rife of the Epicurean philofophy; and Euripides has glanced a remarkable ftroke of fatire againft his nation with regard to this circumftance. HUME.

OBSTINACY.

IT is often from the want of paffions that arifes the obftinacy of perfons of mean parts. Their flender knowledge fuppofes that they never had any defire of inftruction, or, at leaft, that this defire has been always very faint; very much below their fondnefs for floth: now he who is not defirous of inftruction, has never fufficient motives for altering his mind. To fave himfelf the fatigue of imagination, he muft always turn a deaf ear to the remonftrances of reafon; and obftinacy, in this cafe, is the neceffary effect of floth.

HELVETIUS.

OCCULT QUALITIES.

THE doctrine of occult qualities is the wifeft and trueft which antiquity has produced. The formation of the elements, the emiffion of light, animals, vegetables, minerals, our birth, our death, waking, fleeping, fenfation, thought,—

every thing is occult quality. See, feel, separate, measure, weigh, collect, and be assured that you will never do any more. Newton calculated the force of gravitation, but he has not discovered its cause. Why is that cause occult? It is a first principle. We are acquainted with the laws of motion; but the cause of motion being a first principle, will for ever remain a secret. You are alive, but how? You will never know any thing of the matter. You have sensations, ideas; but can you guess by what they are produced? Is not that the most occult thing in the world? Names have been given to a certain number of faculties which display themselves in us, according as our organs acquire some degree of strength, when they are freed from the teguments in which we were inclosed during nine months, without so much as knowing in what that strength consists. If we call any thing to mind, we say it is memory; if we range a few ideas in order, it is judgment; if we form a connected picture of some other scattered ideas, it is called imagination:—and the result or principle of those qualities is named *soul*, a thing still a thousand times more occult.

It is a certain truth, that there does not exist in us one separate being called sensibility, another memory, a third judgment, a fourth imagination; how then can we easily conceive that we have a fifth composed of the four others which are really non-

non-entities ?—What was underſtood by the ancients, when they pronounced the Greek word
Pſyché? Did they mean a property of man, or a
particular being concealed in man? Was it not an
occult expreſſion of a very occult thing? Are not
all the ſyſtems of ontology and pſychology mere
dreams? In our mother's womb we are entirely
unacquainted with ourſelves; yet there our ideas
ought to be the pureſt, becauſe there our attention is the leaſt diſtracted. We are unacquainted
with ourſelves at our birth, in our growth, during our life, and at the hour of death. The firſt
reaſoner who departed from the ancient doctrine
of occult qualities, corrupted the underſtanding
of mankind. He involved us in a labyrinth, from
which it is now impoſſible to extricate ourſelves.

How much wiſer had the firſt man been, who,
ſenſible of his ignorance, had ſaid to that Being
who is the author of the univerſe: "Thou haſt
" made me without my knowing it; and thou
" preſerveſt me without my being able to find out
" the mode of my exiſtence. When I ſuckled my
" nurſe's breaſt, I fulfilled one of the moſt ab-
" ſtruſe laws of natural philoſophy; and I fulfil
" one ſtill more unknown, when I eat and digeſt
" the aliments with which thou feedeſt me. I
" know ſtill leſs, how ſome ideas enter my head
" to quit it the next moment without ever re-
" appearing; and how others remain there du-
                                        " ring

" ring my whole life, notwithstanding my strongest
" efforts to drive them out. I am an effect of thy
" occult and supreme power, which the stars obey
" as well as myself. A particle of dust agitated
" by the wind, saith not, I command the winds.
" *In te vivimus, movemur, et sumus.* Thou art
" the sole *Being*; and the rest is only mode."

VOLTAIRE.

Our OPINIONS DEPEND UPON OUR INTEREST.

ALL men agree in the truth of geometric propositions. Is it because they are demonstrated?
No: but because men have no interest in taking
the false for the true. If they had such interest,
the propositions most evidently demonstrated
would appear to them problematic; they would
prove on occasion, that the contained is greater
than the container: this is a fact of which some
religions afford examples. If a Catholic divine
propose to prove that there are sticks that have not
two ends, nothing is more easy: he will first distinguish sticks into two sorts, the one material,
the other spiritual. He will then deliver an obscure dissertation on the nature of spiritual sticks;
and conclude that the existence of these sticks is
a mystery above, yet not contrary to, reason: and
then this self-evident proposition, that there is no
stick

ftick without two ends, becomes problematic. It
is the fame with the moft obvious truths of morality; the moft evident is, " That, with regard to
" crimes, the punifhment fhould be perfonal, and
" that I ought not to be punifhed for a crime
" committed by my neighbour." Yet how many
theologians are there who ftill maintain, that God
punifhes in the prefent race of mankind the fins
of their firft parents? HELVETIUS.

No SPECULATIVE OPINIONS INJURIOUS TO SOCIETY.

THE moft abfurd opinions in morality, and
from whence the moft deteftable confequences
may be drawn, can have no influence on the manners of a people, if there be no alteration in their
laws. It is not a falfe maxim in morality that will
render us wicked, but the intereft we have to be
fo. In morality, fays Machiavel, whatever abfurd
opinion we advance, we do not thereby injure fociety, provided we do not maintain that opinion
by force. In every fort of fcience, it is by ex-
haufting the errors that we come at laft to the
fpring of truth. In morality, the thing really ufeful, is the inquiry after truth; and the non-in-
quiry that is really detrimental. He that extols
ignorance, is a knave that would make dupes.
Should we deftroy error, compel it to filence?
No:

No: How then? Let it talk on. Error, obscure in itself, is rejected by every sound understanding. If time has not given it credit, and it be not favoured by government, it cannot bear the aspect of examination. Reason will ultimately direct wherever it be freely exercised.

HELVETIUS.

ORACLES.

IT is evident we cannot be acquainted with futurity, because we cannot be acquainted with what does not exist; but it is also clear, that conjectures may be formed of an event.

All predictions are reduced to the calculations of probabilities: there is, therefore, no nation in which some predictions have not been made that have come to pass. The most celebrated and best attested, is that which Flavius Josephus made to Vespasian and Titus his son, the conquerors of the Jews. He saw Vespasian and Titus adored by the Roman armies in the East, and Nero detested by the whole empire. He had the audacity, in order to obtain the good graces of Vespasian, to predict to him, in the name of the God of the Jews (Joseph. Book. iii. ch. 28.), that he and his son would become emperors. They, in effect, were so; but it is evident that Josephus ran no risk. If the day of Vespasian's overthrow

throw had come, he would not have been in a fituation to punifh Jofephus; if he obtained the
imperial throne, he muft recompence his prophet;
and till fuch time as he reigned, he was in hopes
of doing it. Vefpafian informed this Jofephus,
that if he were a prophet, he fhould have foretold him the lofs of Jotapat, which he had inef-
fectually defended againft the Roman army. Jofephus replied, that he had in fact foretold it;
which was not very furprifing. What commander,
who fuftains a fiege in a fmall place againft a numerous army, does not foretell that the place will
be taken.

The moft brilliant function of the oracles was
to infure victory in war. Each army, each nation, had its own peculiar oracles, who promifed
triumphs. The oraculous intelligence of one of
the parties was infallibly true. The vanquifhed,
who had been deceived, attributed their defeat to
fome fault committed towards the gods after the
oracle had been confulted; and they hoped the
oracle's prediction would another time be accom-
plifhed. Thus is almoft the whole earth fed with
illufion.

It was not difficult to difcover, that refpect and
money might be drawn from the multitude by
playing the prophet; and the credulity of the
people muft be a revenue for any who knew how
to cheat them. There were in all places footh-
sayers;

ayers; but it was not sufficient to foretell in their own name, it was necessary to speak in the name of the divinity: and from the time of the prophets of Egypt, who called themselves seers, till the time of Ulpius, who prophesied to the favourite of the empire, Adrian, who became a god, there was a prodigious number of sacred quacks, who made the gods speak to make a jest of man. It is well known how they might succeed; by an ambiguous reply, which they afterwards explained as they pleased.

These prophets were reckoned to know the past, the present, and the future. This is the elogium which Homer makes upon Calchas.

Divinations and auguries were a kind of oracles, and, perhaps, of higher antiquity; for many ceremonies were necessary, much time was required, to draw custom to a divine oracle, that could not do without temple and priests; and nothing was easier than to tell fortunes in the cross ways. This art was subdivided into a thousand shapes; predictions were extracted from the flight of birds, sheeps livers, the lines of the palm of the hand, circles drawn upon the ground, water, fire, small flints, wands; and, in a word, from every thing that could be devised, and frequently from enthusiasm alone, which supplied the place of all rules. But who invented this art? The first rogue that met with a fool.　　　VOLTAIRE.

ORTHODOXY.

ORTHODOXY is a Greek word, which fignifies a right opinion; and hath been ufed by churchmen as a term to denote a foundnefs of doctrine or belief, with regard to all points and articles of faith. But as there have been amongft thefe churchmen feveral fyftems of doctrine or belief, they all affert for themfelves, that they *only* are orthodox, and in the right; and that all others are heterodox, or in the wrong. So that what at one time, and in one place, hath been declared orthodoxy, or found belief, hath at another time, and in another, or even the fame place, been declared to be heterodoxy, or wrong belief. Of this there are numberlefs inftances in ecclefiaftical hiftory; and we need only juft take a tranfient view of the prefent Chriftian world, to perceive many more inftances of it fubfifting at this day. What is orthodoxy at Conftantinople, is heterodoxy or herefy at Rome. What is orthodoxy at Rome, is heterodoxy at Geneva, London, and many other places. What was orthodoxy here in the reign of Edward VI. became herefy in the reign of his fifter Mary; and in Queen Elifabeth's time, things changed their names again. Various was the fate of thefe poor words in the reigns of our fucceeding kings; as the currents of Calvinifm, Arminianifm, and Popery, ebbed and flowed. So uncertain and fluctuating a thing is orthodoxy. To-day it confifts in one fet of principles, to-morrow in another. Were the words orthodoxy, heterodoxy, and herefy, employed, as they ought, in diftinguifhing virtue from vice, and good from evil, they would admit of no variation, and be for ever taken in the fame fenfe. But as they are ufed to denote opinions concerning the moft incomprehenfible fubjects, no wonder that their meaning fhould be fo often miftaken, and occafion fo many endlefs and bitter difputes.

ROBERTSON.

P.

P.

MANKIND GOVERNED BY PAIN AND PLEA-SURE.

NATURE has placed mankind under the governance of two sovereign masters, *pain* and *pleasure*. It is for them alone to point out what we ought to do, as well as to determine what we shall do. On the one hand the standard of right and wrong, on the other the chain of causes and effects, are fastened to their throne. They govern us in all we do, in all we say, in all we think: every effort we can make to throw off our subjection, will serve but to demonstrate and confirm it. In words a man may pretend to abjure their empire; but in reality he will remain subject to it all the while. The *principle of utility*

Cc 2   re-

recognizes this subjection, and assumes it for the foundation of that system, the object of which is, to rear the fabric of felicity by the hands of reason and of law. Systems which attempt to question it, deal in sounds instead of sense, in caprice instead of reason, in darkness instead of light.

The happiness of the individuals, of whom a community is composed, that is, their pleasures and their security, is the end and the sole end which the legislator ought to have in view: the sole standard, in conformity to which each individual ought, as far as depends upon the legislator, to be *made* to fashion his behaviour. But whether it be this or any thing else that is to be *done*, there is nothing by which a man can ultimately be *made* to do it, but either pain or pleasure.

J. BENTHAM.

SANCTIONS, OR SOURCES OF PAIN AND PLEASURE, AND THEIR INFLUENCE IN LEGISLATION.

THERE are four distinguishable sources from which pleasure and pain are in use to flow: Considered separately, they may be termed the *physical*, the *political*, the *moral*, and the *religious*; and inasmuch as the pleasures and pains belonging

ing to each of them are capable of giving a binding force to any law or rule of conduct, they may all of them be termed *sanctions*. If it be in the present life, and from the ordinary course of nature, not purposely modified by the interposition of the will of any human being, nor by any extraordinary interposition of any superior, invisible being, that the pleasure or the pain takes place or is expected, it may be said to issue from or belong to the *physical sanction*. If at the hands of a *particular* person or set of persons in the community, who, under names correspondent to that of *judge*, are chosen for the particular purpose of dispensing it, according to the will of the sovereign or supreme ruling power in the state, it may be said to issue from the *political sanction*. If at the hands of such *chance* persons in the community, as the party in question may happen in the the course of his life to have concerns with, according to each man's spontaneous disposition, and not according to any settled or concerted rule, it may be said to issue from the *moral sanction*. If from the immediate hand of a superior invisible Being, either in the present life, or in a future, it may be said to issue from a *religious sanction*. Pleasures or pains which may be expected to issue from the *physical, political*, or *moral* sanctions, must all of them be expected to be experienced, if ever, in the *present* life: those which may be

ex-

expected to issue from the *religious* sanction, may
be expected to be experienced either in the *present* life or in a *future*.

Those which can be experienced in the present
life, can of course be no other than such as human nature in the course of the present life is suf-
ceptible of; and from each of these sources may
flow all the pleasures or pains of which, in the
course of the present life, human nature is susceptible. With regard to these then (with which
alone we have in this place any concern), those of
them which belong to any one of those sanctions,
differ not ultimately in kind from those which belong to any one of the other three: the only difference there is among them lies in the circumstances that accompany their production. A suffering which befalls a man in the natural and
spontaneous course of things, shall be styled, for
instance, a *calamity*; in which case, if it be supposed to befall him through any imprudence of
his, it may be styled a punishment issuing from
the *physical* sanction. Now this same suffering,
if inflicted by the law, will be what is commonly
called a *punishment*; if incurred for want of any
friendly assistance, which the misconduct, or supposed misconduct, of the sufferer has occasioned
to be withholden, a punishment issuing from the
moral sanction; if through the immediate interposition of a particular providence, a punishment
                                                    issuing

iſſuing from a *religious* ſanction. A man's goods, or his perſon, are conſumed by fire. If this happened to him by what is called an accident, it was a calamity; if by reaſon of his own imprudence (for inſtance, from his neglecting to put his candle out), it may be ſtyled a puniſhment of the phyſical ſanction: if it happened to him by the ſentence of the political magiſtrate, a puniſhment belonging to the political ſanction; that is, what is commonly called a puniſhment: if for want of any aſſiſtance which his *neighbour* withheld from him out of ſome diſlike to his *moral* character, a puniſhment of the *moral* ſanction: if by an immediate act of *God's* diſpleaſure, manifeſted on account of ſome *ſin* committed by him, or through any diſtraction of mind, occaſioned by the dread of ſuch diſpleaſure, a puniſhment of the *religious* ſanction.

As to ſuch of the pleaſures and pains belonging to the religious ſanction as regard a future life, of what kind theſe may be we cannot know. Theſe lie not open to our obſervation. During the preſent life they are matter only of expectation: and, whether that expectation be derived from natural or revealed religion, the particular kind of pleaſure or pain, if it be different from all thoſe which lie open to our obſervation, is what we can have no idea of. Of theſe four ſanctions, the phyſical is altogether, we may obſerve, the groundwork of the political and the moral; ſo is it alſo of the religious, in as far as the latter bears relation to the preſent life. It is included in each of thoſe other three. This may operate in any caſe (that is, any of the pains or pleaſures belonging to it may operate) independently of *them*: none of *them* can operate but by means of this. In a word, the powers of nature may operate of themſelves; but neither the magiſtrate, nor men at large, *can* operate, nor is God in the caſe in queſtion *ſuppoſed* to operate, but through the powers of nature.

For theſe four objects, which in their nature have ſo much in common, it ſeemed of uſe to find a common name. It ſeemed of uſe, in the firſt place, for the convenience of giving a name to certain pleaſures and pains, for which a name equally characteriſtic could hardly otherwiſe have been found: in the ſecond place, for the ſake of holding up the efficacy of certain moral forces, the influence of which is apt not to be ſufficiently attended to. Does the political ſanction exert an influence over the conduct of mankind? The moral, the religious ſanctions do ſo too. In every inch of his career are the operations of the political magiſtrate liable to be aided or impeded by theſe two foreign powers: who, one or other of them, or both, are ſure to be either his rivals or his allies. Does it happen to him to leave them

out

out in his calculations; he will be sure almost to find himself mistaken in the result. It behoves him, therefore, to have them continually before his eyes; and that under such a name as exhibits the relation they bear to his own purposes and designs.

J. BENTHAM.

THE NATURE OF PAIN AND TERROR.

A MAN who suffers under *violent* bodily pain has his teeth set, his eye-brows violently contracted, his forehead wrinkled, his eyes dragged inwards, and rolled with great vehemence, his hair stands an end, the voice is forced out in short shrieks and groans, and the whole fabric totters. Fear or terror, which is an apprehension of pain or death, exhibits exactly the same effects, approaching in violence to those just mentioned, in proportion to the nearness of the cause, and the weakness of the subject.

This is not only so in the human species, but it is observable even in dogs; they, under the apprehension of punishment, writhe their bodies, and yelp, and howl, as if they actually felt blows. From whence we may conclude, that pain and fear act upon the same parts of the body, and in the same manner, though somewhat different in degree: that pain and fear consist in an unnatu-

ral

ral tenſion of the nerves; that this is ſometimes
accompanied with an unnatural ſtrength, which
ſometimes ſuddenly changes into an extraordinary
weakneſs; that the effects often come on alternately, and are ſometimes mixed with each other.
This is the nature of all convulſive agitations,
eſpecially in weaker ſubjects, which are the moſt
liable to the ſevereſt impreſſions of pain and fear.
The only difference between pain and terror is,
that things which cauſe pain operate on the mind
by the intervention of the body; whereas things
that cauſe terror, generally affect the bodily organs by the operation of the mind ſuggeſting the
danger; but both agreeing, either primarily or
ſecondarily, in producing a tenſion, contraction,
or violent emotion of the nerves, they agree likewiſe in every thing elſe. For it appears clearly
from this example, as well as from many others,
that when the body is diſpoſed, by any means
whatſoever, to ſuch emotions as it would acquire
by the means of a certain paſſion, it will of itſelf excite ſomething very like that paſſion in the
mind.

To this purpoſe Mr Spon, in his Recherches
d'Antiquité, gives us a curious ſtory of the celebrated Campanella, a phyſiognomiſt. This
man, it ſeems, had not only made very accurate obſervations on human faces, but was very
expert in mimicking ſuch as were any way remarkable.

markable. When he had a mind to penetrate into the inclinations of those he had to deal with, he composed his face, his gesture, and his whole body, as nearly as he could, into the exact similitude of the person he intended to examine; and then carefully examined what turn of mind he seemed to acquire by this change. So that, says our author, he was able to enter into the dispositions and thoughts of people as effectually as if he had been changed into the very men. We may observe, that on mimicking the looks and gestures of angry, or placid, or frighted, or daring men, our minds are involuntarily turned to that passion whose appearance we endeavour to imitate; nay, it seems hard to avoid it, though one strove to separate the passion from its correspondent gestures. Our minds and bodies are so closely and intimately connected, that one is incapable of pain and pleasure without the other. Campanella, of whom we have been speaking, could so abstract his attention from any sufferings of his body, that he was able to endure the rack itself without much pain; and in lesser pains, every body must have observed, that when we can employ our attention on any thing else, the pain has been for some time suspended: on the other hand, if by any means the body is indisposed to perform such gestures, or to be stimulated into such emotions as any passion usually produces in it, that

passion

paffion itfelf never can arife, though its caufe
fhould be ever fo ftrongly in action; though it
fhould be merely mental, and immediately affecting none of the fenfes: As an opiate, or fpiritu-
ous liquors, fhall fufpend the operation of grief,
or fear, or anger, in fpite of all our efforts to the
contrary; and this, by inducing in the body a difpofition contrary to that which it receives from
thefe paffions.

BURKE.

A PARABLE AGAINST PERSECUTION.

AND it came to pafs after thefe things, that
Abraham fat in the door of his tent, about the
going down of the fun. And behold a man bent
with age, coming from the way of the wildernefs
leaning on a ftaff. And Abraham arofe, and met
him, and faid unto him, Turn in, I pray thee, and
wafh thy feet, and tarry all night; and thou fhalt
arife early in the morning, and go on thy way.
And the man faid, Nay; for I will abide under
this tree. But Abraham preffed him greatly: fo
he turned, and they went into the tent: and A-
braham baked unleavened bread, and they did eat.
And when Abraham faw that the man bleffed not
God, he faid unto him, Wherefore doft thou not
worfhip the moft high God, Creator of heaven
and earth? And the man anfwered and faid, I do

2   not

not worſhip thy God, neither do I call upon his
name; for I have made to myſelf a god, which
abideth always in my houſe, and provideth me
with all things. And Abraham's zeal was kin-
dled againſt the man; and he aroſe, and fell upon
him, and drove him forth with blows into the wilderneſs. And God called unto Abraham, ſaying,
Abraham, where is the ſtranger? And Abraham
anſwered and ſaid, Lord, he would not worſhip
thee, neither would he call upon thy name; therefore have I driven him out from before my face
into the wilderneſs. And God ſaid, Have I borne
with him theſe hundred and ninety and eight
years, and nouriſhed him, and clothed him, not-
withſtanding his rebellion againſt me; and couldſt
not thou, who art thyſelf a ſinner, bear with him
one night?

FRANKLIN.

PARDON of Criminals.

CLEMENCY is a virtue which belongs to the
legiſlator, and not to the executor of the laws; a
virtue which ought to ſhine in the code, and not
in the private judgment. To ſhow mankind, that
crimes are ſometimes pardoned, and that puniſhment is not the neceſſary conſequence, is to nou-
riſh the flattering hope of impunity, and is the
cauſe of their conſidering every puniſhment in-

VOL. II. † D d   flicted

flicted as an act of injuftice and oppreffion. The prince in pardoning, gives up the public fecurity in favour of an individual, and, by his ill-judged benevolence, proclaims a public act of impunity. Let then the executors of the laws be inexorable; but let the legiflator be tender, indulgent, and humane. He is a wife architect, who erects his edifice on the foundation of felf-love, and contrives that the intereft of the public fhall be the intereft of each individual; who is not obliged, by particular laws and irregular proceedings, to feparate the public good from that of individuals, and erect the image of public felicity on the bafis of fear and diftruft; but, like a wife philofopher, he will permit his brethren to enjoy, in quiet, that fmall portion of happinefs which the immenfe fyftem, eftablifhed by the firft caufe, permits them to tafte on this earth. A fmall crime is fometimes pardoned, if the perfon offended choofe to forgive the offender. This may be an act of good-nature and humanity, but it is contrary to the good of the public. For, although a private citizen may difpenfe with fatisfaction for the injury he has received, he cannot remove the neceffity of example. BECCARIA.

PA-

PARENTAL AFFECTION.

IT is the conftant hourly attention that a mother gives to her child, an attention that com-
mences on her part before it is born, and not any
thing properly inftinctive, that is the caufe of the
idea of it becoming affociated with almoft every
idea and affection of her foul, which is the fource
of maternal tendernefs; a kind of tendernefs that
the father feldom feels any thing of till fome
months afterwards, when it is acquired by the
fame attention: hence it is that a fickly child generally gets the largeft fhare of its parents love.
For the fame reafon alfo, nurfes that are not mothers feel more of this tendernefs than the mothers who fend their children out to nurfe. The
fame familiar intercourfe, that endears a child to
a parent, does likewife endear the parent to the
child; and to expect thefe affections without fuch
intercourfe and attention, is the fame thing as ex-
pecting the harveft without a previous feed-time.
This intercourfe, and thofe endearments, which
gradually fupply the affociations that conftitute
parental affection, are mechanical things, and cannot be acquired without the affociation of the proper ideas and fenfations which only time and intercourfe can fupply.

PRIESTLEY.

O-

On the same Subject.

A MOTHER idolizes her fon; I love him, fays fhe, for his own fake. However, one might reply, you take no care of his education, though you are in no doubt that a good one would contribute infinitely to his happinefs: why, therefore, do not you confult fome men of fenfe about him, and read fome of the books written on that fubject? Why, becaufe, fays fhe, I think I know as much of that matter as thofe authors and their works. But how did you get this confidence in your own underftanding? Is it not the effect of your indifference? An ardent defire always infpires us with a falutary diftruft of ourfelves. If we have a fuit at law of confiderable confequence, we vifit counfellors and attorneys, we confult a great number and examine their advice. Are we attacked by any of thofe lingering difeafes, which inceffantly place around us the fhades and horrors of death, we go to phyficians, compare their opinions, read medical books, and in fome degree become phyficians ourfelves. Such is the conduct of a man very much interefted. With refpect to the education of children, if you are not influenced in the fame manner, it is becaufe you do not love your fon fo well as yourfelf. But, adds the mother, What then fhould be the mo-

tive

tive of my tenderneſs? Among fathers and mothers, I reply, fome are influenced by the defire
of perpetuating their name in their children; they
properly **love** only their names: others are fond
of command, and fee in their children their ſlaves.
The animal leaves its young when their weakneſs
no longer keeps them in dependence; and paternal love becomes extinguiſhed in almoſt all hearts,
when children have by their age and ſtation attained to independence. Then, faid the poet
Saadi, The father fees nothing in them but greedy
heirs; and this is the cauſe, adds fome poet, of
the extraordinary love of the grandfather for his
grandchildren; he confiders them as the enemies
of his enemies. There are fathers and mothers
who make their children their play-things and
their paſtime. The loſs of this play-thing would
be infupportable to them; but would their afflic-
tion prove that they loved the child for itſelf?
Every body knows the ſtory of M. de Lauzun;
when he was in the Baſtile, without **books**, without employment, a prey to laſſitude and the horrors of a prifon, he took it into his head to tame
a ſpider. This was the only confolation he had
left in his misfortune. The governor of the Baſtile, from an inhumanity common to men accuſ-
tomed to fee the unhappy, cruſhed the ſpider.
The prifoner felt the moſt cutting grief; and no
mother could be affected by the death of an only

fon with a more violent forrow. Now, whence is derived this conformity of fentiments for fuch different objects? It is becaufe, in the lofs of a child, or in the lofs of the fpider, people frequently weep for nothing but for the laffitude and want of employment into which they fall. If mothers appear, in general, more afflicted at the death of a child, than fathers employed in bufinefs, or given up to the purfuit of ambition, it is not becaufe the mother loves her child more tenderly, but becaufe fhe fuffers a lofs more difficult to be fupplied. Errrors, in this refpect, are very frequent; people rarely cherifh a child for its own fake. That parental affection, of which fo many people make a parade, and by which they believe themfelves fo warmly affected, is moft frequently nothing more than an effect, either of a defire of perpetuating their names, of the pride of command, or the fear of the wearifomenefs of inaction.

HELVETIUS.

THE INDEPENDENCY OF THE PARLIAMENT OF BRITAIN.

MEN are generally more honeft in their private than in their public capacity; and will go greater lengths to ferve a party, than when their own private intereft is alone concerned. Honour is a great check upon mankind: But where a con-

fiderable

fiderable body of men act together, this check is
in a great meafure removed; fince a man is fure
to be approved by his own party for what promotes the common intereft; and he foon learns
to defpife the clamours of adverfaries. When
there offers, therefore, to our cenfure and examination, any plan of government, real or imaginary, where the power is diftributed among feveral courts, and feveral orders of men, we fhould
always confider the private intereft of each court
and each order; and if we find that, by the fkil-
ful divifion of power, private intereft muft neceffarily in its operation concur with public, we may
pronounce that government to be wife and happy.
If, on the contrary, the private intereft of each
order is not checked, and be not directed to public intereft, we ought to look for nothing but fac-
tion, diforder, and tyranny, from fuch a government. The fhare of power allotted by the Britifh
conftitution to the Houfe of Commons is fo great,
that it abfolutely commands all the other parts of
the government. The King's legiflative power is
plainly no proper check to it. For though the
King has a negative in framing laws; yet this, in
fact, is efteemed of fo little moment, that whatever is voted by the two Houfes, is always fure to
be paffed into a law, and the Royal affent is little
better than a form. The principal weight of the
Crown lies in the executive power. But befides
that

that the executive power in every government is
altogether fubordinate to the legiflature; befides
this, I fay, the exercife of this power requires an
immenfe expence; and the Commons have affumed
to themfelves the fole power of granting money.
How eafy, therefore, would it be for that Houfe
to wreft from the Crown all thefe powers, one
after another, by making every grant conditional,
and choofing their time fo well, that their refu-
fal of fubfidies fhould only diftrefs the government, without giving foreign powers any advantage over us?—By what means is this member of
the Britifh conftitution confined within the proper limits, fince, from the very conftitution, it
muft neceffarily have as much power as it de-
mands, and can only be confined by itfelf? How
is this confiftent with our experience of human
nature? I anfwer, that the intereft of the body is
here reftrained by the intereft of individuals; and
that the Houfe of Commons ftretches not its
power, becaufe fuch an ufurpation would be contrary to the intereft of the majority of its members.   The Crown has fo many offices at its difpofal, that, when affifted by the honeft and dif-
interefted part of the Houfe, it will always command the refolution of the whole; fo far, at leaft,
as to preferve the ancient conftitution from danger.   We may therefore give to this influence
what name we pleafe; we may call it by the in-
                                        vidious

vidious appellations of *corruption* and *dependence*;
but fome degree and fome kind of it are infeparable from the very nature of the conftitution, and
neceffary to the prefervation of our mixed government. All queftions concerning the proper medium between extremes are difficult to be deci-
ded; both becaufe it is not eafy to find words to
fix this medium, and becaufe the good and ill, in
fuch cafes, run fo gradually into each other, as
even to render our fentiments doubtful and uncertain. But there is a peculiar difficulty in the
prefent cafe, which would embarrafs the moft
knowing and impartial examiner. The power of
the Crown is always lodged in a fingle perfon, either king or minifter; and as this perfon may
have either a greater or lefs degree of ambition,
capacity, courage, popularity, or fortune, the
power which is too great in one hand, may become too little in another. By that influence of
the Crown, which I would juftify, I mean only
that arifing from the offices and honours which
are at the difpofal of the Crown. As to private
bribery, it may be confidered in the fame light as
employing fpies; which is fcarcely juftifiable in a
good minifter, and is infamous in a bad one:
But to be a fpy, or to be corrupted, is always infamous under all minifters, and is to be regarded as a fhamelefs proftitution. Polybius juftly
efteems the pecuniary influence of the fenate and
cenfors,

cenfors, to be one of the regular and conftitu-
tional weights which preferved the balance of
the Roman government.

HUME.

ON THE SAME SUBJECT.

IT may be queftioned whether the progrefs to
abfolute flavery and infecurity would be more rapid, if the King were *nominally* arbitrary, or only
virtually fo, by uniformly influencing the Houfe
of Commons. In fome refpects, fo large a body
of men would venture upon things which no
fingle perfon would choofe to do of his own authority; and fo long as they had little intercourfe
but with one another, they would not be much
affected with the fenfe of fear or fhame. One
may fafely fay, that no fingle member of the Houfe
would have had the affurance to decide as the majority have often done in cafes of controverted
elections. Whenever the Houfe of Commons
fhall be fo abandonedly corrupt, as to join with
the Court in abolifhing any of the effential forms
of the conftitution, or effectually defeating the
great purpofes of it, let every Englifhman, before
it is too late, reperufe the hiftory of his country,
and do what Englifhmen are renowned for having done formerly in the fame circumftances.—
Where civil liberty is entirely divefted of its natural

tural guard, political liberty, I should not hesitate
to prefer the government of one to that of a number; because a sense of shame would have less influence upon them, and they would keep one another in countenance, in cases in which any single
person would yield to the sense of the majority.

PRIESTLEY.

THE ORIGIN OF THE PASSIONS.

WE must distinguish the passions into two
kinds; those immediately given us by nature, and
those we owe to the establishment of society.
And to know which of these passions has produced the other, let us transport ourselves in idea to
the first ages of the world; and we shall there see
that nature, by hunger, thirst, heat, and cold, informed man of his wants, and added a variety of
pleasing and painful sensations; the former to
the gratifications of these wants, the latter to the
incapacity of gratifying them. There we shall behold man capable of receiving the impressions of
pleasure and pain, and born as it were with a love
for the one and hatred for the other. Such
was man when he came from the hand of nature.
In this state he had neither envy, pride, avarice,
or ambition; sensible only of the pleasure and
pain derived from nature, he was ignorant of all
those artificial pains and pleasures we procure
from

from the above paffions. Such paffions then are not immediately given by nature; but their exiſtence, which ſuppoſes that of ſociety, alſo ſuppoſes that we have in us the latent ſeeds of thoſe paffions. If, therefore, we receive at our birth only wants, in thoſe wants, and in our firſt deſires, we muſt ſeek the origin of theſe artificial paffions.   HELVETIUS.

ON THE SAME SUBJECT.

THEY certainly do not attach clear ideas to the word *paſſions*, who regard them as detrimental. Our deſires are our motives; and it is the force of our deſires which determines that of our virtues and vices. A man without deſire and without want, is without invention and without reaſon. No motive can engage him to combine or compare his ideas with each other. The more a man approaches to that ſtate of apathy, the more ſtupid he becomes. To attempt to deſtroy the paffions of *men*, is to attempt to deſtroy their action. Does the theologian rail at the paffions? He is the pendulum that mocks its ſpring, and the effect that miſtakes its cauſe. By annihilating the deſires, you annihilate the mind; every man without paffions, has within him no principle of action, nor motive to act.

HELVETIUS.

DIF-

DIFFERENT PASSIONS RECIPROCALLY INSULT EACH OTHER.

LET a woman, young, beautiful, and full of gallantry, such as history has painted the celebrated Cleopatra, who by the multiplicity of her charms, the attractions of her wit, the variety of her caresses, makes her lover daily taste all the delights that could be found in inconstancy, and in short, whose first enjoyment was, as Echard says, only the first favour; let such a woman appear in an assembly of prudes, whose age and deformity secure their chastity; they will there despise her charms and her talents: sheltered from seduction by the Medusean shield of deformity, these prudes form no conception of the pleasure arising from the infatuation of a lover; and do not perceive the difficulty a beautiful woman finds in resisting the desire of making him the confident of all her secret charms: they therefore fall with fury upon this lovely woman, and place her weakness among crimes of the blackest die: but let one of these prudes in her turn appear in a circle of coquets, she will there be treated with as little respect as youth and beauty show to old age and deformity. To be revenged on her prudery, they will tell her, that the fair who yields to love, and the disagreeable who resist that pas-

VOL. II. E e † sion,

sion, are both prompted by vanity; that in case
of a lover, one seeks an admirer of her charms,
and the other flies from him who proclaims her
disgrace; and that both being animated by the
same motive, there is no other difference but that
of beauty between the prude and the woman of
gallantry.   HELVETIUS.

THE PASSIONS SOURCES OF ERROR.

THE passions lead us into error, because they
fix our attention to that particular part of the
object they present to us, not allowing us to view
it on every side. A king passionately affects the
title of conqueror; and, inebriated with the hopes
of victory, he forgets that fortune is inconstant,
and that the victor shares the load of misery
almost equally with the vanquished. He does
not perceive, that the welfare of his subjects is
only a pretence for his martial frenzy, and that
pride alone forges his arms, and displays his en-
signs; his whole attention is fixed on the pomp of
the triumph.—Fear, equally powerful with pride,
will produce the same effect: it will raise ghosts
and phantoms, and disperse them among the
tombs; and in the darkness of the woods, present
them to the eyes of the affrighted traveller; seize
on all the faculties of the soul, without leaving
any one at liberty to reflect on the absurdity of
                                          the

the motives for such a ridiculous terror.—The paſſions not only fix the attention on particular ſides
of the objeɛts they preſent to us; but they alſo
deceive us, by exhibiting the ſame objeɛts when
they do not really exiſt. It is common for us to
ſee in things what we are deſirous of finding
there. Illuſion is the neceſſary effeɛt of the paſſions; the ſtrength or force of which is generally meaſured by the degree of obſcurity into
which they lead us. There is no century which
has not by ſome ridiculous affirmation or negation
afforded matter of laughter to the following age.
A paſt folly is ſeldom ſufficient to ſhow mankind their preſent folly. The ſame paſſions, however, which are the germ of an infinity of errors,
are alſo the ſources of our knowlege. If they
miſlead us, they at the ſame time impart to us
the ſtrength neceſſary for walking. It is they
alone that can rouſe us from that ſluggiſhneſs
and torpor always ready to ſeize on the faculties of
the ſoul.   HELVETIUS.

PATRIOTISM.

EVERY particular ſociety, when it is confined
and its members united, alienates itſelf from the
general one of mankind.—A true patriot is in-
hoſpitable to foreigners: they are mere men,
and appear to have no relation to him. This in-

convenience is inevitable, but it is not great. The most essential point is a man's being beneficent and useful to those among whom he lives. The inhabitants of Sparta, when abroad, were ambitious, covetous, and unjust; but disinterestedness, equity, and concord reigned within their walls. Be ever mistrustful of those cosmopolites, who deduce from books the far-fetched and extensive obligations of universal benevolence, while they neglect to discharge their actual duties towards those who are about them. A philosopher of this stamp affects to have a regard for the Tartars, by way of excuse for his having none for his neighbours. Natural man is every thing with him: he is a numerical unit, an absolute integer, that bears no relation but to himself or his species. Civilized man is only a relative unit, the numerator of a fraction, that depends on its denominator, and whose value consists in its relation to the integral body of society. The best political institutions are those which are best calculated to divest mankind of their natural inclinations; to deprive them of an absolute, by giving them a relative, existence, and incorporating distinct individuals in one common whole. A citizen of Rome was neither Caius nor Lucius; he was a Roman; nay, he even loved his country, exclusive of its relation to himself. Regulus pretended himself a Carthaginian, as being become

the

the property of his mafters. In that character he
refufed to take his feat in the Roman fenate,
till a Carthaginian commanded him. He was
filled with indignation at the remonftrances made
to fave his life; and returned triumphant to perifh
in the midft of tortures. This appears to me,
indeed, to have little relation to men with whom
we are at prefent acquainted.—The Lacedemo-
nian, Pedaretes, who prefented himfelf for admiffion into the council of three hundred, was rejected, returned home rejoicing that there were
to be found in Sparta three hundred men better
than himfelf. Suppofing the demonftrations of
his joy fincere, as there is room to believe they
were, this man was a true citizen.—A woman of
Sparta, having five fons in the army, and being
hourly in expectation of hearing of a battle, a
meffenger at length arrived; of whom fhe, trem-
bling, afked the news. Your five fons, fays he,
are killed.—*Vile flave*, who afked you of my
fons?—But we have gained the victory, continued
he. This was enough; the heroic mother ran to
the temple, and gave thanks to the gods. This
woman was a true citizen.—Thofe who would
have man, in the bofom of a fociety, retain the
primitive fentiments of nature, know not what
they want. Ever contradicting himfelf, and wa-
vering between his duty and inclination, he would

neither

neither be the man nor the citizen; he would be good for nothing either to himself or to others.

ROUSSEAU.

PEASANTS AND SAVAGES.

THERE are two kinds of men, who live in a continual exercise of body, and never think of the cultivation of the mind: These are Peasants and Savages. The former nevertheless are clownish, brutal, and dull; while the latter are as remarkable for their strong sense as for their subtlety. Generally speaking, nothing is so stupid as a clown, nor so cunning as a savage. Whence comes this difference? Doubtless it arises hence: the former being accustomed to do what he is bid, or what his father used to do before him, plods on in the same beaten track; and being little better than a mere machine, constantly employed in the same manner, habit and obedience stand with him in the place of reason.—As to the savage, the case is widely different; being attached to no one place, having no settled task, obedient to none, and restrained by no other law than his own will, he is obliged to reason on every action of his life: he makes not a motion nor takes a step without having previously considered the consequences. Thus, the more his body is exercised, the more is his mind enlightened; his mental

and

and corporeal faculties advance together, and reciprocally improve each other.

ROUSSEAU.

ANCIENT GREEK PHILOSOPHY.

THE ancient Greek philosophy was divided into three great branches; Physics, or natural philosophy; Ethics, or moral philosophy; and Logic. This general division seems perfectly agreeable to the nature of things.

The great phenomena of nature, the revolutions of the heavenly bodies, eclipses, comets, thunder, lightning, and other extraordinary meteors; the generation, the life, growth, and dissolution of plants and animals; are objects which, as they necessarily excite the wonder, so they naturally call forth the curiosity of mankind to inquire into their causes. Superstition first attempted to satisfy this curiosity, by referring all those wonderful appearances to the immediate agency of the gods. Philosophy afterwards endeavoured to account for them from more familiar causes, or from such as mankind were better acquainted with, than the agency of the gods. As those great phenomena are the first objects of human curiosity; so the science which pretends to explain them must naturally have been the first branch of philosophy that was cultivated.

The

The firſt philoſophers, accordingly, of whom hiſtory has preſerved any account, appear to have been natural philoſophers.

In every age and country of the world men muſt have attended to the characters, deſigns, and actions of one another; and many reputable rules and maxims for the conduct of human life, muſt have been laid down and approved of by common conſent. As ſoon as writing came into faſhion, wiſe men, or thoſe who fancied themſelves ſuch, would naturally endeavour to increaſe the number of thoſe eſtabliſhed and reſpected maxims, and to expreſs their own ſenſe of what was either proper or improper conduct; ſometimes in the more artifical form of apologues, like what are called the fables of Æſop; and ſometimes in the more ſimple one of apophthegms, or wiſe ſayings, like the Proverbs of Solomon, the verſes of Theognis and Phocyllides, and ſome part of the works of Heſiod. They might continue in this manner for a long time, merely to multiply the number of thoſe maxims of prudence and morality, without even attempting to arrange them in any very diſtinct or methodical order, much leſs to connect them together by one or more general principles, from which they were all deducible, like effects from their natural cauſes. The beauty of a ſyſtematical arrangement of different obſervations connected

nected by a few common principles, was first seen in the rude essays of those ancient times towards a system of natural philosophy. Something of the same kind was afterwards attempted in morals. The maxims of common life were arranged in some methodical order, and connected together by a few common principles, in the same manner as they had attempted to arrange and connect the phenomena of nature. The science which pretends to investigate and explain those connecting principles, is what is properly called Moral Philosophy.

Different authors gave different systems both of natural and moral philosophy. But the arguments by which they supported those different systems, far from being always demonstrations, were frequently at best but very slender probabilities, and sometimes mere sophisms, which had no other foundation but the inaccuracy and ambiguity of common language. Speculative systems have in all ages of the world been adopted; for reasons too frivolous to have determined the judgment of any man of common sense in a matter of the smallest pecuniary interest. Gross sophistry has scarce ever had any influence upon the opinions of mankind, except in matters of philosophy and speculation; and in these it has frequently had the greatest. The patrons of each system of natural and moral philosophy naturally
en-

endeavoured to expose the weaknefs of the arguments adduced to fupport the fyftems which
were oppofite to their own. In examining thofe
arguments, they were neceffarily led to confider
the difference between a probable and a demonftrative argument, between a fallacious and a con-
clufive one; and logic, or the fcience of the general principles of good and bad reafoning, neceffarily arofe out of the obfervations which a fcru-
tiny of this kind gave occafion to. Though in its
origin pofterior both to phyfics and to ethics, it
was commonly taught, not indeed in all, but in
the greater part of the ancient fchools of philo-
fopy, previoufly to either of thofe fciences. The
ftudent, it feems to have been thought, ought to
underftand well the difference between good and
bad reafoning, before he was led to reafon upon
fubjects of fo great importance.

A. SMITH.

MODERN PHILOSOPHY.

IN the ancient philofophy, whatever was taught
concerning the nature either of the human mind
or of the Deity, made a part of the fyftem of phyfics. Thofe beings, in whatever their effence
might be fuppofed to confift, were parts of the
great fyftem of the univerfe, and parts, too, productive of the moft important effects. Whatever

ever human reason could either conclude or conjecture concerning them, made, as it were, two
chapters, though no doubt two very important
ones, of the science which pretended to give an
account of the origin and revolutions of the great
system of the universe. But in the universities
of Europe, where philosophy was taught only as
subservient to theology, it was natural to dwell
longer upon these two chapters than upon any
other of the science. They were gradually more
and more extended, and were divided into many
inferior chapters; till at last the doctrine of spirits, of which so little can be known, came to
take up as much room in the system of philosophy, as the doctrine of bodies, of which so much
can be known. The doctrines concerning those
two subjects were considered as making two distinct sciences. What are called metaphysics or
pneumatics were set in opposition to physics, and
were cultivated, not only as the more sublime,
but, for the purposes of a particular profession,
as the more useful science of the two. The proper subject of experiment and observation, a subject in which a careful attention is capable of
making so many useful discoveries, was almost entirely neglected. The subject in which, after a
few very simple and almost obvious truths, the
most careful attention can discover nothing but
obscurity and uncertainty, and can consequently

produce

produce nothing but fubtleties and fophifms, was greatly cultivated.

When thofe two fciences had thus been fet in oppofition to one another, the comparifon between them naturally gave birth to a third, to what was called Ontology, or the fcience which treated of the qualities and attributes which were common to both the fubjects of the other two fciences. But if fubtleties and fophifms compofed the greater part of the metaphyfics or pneumatics of the fchools, they compofed the whole of this cob-web fcience of ontology; which was likewife fometimes called Metaphyfics.

Wherein confifted the happinefs and perfection of a man, confidered not only as an individual, but as the member of a family, of a ftate, and of the great fociety of mankind, was the object which the ancient moral philofophy propofed to inveftigate. In that philofophy the duties of human life were treated of as fubfervient to the happinefs and perfection of human life. But when moral, as well as natural philofophy, came to be taught only as fubfervient to theology, the duties of human life were treated of as chiefly fubfervient to the happinefs of a life to come. In the ancient philofophy, the perfection of virtue was reprefented as neceffarily productive, to the perfon who poffeffed it, of the moft perfect happinefs in this life. In the modern philofophy, it was frequently reprefented as generally, or rather as almoft always, inconfiftent with any degree of happinefs in this life ; and heaven was to be earned only by penance and mortification, by the aufterities and abafement of a monk ; not by the liberal, generous, and fpirited conduct of a man. Cafuiftry and an afcetic morality made up, in moft cafes, the greater part of the moral philofophy of the fchools. By far the moft important of all the different branches of philofophy, became in this manner by far the moft corrupted.

Such, therefore, was the common courfe of philofophical education in the greater part of the univerfities in Europe. Logic was taught firft : Ontology came in the fecond place : Pneumatology, comprehending the doctrine concerning the nature of the human foul and of the Deity, in the third : In the fourth followed a debafed fyftem of moral philofophy, which was confidered as immediately connected with the doctrines of pneumatology, with the immortality of the human foul, and with the rewards and punifhments which, from the juftice of the Deity, were to be expected in a life to come : A fhort and fuperficial fyftem of phyfics ufually concluded the courfe.

The alterations which the univerfities of Europe thus introduced into the ancient courfe of philofophy, were all meant for the education of ecclefiaftics, and to render it a more proper in-

troduction to the ſtudy of theology. But the additional quantity of ſubtlety and ſophiſtry, the
caſuiſtry and the aſcetic morality which thoſe alterations introduced into it, certainly did not render it more proper for the education of gentlemen or men of the world, or more likely either
to improve the underſtanding, or to mend the
heart.

This courſe of philoſophy is what ſtill continues
to be taught in the greater part of the univerſities
of Europe; with more or leſs diligence, according as the conſtitution of each particular univer-
ſity happens to render diligence more or leſs neceſſary to the teachers. In ſome of the richeſt
and beſt endowed univerſities, the tutors content
themſelves with teaching a few unconnected ſhreds
and parcels of this corrupted courſe; and even
theſe they commonly teach very negligently and
ſuperficially.

The improvements which, in modern times,
have been made in ſeveral different branches of
philoſophy, have not, the greater part of them,
been made in univerſities; though ſome no doubt
have. The greater part of univerſities have not
even been very forward to adopt thoſe improvements after they were made; and ſeveral of thoſe
learned ſocieties have choſen to remain for a long
time the ſanctuaries in which exploded ſyſtems
and obſolete prejudices found ſhelter and protection,

tion, after they had been hunted out of every other corner in the world. In general, the richest and best endowed univerfities have been the flow-eft in adopting thofe improvements, and the moft averfe to permit any confiderable change in the eftablifhed plan of education. Thofe improvements were more eafily introduced into fome of the poorer univerfities, in which the teachers, depending upon their reputation for the greater part of their fubfiftence, were obliged to pay more attention to the current opinions of the world.

But though the public fchools and univerfities of Europe were originally intended only for the education of a particular profeffion, that of churchmen, and though they were not always very diligent in inftructing their pupils even in the fciences which were fuppofed neceffary for that profeffion; yet they gradually drew to themfelves the education of almoft all other people, particularly of almoft all gentlemen and men of fortune. No better method, it feems, could be fallen upon of fpending, with any advantage, the long interval between infancy and that period of life at which men begin to apply in good earneft to the real bufinefs of the world, the bufinefs which is to employ them during the remainder of their days. The greater part of what is taught in fchools and univerfities, however, does not feem to be the moft proper preparation for that bufinefs.

In

In England, it becomes every day more and more the custom to send young people to travel in foreign countries immediately upon their leaving school, and without sending them to any univerfity. Our young people, it is faid, generally return home much improved by their travels. A young man who goes abroad at feventeen or eighteen, and returns home at one and twenty, returns three or four years older than he was when he went abroad; and at that age it is very difficult not to improve a good deal in three or four years. In the courfe of his travels, he generally acquires fome knowledge of one or two foreign languages; a knowledge, however, which is feldom fufficient to enable him either to fpeak or write them with propriety. In other refpects he commonly returns home more conceited, more unprincipled, more diffipated, and more incapable of any ferious application either to ftudy or to bufinefs, than he could well have become in fo fhort a time had he lived at home. By travelling fo very young, by fpending in the moft frivolous diffipation the moft precious years of his life, at a diftance from the infpection and control of his parents and relations, every ufeful habit, which the earlier parts of his education might have had fome tendency to form in him, inftead of being rivetted and confirmed, is almoft neceffarily either weakened or defaced. Nothing but the

discredit

difcredit into which the univerfities are allowing themfelves to fall, could ever have brought into repute fo very abfurd a practice as that of travelling at this early period of life. By fending his fon abroad, a father delivers himfelf, at leaft for fome time, from fo difagreeable an object as that of a fon unemployed, neglected, and going to ruin before his eyes.

Such have been the effects of fome of the modern inftitutions for education.

A. SMITH.

PHYSIOGNOMY.

THE phyfiognomy, or countenance, is formed by a fimple difplay of the traces already fketched out by nature: but befides this natural difplay of the features, they are infenfibly fashioned into phyfiognomy by the frequent impreffion of certain affections of the mind. That thefe affections are impreffed on the vifage, is beyond doubt; and that fuch impreffions, by frequent repetition, muft neceffarily become durable. Hence it is that a man's character may frequently be difcovered in his face, without having recourfe to myfterious explications, which fuppofe a knowledge we are not endowed with.——In the countenance of a child there are only two affections which are ftrongly impreffed, *i. e.* joy and grief: he laughs

or

or he cries: the intermediate affections are nothing. He passes incessantly from one emotion
to another; and this continual change prevents
any permanent impression which might form a
physiognomy: but at an age when, becoming
more sensible, he is more powerfully and frequently affected, the impressions are too deep to
be easily effaced; and from the habitual state of
the mind results a certain arrangement of features, which in time becomes unalterable. Nevertheless, the physiognomy does sometimes change
at different ages: but whenever this happens, it
may be remarked, that there is a change also of
the habitual passions.   ROUSSEAU.

THE LOVE OF PLEASURE AND THE LOVE OF ACTION, PRINCIPLES OF HUMAN NATURE.

THERE are two natural propensities, which we
may distinguish in the most virtuous and liberal
dispositions, the love of pleasure and the love of
action. If the former is refined by art and learning, improved by the charms of social intercourse,
and corrected by a just regard to œconomy, to
health, and to reputation, it is productive of the
greatest part of the happiness of private life. The
love of action is a principle of a much stronger
and more doubtful nature. It often leads to
anger,

anger, to ambition, and to revenge: but when it is
guided by the fenfe of propriety and benevolence,
it becomes the parent of every virtue; and if
thofe virtues are accompanied with equal abilities,
a family, a ftate, or an empire, may be indebted
for their fafety and profperity to the undaunted
courage of a fingle man. To the love of pleafure we may therefore afcribe moft of the agreeable, to the love of action we may attribute
moft of the ufeful and refpectable qualifications.
The character in which both the one and the
other fhould be united and harmonized, would
feem to conftitute the moft perfect idea of human nature. The infenfible and inactive difpofition, which fhould be fuppofed alike deftitute of
both, would be rejected by the common confent
of mankind, as utterly incapable of procuring any
happinefs to the individual, or any public benefit to the world.   GIBBON.

PLEASURES AND PAINS, VALUE OF THEIR KINDS.

PLEASURES and pains are interefting perceptions; and as fuch either *fimple* or *complex*.

The feveral fimple pleafures of which human
nature is fufceptible, feem to be as follows:
1. The pleafures of fenfe. 2. The pleafures of
wealth. 3. The pleafures of fkill. 4. The pleafures

fures of amity. 5. The pleafures of a good name. 6. The pleafures of power. 7. The pleafures of piety. 8. The pleafures of benevolence. 9. The pleafures of malevolence. 10. The pleafures of memory. 11. The pleafures of the imagination. 12. The pleafures of expectation. 13. The pleafures dependent on affociation. 14. The pleafures of relief.

The feveral fimple pains feem to be as follows: 1. The pains of privation. 2. The pains of the fenfes. 3. The pains of aukwardnefs. 4. The pains of enmity. 5. The pains of an ill name. 6. The pains of piety. 7. The pains of benevolence. 8. The pains of malevolence. 9. The pains of the memory. 10. The pains of the imagination. 11. The pains of expectation.

1. The pleafures of fenfe feem to be as follows: 1. The pleafures of the tafte or palate; including whatever pleafures are experienced in fatisfying the appetites of hunger and thirft. 2. The pleafures of the organ of fmelling. 3. The pleafures of the touch. 4. The fimple pleafures of the ear, independent of affociation. 5. The fimple pleafures of the eye, independent of affociation. 6. The pleafure of the venereal fenfe. 7. The pleafure of health; or the internal pleafurable feeling or flow of fpirits (as it is called) which accompanies a ftate of full health and vigour; efpecially at times of moderate bodily exertion.

ertion. 8. The pleasures of novelty; or the pleasures derived from the gratification of the appetite of curiosity, by the application of new objects
to any of the senses.

2. By the pleasures of wealth may be meant
those pleasures which a man is apt to derive from
the consciousness of possessing any article or articles which stand in the list of instruments of enjoyment or security, and more particularly at the
time of his first acquiring them; at which time
the pleasure may be styled a pleasure of gain or
a pleasure of acquisition; at other times a pleasure of possession.

3. The pleasures of skill, as exercised upon particular objects, are those which accompany the
application of such particular instruments of enjoyment to their uses, as cannot be so applied
without a greater or less share of difficulty or exertion.

4. The pleasures of amity, or self-recommen-
dation, are the pleasures that may accompany the
persuasion of a man's being in the acquisition or
the possession of the good-will of such or such assignable person or persons in particular; or, as
the phrase is, of being upon good terms with him
or them; and, as a fruit of it, of his being in a
way to have the benefit of their spontaneous and
gratuitous services.

5. The pleasures of a good name are the pleasures

fures that accompany the perfuafion of a man's being in the acquifition or the poffeffion of the good-will of the world about him; that is, of fuch members of fociety as he is likely to have concerns with; and as a means of it, either their love or their efteem, or both; and as a fruit of it, of his being in the way to have the benefit of their fpontaneous and gratuitous fervices. Thefe may likewife be called the pleafures of good repute, the pleafures of honour, or the pleafures of the moral fanction.

6. The pleafures of power are the pleafures that accompany the perfuafion of a man's being in a condition to difpofe people, by means of their hopes and fears, to give him the benefit of their fervices; that is, by the hope of fome fervice, or by the fear of fome difservice, that he may be in the way to render them.

7. The pleafures of piety are the pleafures that accompany the belief of a man's being in the acquifition or in poffeffion of the good-will or favour of the Supreme Being; and, as a fruit of it, of his being in a way of enjoying pleafures to be received by God's efpecial appointment, either in this life or in a life to come. Thefe may alfo be called the pleafures of religion, the pleafures of a religious difpofition, or the pleafures of the religious fanction.

8. The pleafures of benevolence are the pleafures.

fures refulting from the view of any pleafures fuppofed to be poffeffed by the beings who may be
the objects of benevolence; to wit, the fenfitive
beings we are acquainted with; under which are
commonly included, 1. The Supreme Being.
2. Human beings. 3. Other animals. Thefe
may alfo be called the pleafures of good-will, the
pleafures of fympathy, or the pleafures of the benevolent or focial affections.

9. The pleafures of malevolence are the pleafures refulting from the view of any pain fuppofed
to be fuffered by the beings who may become the
objects of malevolence; to wit, 1. Human beings. 2. Other animals. Thefe may alfo be
ftyled the pleafures of ill-will, the pleafures of the
irafcible appetite, the pleafures of antipathy, or
the pleafures of the malevolent or diffocial affections.

10. The pleafures of the memory are the pleafures which, after having enjoyed fuch and fuch
pleafures, or even in fome cafe after having fuffered fuch and fuch pains, a man will now and
then experience, at recollecting them exactly in
the order and in the circumftances in which they
were actually enjoyed or fuffered. Thefe deriva-
tive pleafures may of courfe be diftinguifhed into
as many fpecies as there are of original perceptions, from whence they may be copied. They
may alfo be ftyled pleafures of fimple recollection.

11. The

11. The pleasures of the imagination are the pleasures which may be derived from the contemplation of any such pleasures as may happen to be suggested by the memory, but in a different order, and accompanied by different groups of circumstances.. These may accordingly be referred to any one of the three cardinal points of time, present, past, or future. It is evident they may admit of as many distinctions as those of the former class.

12. The pleasures of expectation are the pleasures that result from the contemplation of any sort of pleasure, referred to time future, and accompanied with the sentiment of belief. These also may admit of the same distinctions.

13. The pleasures of association are the pleasures which certain objects or incidents may happen to afford, not of themselves, but merely in virtue of some association they have contracted in the mind with certain objects or incidents which are in themselves pleasurable. Such is the case, for instance, with the pleasure of skill, when afforded by such a set of incidents as compose a game of chess. This derives its pleasurable quality from its association partly with the pleasures of skill, as exercised in the production of incidents pleasurable of themselves; partly from its association with the pleasures of power. Such is the case also with the pleasure of good luck, when

2

afforded

afforded by fuch incidents as compofe the game of
hazard, or any other game of chance, when played at for nothing. This derives its pleafurable
quality from its affociation with one of the pleafures of wealth; to wit, with the pleafure of acquiring it.

14. Farther on, we fhall fee pains grounded
upon pleafures; in like manner may we now fee
pleafures grounded upon pains. To the catalogue
of pleafures may accordingly be added the pleafures of relief; or the pleafures which a man experiences when, after he has been enduring a
pain of any kind for a certain time, it comes to
ceafe or to abate. Thefe may of courfe be diftinguifhed into as many fpecies as there are of pains;
and may give rife to fo many pleafures of memory, of imagination, and of expectation.

1. PAINS of privation are the pains that may refult
from the thought of not poffeffing in the time prefent any of the feveral kinds of pleafures. Pains
of privation may accordingly be refolved into as
many kinds as there are of pleafures to which they
may correfpond, and from the abfence whereof
they may be derived.

There are three forts of pains which are only
fo many modifications of the feveral pains of privation. When the enjoyment of any particular
pleafure happens to be particularly defired, but
without any expectation approaching to affurance,

the pain of privation which thereupon results takes a particular name, and is called the pain of *desire,* or of unsatisfied desire. Where the enjoyment happens to have been looked for with a degree of expectation approaching to assurance, and that expectation is made suddenly to cease, it is called a pain of *disappointment.*

A pain of privation takes the name of a pain of regret in two cases: 1. Where it is grounded on the memory of a pleasure, which having been once enjoyed, appears not likely to be enjoyed again. 2. Where it is grounded on the idea of a pleasure which was never actually enjoyed, nor perhaps so much as expected, but which might have been enjoyed (it is supposed) had such or such a contingency happened, which in fact did not happen.

2. The several pains of the senses seem to be as follows: 1. The pains of hunger and thirst; or the disagreeable sensations produced by the want of suitable substances which need at times to be applied to the alimentary canal. 2. The pains of the taste; or the disagreeable sensations produced by the application of various substances to the palate and other superior parts of the same canal. 3. The pains of the organ of smell; or the disagreeable sensations produced by the effluvia of various substances when applied to that organ. 4. The pains of the touch; or the disagreeable

greeable fenfations produced by the application of various fubftances to the fkin. 5. The fimple pains of the hearing; or the difagreeable fenfations excited in the organ of that fenfe by various kinds of founds, independently (as before) of affociation. 6. The fimple pains of the fight; or the difagreeable fenfations, if any fuch there be, that may be excited in the organ of that fenfe by vifible images, independent of the principle of affociation. 7. The pains refulting from exceffive heat or cold, unlefs thefe be referable to the touch. 8. The pains of difeafe; or the acute and uneafy fenfations refulting from the feveral difeafes and indifpofitions to which human nature is liable. 9. The pain of exertion, whether bodily or mental; or the uneafy fenfation which is apt to accompany any intenfe effort, whether of mind or body.

3. The pains of aukwardnefs are the pains which fometimes refult from the unfuccefsful endeavour to apply any particular inftruments of enjoyment or fecurity to their ufes, or from the difficulty a man experiences in applying them.

4. The pains of enmity are the pains that may accompany the perfuafion of a man's being obnoxious to the ill-will of fuch or fuch an affignable perfon or perfons in particular; or, as the phrafe is, of being upon ill terms with him or them; and, in confequence, of being obnoxious

to certain pains of some sort or other, of which he may be the cause.

5. The pains of an ill-name are the pains that accompany the persuasion of a man's being obnoxious, or in a way to be obnoxious to the ill-will of the world about him. These may likewise be called the pains of ill-repute, the pains of dishonour, or the pains of the moral sanction.

6. The pains of piety are the pains that accompany the belief of a man's being obnoxious to the displeasure of the Supreme Being; and in consequence to certain pains to be inflicted by his especial appointment, either in this life or in a life to come. These may also be called the pains of religion, the pains of a religious disposition, or the pains of the religious sanction. When the belief is looked upon as well-grounded, these pains are commonly called religious terrors; when looked upon as ill-grounded, superstitious terrors.

7. The pains of benevolence are the pains resulting from the view of any pains supposed to be endured by other beings. These may also be called the pains of good-will, of sympathy, or the pains of the benevolent or social affections.

8. The pains of malevolence are the pains resulting from the view of any pleasures supposed to be enjoyed by any beings who happen to be the objects of a man's displeasure. These may also be styled the pains of ill-will, of antipathy,

or

or the pains of the malevolent or diſſocial affections.

9. The pains of the memory may be grounded
on every one of the above kinds, as well of pains
of privation as of poſitive pains. Theſe correſpond exactly to the pleaſures of the memory.

10. The pains of the imagination may alſo be
grounded on any one of the above kinds, as well
of pains of privation as of poſitive pains : in other
reſpects they correſpond exactly to the pleaſures
of the imagination.

11. The pains of expectation may be grounded
on each one of the above kinds, as well of pains
of privation as of poſitive pains. Theſe may be
alſo termed pains of apprehenſion.

12. The pains of aſſociation correſpond exactly
to the pleaſures of aſſociation.

Of the above liſt there are certain pleaſures and
pains which ſuppoſe the exiſtence of ſome pleaſure or pain of ſome other perſon, to which the
pleaſure or pain of the perſon in queſtion has regard : ſuch pleaſures and pains may be termed
extra-regarding. Others do not ſuppoſe any
ſuch thing : theſe may be termed *ſelf-regarding*.
The only pleaſures and pains of the extra-regarding claſs are thoſe of benevolence, and thoſe of
malevolence : all the reſt are ſelf-regarding.

Of all theſe ſeveral ſorts of pleaſures and pains
there is ſcarce any one which is not liable, on

more

more accounts than one, to come under the confideration of the law.   Is an offence committed?
it is the tendency which it has to deftroy, in fuch
or fuch perfons, fome of thefe pleafures, or to
produce fome of thefe pains, that conftitutes the
mifchief of it, and the ground for punifhing it.
It is the profpect of fome of thofe pleafures, or of
fecurity from fome of thefe pains, that conftitutes
the motive or temptation ; it is the attainment of
them that conftitutes the profit of the offence. Is
the offender to be punifhed ? it can be only by
the production of one or more of thefe pains that
the punifhment can be inflicted.

It would be a matter not only of curiofity, but
of fome ufe, to exhibit a catalogue of the feveral
complex pleafures and pains, analyfing them at
the fame time into the feveral fimple ones of
which they are refpectively compofed. But fuch
a difquifition would take up too much room to be
admitted here.   A fhort fpecimen, however, for
the purpofe of illuftration, can hardly be difpen-
fed with.

The pleafures taken in at the eye and ear are
generally very complex. The pleafures of a country fcene, for inftance, confift commonly, amongft
others, of the following pleafures:

I. Pleafures of the fenfes.

1. The fimple pleafures of fight, excited by the
perception of agreeable colours and figures, green
fields,

fields, waving foliage, gliftening water, and the like.

2. The fimple pleafures of the ear, excited by the perceptions of the chirping of birds, the murmuring of waters, the ruftling of the wind among the trees.

3. The pleafures of the fmell, excited by the perceptions of the fragrance of flowers, of new-mown hay, or other vegetable fubftances in the firft ftages of fermentation.

4. The agreeable inward fenfation, produced by a brifk circulation of the blood, and the ventilation of it in the lungs by a pure air, fuch as that in the country frequently is in comparifon of that which is breathed in town.

II. Pleafures of the imagination produced by affociation:

1. The idea of the plenty, refulting from the poffeffion of the objects that are in view, and of the happinefs arifing from it.

2. The idea of the innocence and happinefs of the birds, fheep, cattle, dogs, and other gentle or domeftic animals.

3. The idea of the conftant flow of health, fuppofed to be enjoyed by all thefe creatures : a notion which is apt to refult from the occafional flow of health enjoyed by the fuppofed fpectator.

4. The idea of gratitude, excited by the contemplation of the all-powerful and beneficent Being,

ing, who is looked up to as the author of these blessings.

These four last are all of them, in some measure at least, pleasures of sympathy.

The depriving a man of this groupe of pleasures is one of the evils apt to result from imprisonment; whether produced by illegal violence, or in the way of punishment by appointment of the laws.

J. BENTHAM.

VALUE OF A LOT OF PLEASURE AND PAIN,
HOW TO BE MEASURED.

PLEASURES, and the avoidance of pains, are the *ends* which the legislator ought to have in view: it behoves him therefore to understand their *value.* Pleasures and pains are the *instruments* he has to work with: it behoves him therefore to understand their force; which is again, in other words, their value.

To a person considered *by himself*, the value of a pleasure or pain considered *by itself*, will be greater or less, according to the four following circumstances:

1. Its *intensity.*
2. Its *duration.*
3. Its *certainty* or *uncertainty.*
4. Its *proximity* or *remoteness.*

These

These are the circumstances which are to be considered in estimating a pleasure or a pain considered each of them by itself. But when the value of any pleasure or pain is considered for the purpose of estimating the tendency of any *act* by which it is produced, there are two other circumstances to be taken into the account: These are,

5. Its *fecundity*, or the chance it has of being followed by sensations of the *same* kind: that is, pleasures, if it be a pleasure; pains, if it be a pain.

6. Its *purity*, or the chance it has of *not* being followed by sensations of the *opposite* kind: that is, pains, if it be a pleasure; pleasures, if it be a pain.

These two last, however, are in strictness scarcely to be deemed properties of the pleasure or the pain itself; they are not, therefore, in strictness to be taken into the account of the value of that pleasure or that pain. They are in strictness to be deemed properties only of the act, or other event, by which such pleasure or pain has been produced; and accordingly are only to be taken into the account of the tendency of such act or such event.

To a *number* of persons, with reference to each of whom the value of a pleasure or a pain is considered, it will be greater or less, according to seven circumstances: to wit, the six preceding ones, *viz.*

1. Its

1. Its *intensity*.

2. Its *duration*.

3. Its *certainty* or *uncertainty*.

4. Its *proximity* or *remoteness*.

5. Its *fecundity*.

6. Its *purity*.

And one other : to wit,

7. Its *extent ;* that is, the number of persons to whom it *extends*, or (in other words) who are *affected* by it.

To take an exact account then of the general tendency of any act by which the interests of a community are affected, proceed as follows. Begin with any one person of those whose interests seem most immediately to be affected by it ; and take an account,

1. Of the value of each distinguishable *pleasure* which appears to be produced by it in the *first* instance.

2. Of the value of each *pain* which appears to be produced by it in the *first* instance.

3. Of the value of each pleasure which appears to be produced by it *after* the first. This constitutes the *fecundity* of the first *pleasure*, and the *impurity* of the first *pain*.

4. Of the value of each *pain* which appears to be produced by it after the first. This constitutes the *fecundity* of the first *pain*, and the *impurity* of the first pleasure.

5. Sum

5. Sum up all the values of all the *pleasures* on one side, and those of all the *pains* on the other. The *balance*, if it be on the side of pleasure, will give the *good* tendency of the act upon the whole, with respect to the interests of that *individual* person; if on the side of pain, the *bad* tendency of it upon the whole.

6. Take an account of the *number* of persons whose interests appear to be concerned; and repeat the above process with respect to each. *Sum up* the numbers expressive of the degrees of *good* tendency which the act has with respect to each individual, in regard to whom the tendency of it is *good* upon the whole: do this again with respect to each individual, in regard to whom the tendency of it is *bad* upon the whole. Take the *balance*; which, if on the side of *pleasure*, will give the general *good tendency* of the act, with respect to the total number or *community* of individuals concerned: if on the side of pain, the general *evil tendency* with respect to the same community.

It is not to be expected that this process should be strictly pursued previously to every moral judgment, or to every legislative or judicial operation. It may, however, be always kept in view; and as near as the process actually pursued on those occasions approaches to it, so near will such process approach to the character of an exact one.

The

The same procefs is alike applicable to pleafure and pain, in whatever fhape they appear, and by whatever denomination they are diftinguifhed: to pleafure, whether it be called *good* (which is properly the caufe or inftrument of pleafure), or *profit* (which is diftant pleafure, or the caufe or inftrument of diftant pleafure), or *convenience, advantage, benefit, emolument, happinefs,* and fo forth; to pain, whether it be called *evil* (which correfponds to *good*), or *mifchief*, or *inconvenience*, or *difadvantage*, or *lofs*, or *unhappinefs*, and fo forth.

Nor is this a novel and unwarranted, any more than it is a ufelefs, theory. In all this there is nothing but what the practice of mankind, wherefoever they have a clear view of their own intereft, is perfectly conformable to. An article of property, an eftate in land, for inftance, is valuable, on what account? On account of the pleafures of all kinds which it enables a man to produce, and, what comes to the fame thing, the pains of all kinds which it enables him to avert. But the value of fuch an article of property is univerfally underftood to rife or fall according to the length or fhortnefs of the time which a man has in it; the certainty or uncertainty of its coming into poffeffion; and the nearnefs or remotenefs of the time at which, if at all, it is to come into poffeffion. As to the *intenfity* of the pleafures which

a man may derive from it, this is never thought
of, becaufe it depends upon the ufe which each
particular perfon may come to make of it; which
cannot be eftimated till the particular pleafures
he may come to derive from it, or the particular pains he may come to exclude by means of
it, are brought to view. For the fame reafon,
neither does he think of the *fecundity* or *purity*
of thofe pleafures.

J. BENTHAM.

THE DIFFERENCE BETWEEN THE REMOVAL
OF PAIN AND POSITIVE PLEASURE.

PAIN and pleafure are fimple ideas, incapable
of definition. People are not liable to be miftaken
in their feelings; but they are frequently wrong
in the names they give them, and in their reafonings about them. Many are of opinion, that
pain arifes neceffarily from the removal of fome
pleafure; as they think pleafure does from the
ceafing or diminution of fome pain. Pain and
pleafure, in their moft fimple and natural manner
of affecting, are each of a pofitive nature, and
by no means neceffarily dependent on each other
for their exiftence. The human mind is often,
nay for the moft part, in a ftate neither of pain
nor pleafure; which may be called a ftate of indifference. When we are carried from this ftate

VOL. II. 2   H h   †   into

into a state of actual pleasure, it does not appear
that we should pass through the medium of any
sort of pain. If in such a state of indifference, or
ease, or tranquillity, or call it what you please,
you were to be suddenly entertained with a concert of music ; or suppose some object of a fine
shape and bright lively colours to be presented before you; or imagine your smell is gratified with
the fragrance of a rose ; or if without any previous thirst you were to drink of some pleasant
kind of wine; or to taste of some sweet-meat
without being hungry ; in all the several senses, of
hearing, smelling, and tasting, you undoubtedly
find a pleasure ; yet if inquiry be made into the
state of your mind previous to these gratifications,
you will hardly say, that they found you in any
sort of pain; or having satisfied these several
senses with their several pleasures, will you say
that any pain has succeeded, though the pleasure
is absolutely over ? Suppose, on the other hand,
a man in the same state of indifference, to receive
a violent blow, or to drink of some bitter potion,
or to have his ears wounded with some harsh and
grating sound: here is no removal of pleasure ;
and yet here is felt, in every sense which is affected, a pain very distinguishable. It may be said
perhaps that the pain in these cases had its rise
from the removal of the pleasure which the man
enjoyed before, though that pleasure was of so
                                                        low

low a degree as to be perceived only by the removal. But this feems to be a fubtilty that is
not difcoverable in nature. For if, previous to the
pain, I do not feel any actual pleafure, I have no
reafon to judge that any fuch thing exifts; fince
pleafure is only pleafure as it is felt. The fame
may be faid of pain, and with equal reafon.
Pleafure and pain are not mere relations, which
can exift only as they are contrafted. They are
pofitive pains and pleafures, and depend not on
each other. There is nothing to be diftinguifhed
in the mind with more clearnefs than the three
ftates, of indifference, of pleafure, and of pain.
Every one of thefe is to be perceived without
any fort of idea of its relation to any thing elfe.
Caius is afflicted with a fit of the colic; this man
is actually in pain; ftretch Caius upon the rack,
he will feel a much greater pain; but does this
pain of the rack arife from the removal of any
pleafure? or is the fit of the colic a pleafure or
a pain juft as we are pleafed to confider it?

We fhall carry this propofition yet a ftep further, that pain and pleafure are not neceffarily
dependent for their exiftence on their mutual diminution or removal, but that, in reality, the diminution or ceafing of pleafure does not operate
like pofitive pain; and that the removal or diminution of pain, in its effect, has very little refemblance to pofitive pleafure. The former of thefe

propofitions may probably be allowed more readily than the latter; becaufe it is very evident that pleafure, when it has run its career, fets us down very nearly where it found us. Pleafure of every kind quickly fatisfies; and when it is over, we relapfe into indifference, or rather we fall into a foft tranquillity, which is tinged with the agreeable colour of the former fenfation. At the firft view indeed it is not fo apparent, that the removal of a great pain does not refemble pofitive pleafure; but let us recollect in what ftate we have found our minds upon efcaping fome imminent danger, or on being releafed from the feverity of fome cruel pain. We have on fuch occafions found the temper of our minds in a tenor very remote from that which the prefence of pofitive pleafure induces; we have found them in a ftate of great fobriety, impreffed with a fenfe of awe; in fhort, of tranquillity fhadowed with horror. The fafhion of the countenance and the gefture of the body on fuch occafions is fo correfpondent to this ftate of mind, that any perfon, a ftranger to the caufe of the appearance, would rather judge us under the fame confternation, than in the enjoyment of any thing like pofitive pleafure.

As when a wretch, who confcious of his crime,
Purfued for murder from his native clime,
Juft gains fome frontier, breathlefs, pale, amaz'd;
All gaze, all wonder!

This

This striking appearance of the man whom Homer supposes to have just escaped an imminent danger, the sort of mixed passion, of terror, and surprise, with which he affects the spectators, paints very strongly the manner in which we find ourselves affected upon occasions any way similar. For when we have suffered from any violent emotion, the mind naturally continues in something like the same condition, after the cause which first produced it has ceased to operate. The tossing of the sea remains after the storm; and when this remain of horror has entirely subsided, all the passion which the accident raised subsides along with it; and the mind returns to its usual state of indifference. In short, pleasure that is any thing either in the inward sensation or outward appearance, like pleasure from a positive cause, has never its origin from the removal of pain or danger.

But shall we therefore say, that the removal of pain or its diminution is always simply painful? or affirm, that the cessation or the lessening of pleasure is always attended itself with a pleasure? By no means. There are pleasures and pains of a positive and independent nature; and, secondly, the feeling which results from the ceasing or diminution of pain does not bear a sufficient resemblance to positive pleasure, to have it considered as of the same nature, or intitle it to be known

H h 3   by

by the fame name; and, thirdly, upon the fame principle, the removal or qualification of pleafure has no refemblance to pofitive pain. It is certain that the former feeling (the removal or moderation of pain) has fomething in it far from diftreffing or difagreeable in its nature. This feeling, in many cafes fo agreeable, but in all fo different from pofitive pleafure, has no name which I know; but that hinders not its being a very real one, and very different from all others. It is moft certain, that every fpecies of fatisfaction or pleafure, how different foever in its manner of affecting, is of a pofitive nature in the mind of him who feels it. The affection is undoubtedly pofitive; but the caufe may be, and in this cafe it certainly is, a fort of *privation*.

BURKE.

PLEASURE AND PAIN.

GOOD and evil are common to every thing, and affect us only in different proportions. The moft happy are thofe who feel the leaft of pain; the moft miferable thofe who experience the leaft of pleafure. Every one fuffers more from the former than he enjoys of the latter, and this difproportion is common to all mankind. The happinefs of man, in his prefent ftate, is merely negative, and muft be eftimated by the leaft quantity
tity

tity of his fufferings.—Every fenfe of pain is infeparable from the defire of being freed from it;
every idea of pleafure is alike infeparable from
the defire of enjoying it: now every defire fuppofes the privation or abfence of the object defired;
and this circumftance is always in fome degree
painful: In the difproportion, therefore, between
our defires and our abilities confifts our mifery.
A fufceptible being, whofe abilities fhould be equal
to its defires, would be pofitively happy—In what
then confifts human wifdom, or the means of acquiring happinefs? To diminifh our defires is
certainly not the method; for if thefe were lefs
than our abilities, part of our faculties would remain ufelefs and inactive, and we fhould enjoy
but half our being. Nor is it, on the other hand,
to extend our natural capacity for enjoyment; for
if our defires, at the fame time, be extended in a
greater proportion, we fhould only become thereby the more miferable. It muft confift, therefore, in leffening the difproportion between our
abilities and our defires, and in reducing our inclinations and our powers to a perfect equilibrium.
It is in fuch a fituation, and in that only, that all
our faculties may be employed, and yet the mind
preferve its tranquillity, and the body its due regularity and eafe.

ROUSSEAU.

PO-

POLITENESS.

AMONG the arts of conversation, no one pleases
more than mutual deference or civility; which
leads us to resign our own inclinations to those of
our companion, and to curb and conceal that pre-
sumption and arrogance so natural to the human
mind. To correct such gross vices as lead us to
commit real injuries on others, is the part of morals, and the object of the most ordinary education. Where that is not attended to in some degree, no human society can subsist. But in order to render conversation and the intercourse of
minds more easy and agreeable, good manners
have been invented, and have carried the matter
somewhat further. Wherever nature has given
the mind a propensity to any vice, or to any passion disagreeable to others, refined breeding has
taught men to throw the bias on the opposite
side, and to preserve in all their behaviour the
appearance of sentiments different from those to
which they naturally incline. Thus, as we are
commonly proud and selfish, and apt to assume
the preference above others, a polite man learns
to behave with deference towards his companions,
and to yield the superiority to them in all the common incidents of society. In like manner, where-
ever a person's situation may naturally beget any
dif-

difagreeable fufpicion in him, it is the part of good-manners to prevent it, by a ftudied difplay of fentiments directly contrary to thofe of which he is apt to be jealous. Thus old men know their infirmities, and naturally dread contempt from youth: hence well-educated youth redouble the inftances of refpect and deference to their elders. Strangers and foreigners are without protection: hence, in all polite countries, they receive the higheft civilities, and are intitled to the firft place in every company. A man is lord in his own family; and his guefts are, in a manner, fubject to his authority: hence he is always the loweft perfon in the company; attentive to the wants of every one; and giving himfelf all the trouble, in order to pleafe, which may not betray too vifible an affectation, or impofe too much reftraint on his guefts.

HUME.

POLYGAMY.

WITH regard to polygamy in general, independently of the circumftances which may render it tolerable, it is not of the leaft fervice to mankind, nor to either of the two fexes, whether it be that which abufes, or that which is abufed. Neither is it of fervice to the children; for one of its greateft inconveniences is, that the father and
mother

mother cannot have the same affection for their offspring; a father cannot love twenty children with the same tenderness as a mother can love two. It is much worse when a wife has many husbands; for then paternal love is only held by this opinion, that a father may believe that certain children belong to him.

They say, that the emperor of Morocco has women of all colours, white, black, and tawny, in his seraglio. But the wretch has scarce need of a single colour. Besides, the possession of many wives does not always prevent their entertaining desires for those of others; which is the reason why women in the east are so carefully concealed. It is with lust as with avarice, whose thirst increases by the acquisition of treasure.

In the reign of Justinian, many of the philosophers, displeased with the constraint of Christianity, retired into Persia. What struck them the most, says Agathias, was, that polygamy was permitted amongst men, who did not even abstain from adultery.

Does not a plurality of wives lead to that passion which nature disallows? for one depravation always draws on another. It is said, that in the revolution which happenened at Constantinople, when Sultan Achmet was deposed, that the people having plundered the kiaya's house, they found

not

not a single woman. They tell us, that at Algiers, in the greatest part of their seraglios, they have none at all.

MONTESQUIEU.

END OF THE SECOND VOLUME.